T · H · E

SCHOLASTIC

RHYMING

DICTIONARY

T · H · E
SCHOLASTIC
RHYMING
DICTIONARY

SUE YOUNG

SCHOLASTIC
REFERENCE

New York   Toronto   London   Auckland   Sydney

Design: Brock Waldron, Bill Smith Studio
Illustration: David Sheldon

ISBN 0-590-96393-7 (pb) / ISBN 0-590-49461-9 (SSE) / ISBN 0-590-49460-0 (POB)

35 34   5   6   7/0
                             Printed in the U.S.A.   09

Table of Contents

cheer
fear

How to Use this Dictionary

Welcome to the world of rhymes. We encounter rhyming sounds everywhere — in song lyrics, advertising jingles, rap, greeting card messages, poetry, and verse of all kinds. In all of these, the sounds of rhyme can please and tickle our ears. This book helps you write verse that rhymes.

There are different kinds of rhymes: **perfect**, **imperfect**, and **slant**. Some poets use only perfect rhyme, but you can be more casual, especially if you're rhyming for fun.

Words that sound exactly the same, such as *wait* and *weight*, are not considered rhymes at all — even though the two words sound alike and are spelled differently.

A **perfect rhyme** is formed by two words which have different consonant sounds before identical rhyming sounds. *Cake* and *lake* form a perfect rhyme.

An **imperfect rhyme** has the same consonant before the rhyming sound, such as *therefore* and *before*. (The rhyming sound is *ore* and the consonant is *f*.)

A **slant rhyme** is one in which the sounds are pronounced alike even when they are technically different. For instance, the words *daddy* and *chatty* are frequently spoken with the same rhyming sound: *addy*. Slant rhymes are not true rhymes, but they often sound the same to our ears.

Locating a Rhyming Sound

Unlike other dictionaries which list words by the beginning letter of the word, a rhyming dictionary lists words by the beginning vowel of the rhyming sound.

RHYMING SOUNDS ALWAYS START WITH A VOWEL. The vowels are *A, E, I, O, U,* and sometimes *Y*. All rhyming sounds will start with one of these vowels. Therefore, the main part of this book is divided into six sections — one for each vowel. The sounds are listed alphabetically under the starting vowel.

There are two ways to locate a rhyme in this book. For instance, if you are looking for a rhyme for the word *self,* you can do one of two things:

1. Go directly to the *elf* sound in the rhyming dictionary.

2. Look up the word *self* in the **index** at the back of the book. There the words are listed alphabetically by the beginning letter of the word. There you will see: self/elf.

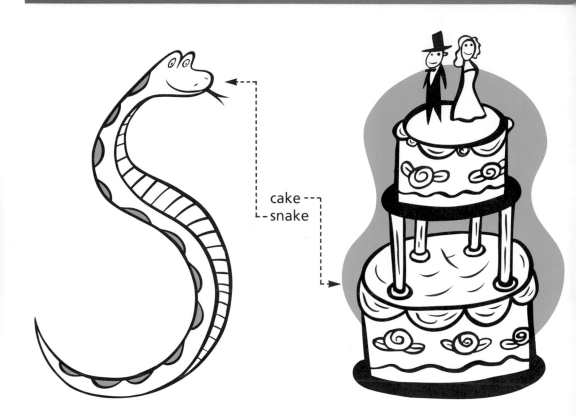

cake
snake

What is the rhyming sound of a word?

Which sound toward the end of the word is louder, or has more stress? One-syllable words have only one sound in them, like *snake* and *cake.* Their rhyming sound is *ake.* But, what if you wanted something to rhyme with a two-syllable word like *silly*? Listen to the sound that you stress the most in *silly — ill.* The rhyming sound includes the stressed syllable plus the rest of the word. So, to rhyme *silly,* you would look up the sound *illy* in the **I** section. There you would find words which end with the same sound, such as *chili, frilly,* and *hilly.*

One sound, different spellings

Sometimes you might look up a rhyming sound in the dictionary, but instead of finding a list of words that rhyme, you are sent to another sound. This is a **cross-reference**. For instance, if you are looking for words that rhyme with *jacks* and you go to *acks* in the dictionary, you won't find a list. Instead you'll find a cross-reference:

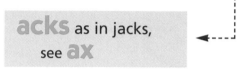

acks as in jacks,
see **ax**

The *ax* list contains *jacks, tax, kayaks, lilacs*—all the words with different spellings of the same sound. Without cross-references, the dictionary would contain many duplicated lists. It would be a very heavy book!

One word, many sounds

Some words end in the same spelling but have totally different sounds. When this happens, the spelling may be listed two or three times, once for each pronunciation of the sound. Each sound will be marked with a number. For instance, you will find three listings for the spelling *ard*. Each stands for a different sound that **ard** makes:

ard 1 stands for sounds like *card* and *guard*.

ard 2 stands for sounds like *reward* and *cord*.

ard 3 stands for sounds like *backward* and *bird*.

The way you hear a word's sound may depend on the region of the country in which you live. That's why in this dictionary you may find some words on a list that don't seem to you to rhyme. The same word may appear on another list under the sound familiar to you.

The point of this book is that you can have fun writing rhymes. As you begin to write your own verse, you may think of rhymes that are not in this or any other book. We encourage you to use your imagination to its fullest.

One word, no rhyme

What if the word you want to rhyme with has no rhyme? *Orange* and *point* don't have a rhyme. It would be very difficult to complete a two-line rhyme which began:

> **Every day I eat an orange**

If you wanted a rhyme, you could try instead:

> **I always eat an orange a day**
> **It's good for me, or so they say**

By not placing the hard-to-rhyme word at the end, you made it easier to find a rhyme.

Whether you want to write a rap or a sonnet, the world of verse is yours for the rhyming. Rhyming sounds, together with the melody of meter, ensure that what we write will be pleasing to the ear.

Sue Young

a 1 as in USA, see **ay**

a 2 as in spa, see **aw**

ab 1

blab
cab
crab
dab
drab
fab
flab
gab
grab
jab
lab
nab
scab
stab
tab

backstab
rehab
sand crab

taxicab

ab 2 as in swab, see **ob**

abber

blabber
drabber
gabber
grabber

jabber
backstabber
money grabber

abble

babble
dabble
rabble
Scrabble

Tower of Babel

abby

abbey
blabby
cabby
crabby
drabby
flabby
gabby
grabby
shabby
tabby

Dear Abby

able

able
cable
fable
label
sable
stable
table

disable
enable
mislabel
times table
timetable

unable
unstable

Aesop's fable
Cain and Abel
warning label

willing and able

aby

baby
maybe

ac as in almanac, see **ack**

ace

ace
base
bass
brace
case
chase
face
grace
lace
pace
place
race
space
trace
vase

birthplace
bookcase
briefcase
deface
disgrace
embrace

erase
fireplace
home base
horse race
misplace
neck brace
replace
retrace
sack race
shoelace
staircase
suitcase
unlace
workplace

anyplace
breathing space
change of pace
data base
double-space
everyplace
face to face
freckle face
human race
just in case
outer space
out of place
poker face
saving grace
wild-goose chase

aced as in laced, see aste

ach as in attach, see atch 1

ache 1 as in headache, see ake

ache 2 as in moustache, see ash 1

acial

facial
glacial
racial
spatial

interracial

acious

gracious
spacious

audacious
curvacious
flirtatious
Horatius
loquacious
tenacious
vivacious

ostentatious

acity

audacity
capacity
sagacity
tenacity
veracity

ack

back
black
crack
flack
hack
jack
knack
lack
pack
plaque
quack
rack
sack
shack
slack
smack
snack
stack
tack
track
whack
yak

attack
backpack
backtrack
blackjack
drawback
feedback
flapjack
flashback
fullback
haystack
hijack
icepack
Iraq
kayak
knapsack
laugh track

3

offtrack
one-track
racetrack
ransack
setback
sidetrack
six-pack
soundtrack
thumbtack
Tic Tac
unpack
wisecrack
wrong track

almanac
back to back
Cadillac
camelback
crackerjack
cul-de-sac
gunnysack
heart attack
hit the sack
jumping jack
lumberjack
maniac
paperback
piggyback
quarterback
railroad track

amnesiac
insomniac
panic attack
yakkity-yak

acked as in cracked, see act

ackle
cackle
crackle
jackal
shackle
spackle
tackle

debacle
ramshackle

fishing tackle
tabernacle

acks as in jacks, see ax

acs as in maniacs, see ax

act
act
backed
cracked
fact
lacked
packed
pact
quacked
sacked
smacked
snacked
stacked
tacked
tact
tracked
tract
whacked

yakked

abstract
attacked
attract
backpacked
compact
contract
distract
enact
exact
extract
hijacked
impact
in fact
jam-packed
ransacked
react
sidetracked
subtract
transact
unpacked
wisecracked

artifact
interact
overact
riot act
vacuum-packed

matter of fact
overreact

actical
practical
tactical

impractical

action
action
faction

fraction
traction

abstraction
attraction
contraction
distraction
extraction
inaction
infraction
reaction
subtraction
transaction

chain reaction
interaction
satisfaction
star attraction

dissatisfaction

affirmative action

active

active

attractive
inactive
reactive

hyperactive
overactive
retroactive

radioactive ------¬

acts as in facts, see **ax**

acy
Casey
Gracie
lacy
spacey
Tracy

ad 1
ad
add
bad
cad
Chad
clad
dad
fad
grad
had
lad
mad
pad
plaid
sad
tad

comrade
doodad
egad
granddad
ink pad
nomad
Sinbad
too bad

Galahad
ironclad
launching pad
mom and dad
not so bad
shoulder pad
Trinidad

undergrad
Olympiad
stark raving mad

ad 2 as in squad, see **awed**

ada
armada
cicada
Granada
piñata
regatta
tostada

enchilada

aficionada

adder as in ladder, see **atter**

addle as in paddle, see **attle**

addy as in daddy, see **atty**

ade 1
aid
aide
blade
braid
fade
frayed
grade

grayed
jade
laid
made
maid
neighed
paid
played
prayed
raid
shade
spade
sprayed
stayed
suede
swayed
trade
wade
weighed

afraid
arcade
Band-aid
betrayed
blockade
bridesmaid
charade
crusade
decade
decayed
delayed
displayed
first aid
grenade
homemade
invade
Kool-Aid
lampshade
mermaid

nursemaid
obeyed
okayed
outweighed
parade
persuade
portrayed
repaid
surveyed
tirade
unmade
unpaid
upgrade
x-rayed

accolade
barricade
cavalcade
centigrade
custom-made
disobeyed
escapade
foreign aid
Gatorade
hearing aid
hit parade
lemonade
make the grade
marmalade
masquerade
overpaid
promenade
razor blade
ready-made
renegade
ricocheted
Rose Parade
serenade
shoulder blade

unafraid
underpaid

penny arcade
visual aid

ade 2 as in facade,
see **awed**

ader

cater
crater
freighter
gator
greater
hater
later
nadir
raider
skater
straighter
trader
traitor
waiter

creator
crusader
debater
dictator
equator
ice skater
invader
narrator
persuader
spectator
tailgater
translator

agitator

alligator
animator
aviator
calculator
decorator
demonstrator
detonator
duplicator
educator
elevator
escalator
generator
illustrator
imitator
indicator
innovator
instigator
legislator
liberator
masquerader
mediator
moderator
navigator
operator
perpetrator
radiator
regulator
roller skater
see you later
serenader
speculator
terminator
ventilator

assassinator
coordinator
exaggerator
exterminator

facilitator
impersonator
investigator
manipulator
negotiator
procrastinator
refrigerator

sooner or later

ady
eighty
Haiti
Katie
lady
matey
shady
weighty

aff
calf
graph
half
laugh
staff

behalf
decaf
giraffe
riffraff

autograph
belly laugh
better half
chief of staff
paragraph
phonograph
photograph
telegraph

aft
craft
draft
graft
laughed
raft
shaft
staffed

aircraft
life raft
mine shaft
spacecraft
witchcraft

autographed
fore and aft
photographed

after
after
drafter
laughter
rafter

hereafter
thereafter

forever after

afty
crafty
drafty

7

ag

bag
brag
drag
flag
gag
jag
lag
nag
rag
sag
shag
snag
stag
tag
wag
zag

beanbag
dishrag
dog tag
grab bag
jet lag
mailbag
name tag
price tag
ragtag
sandbag
tea bag
trash bag
washrag
windbag
zigzag

doggie bag
litterbag
lollygag
saddlebag
sleeping bag

age 1

age
cage
gauge
page
rage
sage
stage
wage

backstage
bird cage
Bronze Age
engage
enrage
front page
Ice Age
offstage
old age
outrage
rampage
rib cage
space age
Stone Age
teenage
upstage

middle age
under age

minimum wage

age 2

barrage
collage
corsage
garage
massage
mirage

bon voyage
camouflage
entourage
sabotage

espionage

ageous

contagious
courageous
enrage us
outrageous
rampageous
upstage us

advantageous

aggy

baggy
draggy
Maggie
saggy
shaggy

ah as in hah, see aw

ai as in bonzai, see y

aid as in paid, see ade 1

aider as in raider, see ader

ail as in mail, see ale 1

aily
daily
gaily
scaly

Israeli
shillelagh
ukulele

Barnum and Bailey

aim
aim
blame
came
claim
fame
flame
frame
game
lame
maim
name
same
shame
tame

acclaim
aflame
ball game
became
defame
exclaim
for shame
inflame
nickname

reclaim
surname
take aim

claim to fame
Hall of Fame
Notre Dame
overcame
put to shame

ain
brain
cane
chain
crane
drain
gain
grain
Jane
lane
main
Maine
mane
pain
pane
plain
plane
rain
reign
rein
sane
slain
Spain
sprain
stain
strain
train
vain
vane
vein

wane
abstain
airplane
birdbrain
bloodstain
campaign
champagne
chow mein
complain
contain
disdain
domain
Elaine
explain
freight train
Great Dane
humane
insane
in vain
Lorraine
maintain
Mark Twain
migraine
mundane
obtain
profane
refrain
regain
remain
restrain
retain
sustain
tearstain
terrain
Ukraine
unchain

acid rain
ascertain

candy cane
cellophane
down the drain
entertain
featherbrain
hurricane
inhumane
lovers' lane
Novocain
potty-train
scatterbrain
Solarcaine
wagon train
weathervane
windowpane

memory lane
no pain, no gain

air
air
bare
bear
blare
care
chair
dare
fair
fare
flair
flare
glare
hair
hare
heir
lair
mare
pair

pear
prayer
rare
scare
share
snare
spare
square
stair
stare
swear
tear
their
there
ware
wear
where

affair
airfare
aware
Bel-Air
beware
bus fare
child care
compare
declare
despair
elsewhere
fanfare
fresh air
health care
high chair
impair
midair
nightmare
no fair
nowhere
outwear

Pierre
prepare
repair
somewhere
threadbare
Times Square
unfair
warfare
welfare
wheelchair

anywhere
billionaire
county fair
debonair
Delaware
dentist chair
everywhere
fair and square
here and there
millionaire
not all there
on the air
over there
questionnaire
rocking chair
silverware
solitaire
teddy bear
unaware
underwear
wash and wear

electric chair
intensive care
Smokey the Bear

aire as in millionaire, see **air**

airy as in fairy,
see **ary**

aise as in praise,
see **aze**

ait as in bait,
see **ate**

ak as in yak,
see **ack**

ake

ache
bake
Blake
brake
break
cake
fake
flake
Jake
lake
make
quake
rake
sake
shake
snake
stake
steak
take
wake

awake
backache
beefsteak

cheesecake
clambake
cupcake
daybreak
earache
earthquake
fruitcake
handshake
headache
heartache
heartbreak
housebreak
intake
jailbreak
keepsake
milk shake
mistake
namesake
newsbreak
opaque
outbreak
pancake
remake
shortcake
snowflake
toothache

bellyache
birthday cake
coffee break
double take
give and take
make or break
overtake
pat-a-cake
rattlesnake
Shake 'n Bake
stomachache
take a break

wide-awake

for goodness' sake
for pity sake
gimme a break
jump in the lake

aks as in kayaks,
see **ax**

al

Al
gal
Hal
pal
shall

canal
chorale
corral
decal
locale
low-cal
morale
pen pal

musicale
rationale
root canal

ald as in bald,
see **alled**

ale 1

ail
ale
bail
Braille

fail
frail
gale
hail
jail
mail
male
nail
pail
pale
quail
rail
sail
sale
scale
snail
stale
tail
tale
trail
veil
wail
whale
Yale

airmail
blackmail
cocktail
curtail
derail
detail
dovetail
exhale
fan mail
female
for sale
hangnail
impale
inhale

pigtail
prevail
retail
shirttail
telltale
thumbnail
toenail
unveil
upscale
wholesale

Abigail
cottontail
fairy tale
fingernail
garage sale
ginger ale
Holy Grail
killer whale
monorail
nature trail
nightingale
rummage sale
tattletale
without fail

ale 2 as in morale, see al

ale 3 as in finale, see olly

alf as in calf, see aff

ality 1

brutality
fatality
finality
formality
legality
locality
mentality
morality
mortality
neutrality
normality
reality
totality
vitality

abnormality
hospitality
illegality
immorality
immortality
informality
joviality
nationality
personality
practicality
principality
punctuality
rationality
technicality
triviality

congeniality
municipality
originality
sentimentality

confidentiality
constitutionality
individuality

ality 2
quality
equality
frivolity
inequality

alk as in talk,
see **ock**

alker as in walker,
see **ocker**

alks as in walks,
see **ox**

all
all
ball
bawl
brawl
call
crawl
doll
drawl
fall
gall
hall
haul
loll
mall
maul
Paul
Saul
scrawl
shawl

small
sprawl
squall
stall
tall
wall

appall
baseball
birdcall
blackball
close call
downfall
enthrall
eyeball
football
free fall
goofball
gum ball
handball
install
meatball
nightfall
oddball
phone call
pinball
pitfall
rag doll
rainfall
recall
snowball
snowfall
spitball
stonewall
toll call

aerosol
alcohol
Barbie doll
basketball

butterball
cannonball
caterwaul
city hall
cotton ball
crystal ball
curtain call
free-for-all
know it all
Montreal
off-the-wall
overall
overhaul
paper doll
parasol
protocol
shopping mall
study hall
Taj Mahal
Tylenol
volleyball
wake-up call
wall-to-wall
waterfall

cholesterol
justice for all
Neanderthal

alled
bald
bawled
brawled
called
crawled
drawled
hauled
lolled
mauled

scald
scrawled
sprawled
squalled
stalled
walled

appalled
blackballed
enthralled
installed
recalled
snowballed
so-called

overhauled

aller

brawler
caller
collar
dollar
holler
scholar
smaller
squalor
taller

bird caller
blue-collar
flea collar
free-faller
installer
name-caller
white-collar

creepy crawler
hoot and holler
million-dollar ------>

alley

alley
Bali
dally
galley
rally
Sally
tally
valley

blind alley
Death Valley
pep rally

allow 1

aloe
hallow
shallow

marshmallow

allow 2

follow
hollow
swallow
wallow

Apollo

ally as in rally, see alley

alm

balm
calm
palm
psalm
qualm

embalm
napalm

alt

fault
halt
malt
salt
vault

asphalt
assault
default
exalt
pole-vault

somersault

alter

altar
alter
falter
halter
vaulter
Walter

assaulter
Gibraltar

alts

faults
halts
malts
salts

vaults
waltz

assaults
defaults

smelling salts
somersaults

am
am
clam
cram
dam
gram
ham
jam
lamb
ma'am
Pam
ram
Sam
scam
scram
sham
slam
swam
tram
wham
yam

exam
flimflam
grand slam
madame
outswam
program
toe jam

Abraham
Amsterdam

anagram
Birmingham
diagram
in a jam
leg of lamb
milligram
telegram
traffic jam
Uncle Sam

ama 1
comma
drama
llama
mama
Rama
trauma

pajama

cinerama
melodrama
Yokohama

ama 2
pajama

Alabama
cinerama
panorama

ame as in fame, see aim

ami as in pastrami, see ommy

ammy
clammy
Grammy
Tammy
whammy

Miami

amp
amp
camp
champ
clamp
cramp
damp
lamp
ramp
scamp
stamp
tramp
vamp

postage stamp
summer camp
writer's cramp

amper
camper
damper
hamper
pamper
scamper
tamper

an 1
an
Anne
ban
bran

15

can
clan
fan
Fran
Jan
man
Nan
pan
plan
ran
scan
span
Stan
tan
than
van

Batman
began
cancan
caveman ----
Chopin
deadpan
dishpan
dustpan
hangman
Japan
lawman
life span
madman
oat bran
outran
Pac-Man
sandman
sedan
Spokane
suntan
time span
trashcan

caravan
frying pan
handyman
man-to-man
moving van
overran
Pakistan
Peter Pan
spic-and-span
Superman

Afghanistan
attention span
catamaran
flash-in-the-pan
medicine man
orangutan

an 2 as in pecan, see awn

ana 1
Anna

banana
bandanna
Diana
Havana
Montana
Savannah
Susanna

Indiana
Pollyanna

Louisiana

ana 2 as in iguana, see onna

ance
ants
aunts
chance
chants
dance
France
glance
grants
lance
pants
plants
prance
stance
trance

advance
break dance
by chance
enchants
enhance
entrance
expanse
fat chance
finance
folk dance
free-lance
last chance
rain dance
romance
square dance
sweat pants
tap dance
transplants

circumstance
disenchants
fighting chance
song and dance
underpants

and

and
band
banned
bland
brand
canned
fanned
gland
grand
hand
land
panned
planned
sand
spanned
stand
strand
tanned

armband
backhand
bandstand
command
cowhand
crash-land
demand
disband
dreamland
expand
firsthand
grandstand
handstand
headband
homeland
kickstand
Lapland
longhand
name-brand

offhand
quicksand
shorthand
suntanned
Thailand
wasteland

baby grand
beforehand
close-at-hand
contraband
Disneyland
Dixieland
fairyland
hand-in-hand
helping hand
Holy Land
hot dog stand
no man's land
reprimand
Rio Grande
rubber band
secondhand
sleight of hand
understand

chain of command
fantasyland
law of the land
misunderstand

supply and demand

ane as in lane,
see **ain**

ang

bang
clang
dang

fang
gang
hang
rang
sang
slang
sprang
Tang
twang

chain gang
harangue
meringue
mustang

boomerang ------
overhang

orangoutang

ange

change
range
strange

arrange
downrange
exchange
long-range
shortchange

interchange
prearrange
rearrange

ank

bank
blank
clank
crank
dank
drank

17

frank
plank
prank
rank
sank
shrank
spank
tank
thank
yank

blood bank
fish tank
gangplank
outrank
point-blank
think tank

data bank
draw a blank
savings bank
walk the plank

blankety-blank

military rank

anky
blanky
clanky
cranky
Frankie
hankie
lanky
swanky
Yankee

hanky-panky

anned as in banned, see and

anner
banner
manner
manor
planner
scanner
tanner

anny
Annie
Danny
granny
nanny

uncanny

ans as in swans, see ons

ant 1
ant - - - - - - - - - - -
aunt
can't
chant
grant
pant
plant
rant
scant
slant

eggplant
enchant

implant
Rembrandt
supplant
transplant

disenchant
gallivant
power plant

ant 2 as in want, see aunt

ante as in confidante, see aunt

antic
antic
frantic

Atlantic
gigantic
romantic

transatlantic
unromantic

ants as in pants, see ance

any as in many, see enny

ap
cap
chap
clap
flap

gap
lap
map
nap
rap
sap
scrap
slap
snap
strap
tap
trap
wrap
yap
zap

backslap
burlap
catnap
dunce cap
firetrap
giftwrap
hubcap
kidnap
kneecap
madcap
mishap
mousetrap
recap
road map
unwrap
wiretap

baseball cap
beat the rap
booby trap
bottlecap
gender gap
gingersnap
handicap

overlap
thinking cap
tourist trap

generation gap

ape

ape
cape
drape
gape
grape
scrape
shape
tape

agape
egg-shape
escape
go ape
landscape
red tape
reshape
shipshape

fire escape
out of shape
ticker tape

aph as in graph, see aff

aphed as in autographed, see aft

aphic

graphic
traffic

geographic
one-way traffic
photographic

apple

apple
chapel
grapple

appy

happy
pappy
sappy
scrappy
snappy

grandpappy
slaphappy
unhappy

make it snappy
trigger-happy

ar

are
bar
car
czar
far
jar
mar
par
scar
spar
star
tar

19

ajar
all-star
bazaar
bizarre
boxcar
cigar
costar
disbar
guitar
jaguar
memoir
Renoir
snack bar
so far
streetcar

cable car
candy bar
caviar
cookie jar
CPR
falling star
handlebar
movie star
near and far
registrar
reservoir
salad bar
seminar
superstar
VCR
Zanzibar

ara
Clara
Sarah

mascara
Sahara

arch
arch
March
march
parch
starch

ard 1
bard
barred
card
charred
guard
hard
jarred
lard
marred
scarred
sparred
starred
tarred
yard

armed guard
backyard
barnyard
Bernard
blowhard
bombard
Coast Guard
costarred
cue card
diehard
discard
flash card
graveyard
junkyard
lifeguard
postcard

regard
safeguard
scorecard
shipyard
vanguard

avant-garde
baseball card
battle-scarred
birthday card
bodyguard
boulevard
credit card
crossing guard
disregard
leotard
report card
St. Bernard

ard 2 as in reward, see ord

ard 3 as in backward, see erd

arder as in harder, see arter

ardy
arty
hardy
hearty
Marty
party
smarty

tardy

foolhardy
search party
tea party

birthday party

are as in care,
see **air**

area
area

Bavaria
Bulgaria
hysteria
malaria

arent
parent

apparent
grandparent
inherent
transparent

unapparent

arer
barer
error
fairer
rarer
terror

pallbearer
seafarer
torchbearer
wayfarer

holy terror
trial and error

arf 1
arf
barf
scarf

arf 2
dwarf
wharf

arge
barge
charge
large
Marge
sarge

discharge
enlarge
recharge
take charge

overcharge

ari as in safari,
see **arry** 2

arious 2/3
various

Aquarius
gregarious
hilarious
precarious
vicarious

Sagittarius

arity
charity
clarity
rarity

barbarity
dexterity
disparity
hilarity
posterity
prosperity
severity
sincerity
vulgarity

insincerity
popularity
regularity
similarity
solidarity

familiarity
irregularity
peculiarity

ark
arc
ark
bark
Clark
dark
hark
lark
mark
park
shark
spark
stark

aardvark

ballpark
birthmark
bookmark
check mark
Denmark
earmark
footmark
landmark
monarch
postmark
remark
skylark
theme park
trademark

baseball park
Central Park
disembark
double-park
Joan of Arc
Noah's ark
question mark

arm 1

arm
charm
farm
harm

alarm
disarm
firearm

arm in arm
false alarm
fire alarm
lucky charm
underarm

arm 2 as in warm, see orm

arn

barn
darn
yarn

aron

Aaron
baron
barren
heron
Karen
Sharon

arred as in barred, see ard 1

arrot

bear it
carat
carrot
dare it
ferret
merit
parrot
scare it
share it
swear it
wear it

demerit
inherit
prepare it
repair it

disinherit

arrow

arrow
marrow
narrow
pharaoh
sparrow

bolero
bone marrow
Camaro
dinero
sombrero
wheelbarrow

bow and arrow
caballero
straight and narrow

Rio de Janeiro

arry 1 as in carry, see ary

arry 2

sari
sorry
starry

Ferrari
safari

calamari

art 1

art
cart
chart

dart
heart
mart
part
smart
start
tart

apart
depart
eye chart
false start
folk art
go cart
golf cart
head start
impart
jump-start
K Mart
Mozart
outsmart
Pop Tart
restart
street smart
sweetheart
upstart

à la carte
applecart
change of heart
counterpart
fall apart
heart to heart
lonely heart
martial art
minimart
Purple Heart
running start
shopping cart
work of art

art 2 as in wart,
see **ort**

arter
ardor
barter
charter
garter
harder
martyr
smarter
starter
Tartar
tarter

self-starter
slow starter

arty as in party,
see **ardy**

arve
carve
Marv
starve

ary
airy
Barry
berry
bury
Carrie
carry
cherry
dairy
fairy
ferry

Gary
hairy
Harry
Larry
marry
Mary
merry
prairie
scary
tarry
Terry
vary
very
wary

canary
contrary
library
primary
raspberry
remarry
Rosemary
strawberry
tooth fairy

adversary
arbitrary
aviary
cemetery
commentary
culinary
customary
dictionary
dietary
dignitary
dromedary
February
fragmentary
honorary
January

legendary
literary
mercenary
military
missionary
momentary
monastery
mortuary
necessary
ordinary
planetary
sanctuary
sanitary
secondary
secretary
sedentary
solitary
stationary
stationery
temporary
visionary
voluntary

contemporary
disciplinary
extraordinary
hereditary
imaginary
itinerary
obituary
precautionary
preliminary
sugarplum fairy
unnecessary
vocabulary

revolutionary

as as in has,
see **azz**

asco
fiasco
Tabasco

ase 1 as in case,
see **ace**

ase 2 as in phase,
see **aze**

ased as in chased,
see **aste**

ash 1
ash
bash
brash
cache
cash
clash
crash
dash
flash
gash
gnash
hash
lash
mash
rash
sash
slash
smash

splash
stash
thrash
trash

backlash
eyelash
mishmash
mustache
news flash
whiplash

balderdash
corned beef hash
diaper rash
succotash

ash 2 as in wash,
see **osh**

ashy
flashy
splashy
trashy

asion
Asian

abrasion
Caucasian
equation
Eurasian
evasion
invasion
occasion
persuasion

ask

ask
bask
cask
flask
mask ---→
task

asket

basket
casket
gasket

asm

chasm
spasm

sarcasm

enthusiasm

ason

basin
chasten
hasten
Jason
mason

asp

clasp
gasp
grasp
rasp

ass

ass
bass
brass
class

crass
gas
glass
grass
lass
mass
pass
sass

amass
bypass
first class
harass
hourglass
impasse
spyglass
surpass
tear gas
trespass

boarding pass
bonny lass
laughing gas
looking glass
middle-class
out of gas
overpass
sassafras
smooth as glass

head of the class
snake in the grass

magnifying glass

assed as in passed, see ast

assy

brassy
chassis
classy
glassy
grassy
sassy

Tallahassee

ast

blast
cast
caste
fast
gassed
last
mast
passed
past
sassed
vast

aghast
amassed
at last
bombast
broadcast
contrast
downcast
forecast
full blast
gymnast
halfmast
harassed
miscast
newscast
outcast
outclassed
outlast

sandblast
steadfast
surpassed
typecast

all-star cast
flabbergast
overcast
telecast
unsurpassed

enthusiast
iconoclast

aste

aced
baste
braced
chased
chaste
faced
graced
haste
laced
paced
paste
placed
raced
spaced
taste
traced
waist
waste

bad taste
defaced
disgraced
displaced
distaste
embraced
erased

fast paced
good taste
misplaced
red-faced
replaced
retraced
straitlaced
toothpaste
two-faced
unlaced

aftertaste
baby-faced
cut-and-paste
freckle-faced
haste makes waste
interlaced
interspaced

hazardous waste

asten as in chasten, see ason

aster

blaster
faster
master
pastor
plaster
vaster

bandmaster
broadcaster
disaster
forecaster
headmaster
newscaster - - - - ▶
postmaster
sandblaster

schoolmaster
scoutmaster

alabaster

astic

drastic
plastic
spastic

bombastic
elastic
fantastic
gymnastic
sarcastic
scholastic

ecclesiastic
enthusiastic
interscholastic

asty

hasty
tasty

at 1

at
bat
brat
cat
chat
fat

flat
gnat
hat
mat
pat
rat
sat
spat
splat
that
vat

chitchat
combat
dingbat
doormat
fat cat
format
hardhat
muskrat
nonfat
pack rat
place mat
tomcat
wildcat
wombat

acrobat
alley cat
army brat
baby fat
baby-sat
bureaucrat
copy cat
cowboy hat
democrat
diplomat
dirty rat
fraidy cat
habitat

laundromat
pussycat
smell a rat
thermostat
this and that
tit for tat
welcome mat

aristocrat
blind as a bat
calico cat

at 2 as in swat, see ot

atch 1

batch
catch
hatch
latch
match
patch
scratch
snatch
thatch

arm patch
attach
detach
dispatch
knee patch
mismatch
unlatch

boxing match
cabbage patch
mix and match
reattach

atch 2 as in watch, see otch

atchy

catchy
patchy
scratchy

Apache

ate

ate
bait
crate
date
eight
fate
freight
gait
gate
grate
great
hate
Kate
late
mate
plate
rate
skate
slate
state
straight
strait
trait
wait
weight

await
birthrate

27

blind date
cellmate
cheapskate
checkmate
classmate
Colgate
create
debate
deflate
donate
elate
equate
estate
first-rate
frustrate
gyrate
helpmate
ice skate
inflate
ingrate
inmate
innate
locate
mandate
migrate
narrate
ornate
playmate
primate
prom date
pulsate
rebate
relate
rotate
sedate
stagnate
stalemate
tailgate
translate

update
vacate
vibrate

activate
advocate
aggravate
agitate
allocate
amputate
animate
calculate
candidate
captivate
celebrate
chief of state
circulate
complicate
concentrate
confiscate
contemplate
cultivate
decorate
dedicate
delegate
demonstrate
detonate
devastate
deviate
dislocate
dominate
double-date
duplicate
educate
elevate
emigrate
escalate
estimate
excavate

fascinate
fluctuate
formulate
fumigate
generate
Golden Gate
graduate
gravitate
heavyweight
hesitate
hibernate
hyphenate
illustrate
imitate
immigrate
indicate
infiltrate
instigate
integrate
irrigate
irritate
isolate
legislate
liberate
liquidate
lubricate
medicate
meditate
motivate
mutilate
nauseate
navigate
nominate
operate
out-of-date
overate
overrate
overstate
overweight

paperweight
penetrate
percolate
populate
punctuate
radiate
real estate
regulate
roller skate ----------
second-rate
segregate
separate
situate
speculate
stimulate
strangulate
suffocate
terminate
tolerate
underrate
underweight
up-to-date
vaccinate
validate
vindicate
violate

abbreviate
accelerate
accommodate
accumulate
alienate
alleviate
annihilate
anticipate
appreciate
asphyxiate
assassinate
associate

at any rate
carbohydrate
communicate
congratulate
contaminate
cooperate
coordinate
deliberate
discriminate
elaborate
eliminate
emancipate
evacuate
evaluate
evaporate
exaggerate
exasperate
exhilarate
exterminate
hallucinate
humiliate
illuminate
impersonate
initiate
inoculate
insinuate
interrogate
intimidate
intoxicate
investigate
invigorate
manipulate
officiate
participate
procrastinate
recuperate
reiterate
retaliate
reverberate

ater 1 as in later, see ader

ater 2 as in water, see otter

ath
bath
math
path
wrath

birdbath
steam bath
warpath

aftermath
bubble-bath ----------
psychopath

ather 1
gather
lather
rather

ather 2
bother
father

godfather
grandfather
no bother

atial as in spatial, see acial

atic

attic
static

asthmatic
dramatic
ecstatic
erratic
fanatic
traumatic

acrobatic
Adriatic
aromatic
Asiatic
autocratic
automatic
bureaucratic
charismatic
democratic
diplomatic
Instamatic
mathematic
problematic
symptomatic
systematic

aristocratic
melodramatic
psychosomatic

idiosyncratic
semiautomatic

atin

fatten
flatten

Latin
satin

Manhattan
pig Latin

ation

nation
station

citation
creation
Dalmatian ------
dictation
donation
duration
elation
fire station
fixation
flirtation
formation
foundation
frustration
inflation
location
migration
ovation
plantation
probation
quotation
relation
rotation
starvation
summation
taxation
vacation
vibration

adaptation
admiration

aggravation
agitation
animation
application
aviation
calculation
cancellation
celebration
circulation
combination
complication
concentration
confirmation
congregation
consolation
conversation
corporation
declaration
decoration
dedication
dehydration
demonstration
desperation
destination
devastation
duplication
elevation
expectation
explanation
exploration
fabrication
fascination
generation
graduation
hesitation
illustration
imitation
immigration
inflammation

information
innovation
inspiration
integration
irritation
isolation
legislation
liberation
limitation
medication
meditation
moderation
motivation
mutilation
nomination
obligation
observation
occupation
operation
perspiration
population
preparation
presentation
preservation
punctuation
radiation
recreation
registration
regulation
relaxation
reputation
reservation
resignation
revelation
segregation
separation
situation
speculation
stimulation

transportation
variation
violation

abbreviation
acceleration
anticipation
appreciation
assassination
civilization
communication
consideration
cooperation
coordination
determination
discrimination
elimination
evaluation
exasperation
extermination
hallucination
humiliation
imagination
impersonation
initiation
interpretation
interrogation
intimidation
intoxication
investigation
justification
manipulation
multiplication
notification
organization
participation
procrastination
pronunciation
qualification
realization

recommendation
retaliation
sophistication
verification

atious as in flirtatious, see **acious**

ator as in narrator, see **ader**

atten as in flatten, see **atin**

atter
batter
bladder
chatter
clatter
fatter
flatter
gladder
ladder
latter
madder
matter
platter
sadder
scatter
shatter
splatter
tatter

gallbladder
gray matter
Mad Hatter

31

no matter

hook and ladder
pitter-patter

attery
battery
flattery

attle
battle
cattle
paddle
prattle
rattle
saddle
straddle
tattle

dog paddle
Seattle
sidesaddle
skedaddle

atty
batty
bratty
caddie
catty
chatty
daddy
faddy
fatty
patty
ratty

granddaddy
rice paddy

Cincinnati

aud as in fraud, see awed

aught as in taught, see ot

aughter as in daughter, see otter

aughty as in naughty, see ody

aul as in haul, see all

auled as in hauled, see alled

ault as in fault, see alt

aulter as in vaulter, see alter

aults as in faults, see alts

aunch
conch
haunch

launch
paunch
staunch

aunder as in launder, see onder

aunt
aunt
daunt
flaunt
gaunt
haunt
jaunt
taunt
want

bouffant --
Vermont

confidante
debutante
dilettante
nonchalant
restaurant

aur as in dinosaur, see ore

ause
cause
clause
claws

flaws
gauze
jaws
laws
pause
paws
straws
vase

applause
because
jigsaws
lost cause
outlaws
seesaws

Santa Claus
Wizard of Oz

aust as in exhaust, see ost 2

aut as in taut, see ot

avage
ravage
savage

ave
brave
cave
crave
gave
grave
knave
pave
rave

save
shave
slave
waive
wave

behave
brainwave
engrave
forgave
heat wave
shockwave

aftershave
galley slave
microwave
misbehave
rant and rave
tidal wave

avel
gavel
gravel
travel

unravel

aver
braver
favor
flavor
savor
shaver
waiver
waver

disfavor
flag-waver
lifesaver
time-saver

avery
Avery
bravery
savory
slavery

unsavory

avity
cavity
gravity

depravity

law of gravity

avor as in favor, see aver

avy
gravy
navy
wavy

aw
ah
awe
blah
claw
draw
flaw
gnaw
hah
jaw
law
ma
pa
paw
raw

awed to awled

saw
spa
straw
thaw

ga-ga
grandma
grandpa
ha ha
hoopla
hurrah
jigsaw
last straw
outdraw
outlaw
seesaw
southpaw
Utah
withdraw

Arkansas
hem and haw
la de da
Mardi Gras
Omaha
Panama
Wichita

awed

awed
broad
Claude
clawed
clod
flawed
fraud
gnawed
God
mod
nod

odd
pawed
plod
pod
prod
quad
rod
sawed
squad
Todd
trod
wad

abroad
applaud
Cape Cod
facade
hot rod
outlawed
pea pod
seesawed
slipshod
spit-wad
tightwad
tripod
vice squad

act of God
cattle prod
firing squad
fishing rod
goldenrod
hemmed and hawed
land of Nod
lightning rod
promenade
riot squad

awful

awful
lawful
waffle

falafel
unlawful

awk as in hawk, see ock

awks as in hawks, see ox

awky

cocky
gawky
hockey
jockey
rocky
stocky

disc jockey
ice hockey
Milwaukee

Jabberwocky
teriyaki
walkie-talkie

awl as in crawl, see all

awled as in crawled, see alled

awler as in brawler, see **aller**

awly as in crawly, see **olly**

awn

con
dawn
don
drawn
fawn
gone
John
lawn
on
pawn
Ron
spawn
swan
yawn

Antoine
baton
bon-bon
Cézanne
chiffon
coupon
doggone
Don Juan
ex-con
Iran
long gone
pecan
python
run-on
Saigon
salon

Szechwan
Taiwan
Tucson
upon
withdrawn
won ton
Yukon
Yvonne

Amazon
Audubon
Avalon
Babylon
crack of dawn
decathlon
Genghis Khan
hanger-on
hexagon
leprechaun
liaison
marathon
Mazatlán
octagon
off and on
overdrawn
paragon
parmesan
pentagon
pro and con
silicon
talkathon
woebegone

phenomenon
Saskatchewan

awned as in dawned, see **ond**

awns as in lawns, see **ons**

awny

bonny
brawny
Connie
Johnny
scrawny
tawny

aws as in claws, see **ause**

ax

acts
ax
backs
cracks
facts
fax
jacks
lacks
lax
packs
plaques
quacks
racks
sacks
sax
shacks
slacks

35

smacks
snacks
stacks
tax
tracks
wax
yaks

attacks
attracts
climax
contacts
distracts
drawbacks
earwax
haystacks
ice packs
kayaks
lilacs
reacts
relax
subtracts
thumbtacks
unpacks
wisecracks

artifacts
Cadillacs
candle wax
Cracker Jacks
heart attacks
income tax
interacts
jumping jacks
maniacs
overacts
railroad tracks

overreacts

axi

taxi
waxy

ay

bay
bray
clay
day
fray
gay
gray
hay
hey
lay
may
nay
neigh
pay
play
pray
prey
ray
say
slay
sleigh
spray
stay
stray
sway
they
tray
way
weigh

away
ballet
birthday
blue jay

bouquet
cafe
croquet
decay
delay
display
essay
gangway
halfway
hallway
headway
highway
ice tray
Norway
obey
okay
one-way
railway
relay
repay
role-play
runway
someway
stairway
stingray
subway
survey
Taipei
today
weekday
x-ray

by the way
day by day
disobey

everyday
faraway
holiday
matinee
Milky Way
night and day
play-by-play
protégé
PTA
right-of-way
runaway
San Jose
Santa Fe
stowaway
throwaway
tooth decay
underway
USA
yesterday

any which way
April Fools' Day
day after day
far and away
happy birthday
out of the way
rub the wrong way
St. Patrick's Day
vitamin A

TWA

ayed as in played,
see **ade** 1

ayer
grayer
layer
mayor

player
betrayer
conveyor
soothsayer
surveyor
taxpayer

ays as in days,
see **aze**

aze
bays
blaze
craze
days
daze
faze
gaze
glaze
graze
haze
laze
maze
nays
pays
phase
phrase
plays
praise
prays
raise
rays
slays
sprays
stays
strays
sways

trays
ways
weighs

ablaze
always
amaze
ballets
betrays
birthdays
blue jays
bouquets
cafes
decays
delays
displays
essays
hallways
obeys
okays
outweighs
portrays
railways
repays
rephrase
school days
sideways
stargaze
subways
surveys
trailblaze
x-rays

disobeys
gamma rays
holidays
mayonnaise
nowadays
paraphrase
runaways

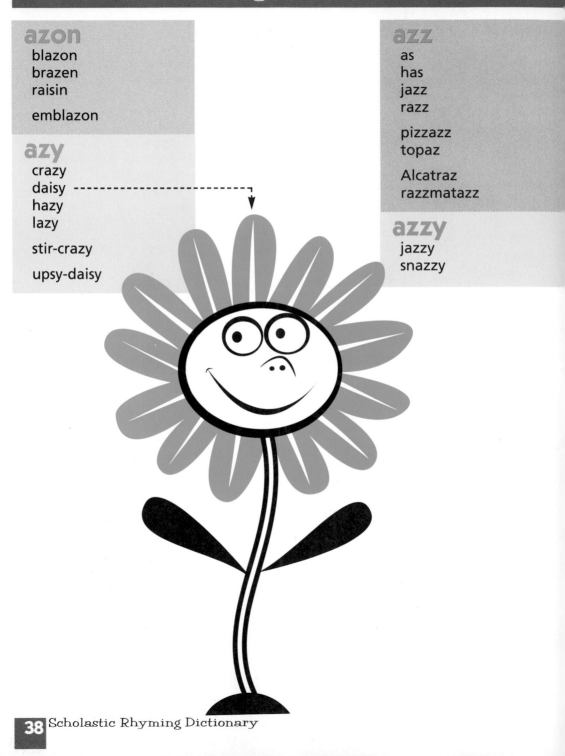

azon
blazon
brazen
raisin

emblazon

azy
crazy
daisy
hazy
lazy

stir-crazy

upsy-daisy

azz
as
has
jazz
razz

pizzazz
topaz

Alcatraz
razzmatazz

azzy
jazzy
snazzy

e as in be,
see **ee**

ea as in flea,
see **ee**

each
beach
bleach
each
leech
peach
preach
reach
screech
speech
teach

free speech
impeach
outreach

figure of speech

eacher
bleacher
creature
feature
preacher
screecher
teacher

ead 1 as in plead,
see **eed**

ead 2 as in bread,
see **ed**

eader 1 as in leader
see **eeder**

eader 2
as in deader,
see **etter**

eady as in ready,
see **etty**

eager
eager
meager

little leaguer
overeager

eagle as in beagle,
see **egal**

eague
league

big league
blitzkrieg
colleague
fatigue
intrigue

Little League

eak 1 as weak,
see **eek**

eak ½ as in break,
see **ake**

eaker
beaker
peeker
sneaker
speaker
weaker

loudspeaker

eaky
creaky
freaky
geeky
leaky
sneaky
squeaky

eal as in real,
see **eel**

ealed as in healed,
see **ield**

eally
freely
really
wheelie

ideally
Swahili

ealous
jealous
tell us
zealous

expel us

overzealous

eam as in dream, see eem

eamy
creamy
dreamy
Mimi
preemie
steamy

sashimi

ean as in bean, see een

eap as in leap, see eep

eaper as in cheaper, see eeper

ear 1 as in pear, see air

ear 2 as in year, see eer

earch as in search, see urch

earer
clearer
dearer
mirror
nearer

severer
sincerer

interferer

earful
cheerful
earful
fearful
tearful

earl as in pearl, see url

early as in pearly, see urly

earn as in learn, see urn

earse as in hearse, see erse

earth as in earth, see irth

eary as in weary, see eery

eas as in fleas, see eeze

ease 1 as in please, see eeze

ease 2
cease
crease
fleece
geese
grease
Greece
lease
niece
peace
piece

apiece
caprice
Clarisse
Cochise
decease
decrease
hairpiece
increase
Matisse
Maurice
obese
police
release
timepiece
wild geese
world peace

centerpiece
elbow grease
Golden Fleece
masterpiece -------
piece by piece
press release
time-release

all in one piece
gaggle of geese
secret police

justice of the peace

eason
reason
season
treason

out of season
stands to reason

east
beast
ceased
creased
east
feast
greased
least
pieced
priest
yeast

deceased
decreased
Far East
increased
Near East
policed
released

Middle East
wildebeest

last but not least

beauty and the beast

easure
measure
pleasure
treasure

displeasure
tape measure

easy
breezy
cheesy
easy
queasy
sneezy

Parcheesi
uneasy
Zambezi

eat 1 as in beat, see eet

eat 2 as in great, see ate

eat 3 as in sweat, see et

eaten
beaten
cretin
eaten
neaten
sweeten

browbeaten
moth-eaten -----------

weatherbeaten

eater as in heater, see eeder

eath 1
breath
death

bad breath
Macbeth

kiss of death
out of breath
scared to death
starve to death

Elizabeth
tickled to death

eath 2

Keith
teeth
wreath

beneath
bequeath
false teeth

underneath

eather

feather
Heather
leather
tether
weather
whether

fair-weather
together

altogether
get-together
tar and feather

birds of a feather
light as a feather
under the weather

eature as in

creature,
see eacher

eaty as in meaty,

see eedy

eave

eve
grieve
heave
leave
sleeve
Steve
weave
we've

achieve
believe
conceive
deceive
naive
perceive
pet peeve
receive
relieve
retrieve
shirtsleeve
sick leave

Christmas Eve
make believe
Tel Aviv

Adam and Eve

eaver

beaver
cleaver
fever
weaver

achiever
believer
hay fever
meat cleaver
receiver

spring fever

basket weaver
eager beaver
nonbeliever
scarlet fever

golden retriever
overachiever
underachiever

ebble

pebble
rebel
treble

eck

check
Czech
deck
fleck
heck
neck
peck
speck
trek
wreck

Aztec
hi-tech
paycheck
Quebec
raincheck

roughneck
shipwreck
spot-check
Star Trek

bottleneck
discotheque
double-check
hit the deck
hunt and peck
leatherneck
neck and neck
rubberneck
turtleneck

pain in the neck

ecked as in

checked,
see **ect**

eckle

freckle
heckle
Jekyll

ecks as in decks,
see **ex**

ecord

checkered
record

ect

checked
decked
flecked

sect
trekked
wrecked

affect
collect
connect
correct
defect
detect
direct
dissect
effect
eject
elect
erect
expect
infect
inject
insect
inspect
neglect
object
perfect
project
prospect
protect
reflect
reject
respect
select
shipwrecked
subject
suspect

architect
disconnect
disinfect
disrespect
double-checked

incorrect
indirect
intellect
intersect
recollect
reelect
self-respect
sound effect

cause and effect

ection

section

affection
collection
complexion
conception
connection
correction
cross-section
dejection
direction
ejection
election
infection
inflection
injection
inspection
objection
perfection
protection
reflection
rejection
selection

imperfection
interjection
intersection
recollection

resurrection
house of correction
sense of direction

ective

defective
detective
effective
elective
objective
perspective
reflective
selective
subjective

ineffective
retrospective

overprotective

ector

Hector
nectar
specter

collector
connector
defector
detector
director
inspector
projector
protector
reflector

ects as in insects,
see **ex**

ed

bed
bled
bread
bred
dead
dread
Ed
fed
fled
head
lead
led
read
red
said
shed
shred
sled
sped
spread
Ted
thread
tread
wed

ahead
bald head
behead
biped
blockhead
bloodshed
bobsled
bonehead

bunkbed
Club Med
coed
deathbed
drop dead
egghead
forehead
French bread
hardhead
homestead
ill-bred
inbred
instead
misread
moped
proofread
purebred
redhead
sickbed
spoonfed
spearhead
unsaid
unwed
well-bred
well-fed
widespread

arrowhead
bottlefed
city-bred
figurehead
gingerbread
Grateful Dead
infrared
knucklehead
letterhead
newlywed
overfed
overhead

sleepyhead
straight ahead
Sudafed
thoroughbred
underfed
waterbed

early to bed
full speed ahead
hole in the head
out of your head

edal as in pedal, see eddle

edder as in shredder, see etter

eddle

Gretel
kettle
medal
meddle
metal
pedal
peddle
petal
settle

backpedal
gold medal
rose petal
teakettle
unsettle

heavy metal

Hansel and Gretel

ede as in proceed, see eed

edge

dredge
edge
hedge
ledge
pledge
veg
wedge

allege
on edge

edic

comedic

orthopedic

edicate

dedicate
medicate

edo

Frito
neat-o
veto

bandito
Benito
burrito
Toledo
torpedo
tuxedo

incognito

ee

be
bee
fee
flea
flee
free
gee
glee
he
key
knee
me
pea
plea
sea
see
she
ski
spree
tea
tee
three
tree
we

agree
carefree
deep-sea
degree
emcee
home free
ID
M.D.
Marie
monkey
off-key
peewee
queen bee

RV
sightsee
sweet pea
tax-free
tee hee
teepee

absentee
bumblebee
caffeine-free
chimpanzee
Christmas tree
disagree
employee
fancy free
guarantee
jamboree
nominee
oversee
pardon me
pedigree
Ph.D.
referee
refugee
Rosemarie
shopping spree
spelling bee
sugar-free
Tennessee
VIP
water ski
worry-free

college degree
family tree
fiddle-de-dee
land of the free

under lock and key
Washington, D.C.

eech as in speech, see each

eed

bead
bleed
breed
creed
deed
feed
freed
greed
heed
knead
kneed
lead
need
plead
read
reed
seed
skied
speed
steed
treed
tweed
weed

agreed
concede
exceed
force-feed
full speed
impede
indeed
lip-read
mislead
nosebleed

precede
proceed
proofread
recede
seaweed
speed-read
stampede
succeed

centipede
disagreed
guaranteed
overfeed
refereed
supersede
tumbleweed
up to speed

eeder

beater
bleeder
cedar
cheater
eater
feeder
heater
leader
liter
meter
neater
Peter
reader
speeder
sweeter
teeter
weeder

anteater
bandleader
born leader

cheerleader
fire eater
gang leader
impeder
mind-reader
proofreader
repeater
ringleader
Saint Peter
two-seater

centimeter
kilometer
meter reader
overeater
parking meter
trick-or-treater

eedle

beetle
needle
wheedle

eedy

beady
greedy
meaty
needy
seedy
speedy
sweetie
treaty
weedy

entreaty
graffiti
peace treaty
Tahiti

eef as in beef, see ief

eek

beak
bleak
cheek
creak
creek
freak
geek
Greek
leak
meek
peak
peek
pique
reek
seek
shriek
sleek
sneak
speak
squeak
streak
tweak
weak
week

antique
boutique
critique
midweek
misspeak
mystique
oblique
physique
pip-squeak

technique
unique

cheek-to-cheek
Chesapeake
hide-and-seek
so to speak
tongue in cheek

eeker as in peeker, see eaker

eel

deal
eel
feel
heal
heel
keel
kneel
meal
peel
real
reel
seal
squeal
steal
steel
teal
veal
wheel
zeal

appeal
bastille
big deal
cartwheel
chenille
conceal

congeal
fair deal
for real
genteel
high heel
ideal
misdeal
mobile
newsreel
oatmeal
ordeal
piecemeal
reveal
unreal

bookmobile
Ferris wheel
glockenspiel
no big deal
Oldsmobile

automobile

eeled as in peeled, see ield

eem

beam
cream
deem
dream
gleam
ream
scheme
scream
seam
seem
steam
stream

team
teem
theme

bloodstream
daydream
downstream
drill team
esteem
extreme
ice cream
mainstream
moonbeam
pipe dream
redeem
regime
sunbeam
supreme
whipped cream

color scheme
double-team
let off steam
self-esteem
sour cream

een

bean
clean
dean
gene
glean
green
Jean
keen
lean
mean
queen - - - - - - - - -
scene
screen

seen
sheen
teen

Bactine
between
caffeine
canteen
chlorine
Colleen
convene
cuisine
Darlene
dry clean
eighteen
Eugene
fifteen
fourteen
green bean
hygiene
Irene
Kathleen
machine
marine
Marlene
Maxine
mob scene
obscene
preteen
prom queen
protein
ravine
routine
sardine
serene
sixteen
smokescreen
sunscreen
thirteen

unseen
vaccine

evergreen
fairy queen
gasoline
go-between
guillotine
Halloween
intervene
jelly bean
Josephine
kerosene
lean and mean
limousine
magazine
Maybelline
mezzanine
movie screen
nectarine
nicotine
quarantine
serpentine
seventeen
squeaky clean
submarine
sweet sixteen
tambourine
tangerine
trampoline
Vaseline

eep

beep
bleep
cheap
creep
deep
heap

jeep
keep
leap
peep
reap
seep
sheep
sleep
steep
sweep
weep

asleep
Bo Peep
junkheap
knee-deep
skin-deep

beauty sleep
oversleep

eeper

beeper
cheaper
creeper
deeper
keeper
reaper
sleeper
steeper
sweeper
weeper

housekeeper
timekeeper

eepy

creepy
sleepy
tepee
weepy

eer

beer
cheer
clear
dear
deer
ear
fear
gear
hear
here
jeer
leer
mere
near
peer
pier
rear
sheer
smear
sneer
spear
sphere
steer
tear
tier
veer
year

adhere
all clear
appear
career
cashier
cashmere
frontier
leap year
pierced ear
premier

reindeer
root beer
severe
Shakespeare
sincere
unclear

atmosphere
auctioneer
buccaneer
cavalier
chandelier
crystal-clear
disappear
engineer
far and near
free and clear
hemisphere
insincere
interfere
loud and clear
mouseketeer
musketeer
mutineer
never fear
overhear
Paul Revere
persevere
pioneer
racketeer
reappear
souvenir
stratosphere
volunteer

eery

cheery
dearie
dreary

eerie
leery
query
teary
theory
weary

hara-kiri

ees as in bees, see eeze

eese as in geese, see ease 2

eet

beat
beet
bleat
cheat
eat
feat
feet
fleet
greet
heat
meat
meet
neat
Pete
pleat
seat
sheet
sleet
street
suite
sweet
treat

tweet
wheat

athlete
backseat
browbeat
cold feet
compete
complete
conceit
concrete
deadbeat
deceit
defeat
delete
discreet
discrete
elite
excrete
flat feet
heartbeat
mistreat
off-beat
petite
receipt
repeat
retreat
secrete
upbeat
Wall Street

bittersweet
incomplete
indiscreet
overeat
parakeet
short and sweet
shredded wheat
stocking feet
trick or treat

two left feet

red as a beet
Sesame Street

eeter as in sweeter, see eeder

eethe
breathe
seethe
teethe

eeve as in sleeve, see eave

eeze
bees
breeze
cheese
ease
fees
fleas
flees
frees
freeze
keys
knees
peas
pleas
please
seas
sees
seize
skis
sneeze
sprees

teas
tease
these
trees
wheeze

agrees
big cheese
Chinese
cream cheese
deep freeze
degrees
disease
displease
foresees
high seas
Louise
monkeys
sea breeze
sweet peas
tepees
trapeze
TVs

ABCs
Androcles
antifreeze
bumblebees
chickadees
chimpanzees
cottage cheese
disagrees
dungarees
guarantees
Hercules
ill at ease
jamborees
Japanese
nominees
overseas

oversees
pedigrees
pretty please
referees
shopping sprees
Siamese
Socrates
water skis

eezer
Caesar
freezer
geezer
squeezer
tweezer

eezy as in breezy, see easy

ef
chef
clef
deaf
Jeff
ref

eft
deft
left
theft

eg
beg
egg
Greg
keg
leg

Meg
peg

nest egg
renege

Winnipeg

egal
beagle
eagle
legal
regal

bald eagle - - - - - -
illegal

egion
legion
region

collegian
Norwegian

eigh as in sleigh,
see **ay**

eight as in weight,
see **ate**

eighty as in weighty,
see **ady**

eir as in their,
see **air**

eist as in heist,
see **iced**

eit as in conceit,
see **eet**

eive as in receive,
see **eave**

el as in hotel,
see **ell**

elch
belch
squelch
welch

eld
held
jelled
meld
quelled
shelled
spelled
weld
yelled

beheld
compelled
excelled
expelled
hand-held
misspelled
propelled
rebelled
repelled
upheld
withheld

unparalleled

elf
elf
self
shelf

bookshelf
herself
himself
itself
myself
yourself

ell
bell
belle
cell
dwell
fell
gel
hell
jell
Nell
sell
shell
smell
spell
swell
tell
well
yell

Adele
bombshell
compel
doorbell
dumbbell
eggshell
excel
expel

farewell
gazelle
hotel
inkwell
jail cell
lapel
Maxwell
misspell
motel
Noel
nutshell
pastel
propel
Raquel
rebel
repel
retell
schoolbell
sleighbell
unwell

carousel
clientele
dinner bell
Isabel
magic spell
NFL
oil well
parallel
personnel
Raphael
show and tell
Tinker Bell
very well
William Tell
wishing well

clear as a bell
mademoiselle

ella

Della
Ella
fella
Stella

umbrella

a cappella
Cinderella
Isabella
mozzarella

ellar as in stellar, see eller

elle as in belle, see ell

elled as in spelled, see eld

eller

cellar
dweller
feller
seller
speller
stellar
teller
yeller

cave dweller
propeller
storm cellar

fortune-teller ----------→
interstellar
Rockefeller

ello as in cello, see ellow

ellow

bellow
cello
fellow
hello
Jell-O
mellow
yellow

Longfellow
marshmallow

elly

belly
deli
jelly
Kelly
Nellie
Shelley
smelly

New Delhi
potbelly

elp

help
kelp
yelp

elt
belt
Celt
dealt
felt
knelt
melt
pelt
svelte
welt

heartfelt
seat belt

elter
shelter
smelter
swelter

helter-skelter

elve
delve
shelve
twelve

em
gem
hem
stem
them

A.M.
condemn
FM
P.M.

ember
ember
member

December
gang member
November
remember
September

emble
tremble

assemble
resemble

eme as in theme, see eem

empt
dreamt
tempt

attempt
contempt
exempt

en
Ben
den
hen
men
pen
ten
than
then
when
yen

again
amen
bullpen
Cheyenne
hang ten
pigpen
playpen

Adrienne
lion's den
mother hen
now and then
poison pen

ena
Gina
Tina

arena
cantina
Christina
hyena
marina
subpoena

Argentina
ballerina
Pasadena

ence as in fence, see ense

ench

bench
clench
drench
French
quench
stench
trench
wrench

park bench
unclench

monkey wrench

encher as in

quencher,
see **enture**

encil

pencil
stencil

utensil

end

bend
blend
end
friend
lend
mend
penned
send
spend
tend
trend

amend

ascend
attend
best friend
boyfriend
dead end
defend
depend
descend
extend
girlfriend
intend
offend
pretend
suspend
transcend
unbend
upend
wit's end

apprehend
bitter end
comprehend
dividend
end-to-end
man's best friend
overspend
recommend

fair-weather friend

ender

blender
fender
gender
lender
render
sender
slender
splendor
tender

vendor

bartender
contender
defender
goaltender
offender
pretender
surrender
suspender

endor as in splendor,
see **ender**

ene as in gene,
see **een**

ength

length
strength

enny

any
Benny
Denny
Jenny
Kenny
many
penny

55

ense

cents
dense
dents
fence
gents
scents
sense
tense
tents
vents

commence
condense
defense
dispense
expense
good sense
immense
incense
intense
make sense
nonsense
offense
percents
presents
pretense
resents
sixth sense
suspense

common sense
compliments
consequence
evidence
false pretense
no-nonsense
represents
self-defense

dollars and cents

ension as in tension, see ention

ensity

density

immensity
intensity

ensive

pensive

defensive
expensive
extensive
intensive
offensive

apprehensive
comprehensive
inexpensive

labor-intensive

ent

bent
cent
dent
gent
Lent
meant
rent
scent
sent
spent
tent
vent
went

air vent

cement
consent
content
descent
dissent
event
extent
for rent
frequent
indent
intent
invent
lament
misspent
percent
present
prevent
repent
resent
torment
well-spent

came and went
circus tent
compliment
discontent
evident
heaven sent
implement
malcontent
represent
underwent

blessed event
experiment
misrepresent

ental

dental
gentle
lentil
mental
rental

judgmental
parental

accidental
continental
departmental
detrimental
elemental
fundamental
governmental
incidental
instrumental
monumental
ornamental
sentimental
temperamental
transcendental

coincidental
environmental
experimental

enter

center
enter
mentor

dissenter
inventor
off center
presenter
reenter
tormentor

civic center
do not enter
front and center
shopping center

ential

credential
essential
potential
torrential

confidential
deferential
influential
preferential
presidential
residential

ention

mention
pension
tension

attention
convention
detention
dimension
dissension
extension
intention
invention
pretension
prevention
suspension

apprehension
comprehension
hypertension
inattention
intervention

not to mention
three dimension

misapprehension
ounce of prevention

honorable mention

entive

attentive
incentive
inventive
preventive

ently

gently

contently
intently

consequently
evidently
incidentally

entor as in mentor, see enter

ents as in cents, see ense

enture

censure
denture
quencher
venture

adventure
fist clencher
joint venture
thirst quencher

ep

pep
prep
schlep
step
strep
yep

bicep
doorstep
sidestep

overstep

epped as in stepped,

see **ept**

ept

crept
kept
pepped
slept
stepped
swept
wept

accept
concept
except
inept
rainswept
sidestepped
windswept

intercept
overslept
overstepped

eption

conception
deception
exception
perception
reception

depth perception
interception
misconception

er

blur
burr
err
fir
fur
gr-r-r
her
per
purr
sir
slur
spur
stir
were

astir
Ben Hur
concur
confer
defer
demur
deter
infer
occur
prefer
refer
yes sir

emperor
him and her

erb as in verb,

see **urb**

erce as in coerce,

see **erse**

erd

bird
blurred
erred
heard
herd
purred
slurred
spurred
stirred
third
word

absurd
backward
Big Bird
blackbird

buzzword
code word
concurred
conferred
crossword
deferred
deterred
forward
inferred
jailbird
lovebird - - - - - -
occurred
one-third
password
preferred
referred
songbird
swearword
transferred
unheard
watchword

afterward
early bird
hummingbird
ladybird
massacred
mockingbird
overheard
reoccurred
self-assured
solemn word
word for word

four-letter word
free as a bird

ere 1 as in sphere, see eer

ere 2 as in there, see air

erer as in sincerer, see earer

erge
merge
purge
splurge
surge
urge
verge

converge
diverge
emerge
submerge

ergent
urgent

detergent
divergent
emergent
insurgent

eria
Syria

Algeria
bacteria
diphtheria
Nigeria
Siberia

cafeteria

erious
serious

delirious
mysterious

erish
bearish
cherish
garish
perish

erit as in merit, see arrot

erity as in sincerity, see arity

erk
clerk
irk
jerk
Kirk
lurk
perk
quirk
shirk
smirk
Turk
work

berserk
brain-work
clockwork
footwork
framework
groundwork
guesswork

homework
housework
legwork
network
patchwork
schoolwork
teamwork
woodwork

dirty work
handiwork
out of work
overwork

erky

jerky
murky
perky
quirky
turkey

beef jerky
cold turkey

Albuquerque

erm

firm
germ
perm
squirm
term
worm

affirm
bookworm
confirm
earthworm
glowworm
long-term
midterm

silkworm

pachyderm
wiggle worm

ern as in stern, see urn

ernal

colonel
journal
kernel

eternal
external
fraternal
internal
maternal
nocturnal
paternal

ero 1

hero
Nero
zero

ero 2 as in sombrero, see arrow

erred as in transferred, see erd

error as in terror, see arer

erry as in cherry, see ary

erse

curse
hearse
nurse - - - →
purse
terse
verse
worse

adverse
coerce
commerce
converse
disperse
diverse
immerse
inverse
rehearse
reverse
submerse
transverse

intersperse
reimburse
universe

ersed as in conversed, see irst

ersion

Persian
version

aversion

coercion
conversion
diversion
excursion
immersion
submersion

ersity
adversity
diversity

university

erson
person
worsen

layperson
spokesperson

ert
Bert
blurt
curt
dirt
flirt
hurt
pert
shirt
skirt
spurt
squirt

alert
assert
avert
convert
covert
desert
dessert

divert
exert
Frankfurt
insert
invert
nightshirt
overt
pay dirt
redshirt
stuffed shirt
subvert
unhurt

extrovert
hula skirt
introvert
miniskirt
smog alert
undershirt

overexert

erter
herder
murder
squirter

absurder
converter
deserter
frankfurter

erve
curve
nerve
serve
swerve
verve
conserve
deserve

hors d'oeuvre
observe
preserve
reserve
self-serve
unnerve

brown-and-serve

ery as in very,
see ary

escent
crescent

fluorescent
incessant

adolescent
convalescent
effervescent
iridescent

esh
flesh
fresh
mesh

enmesh
gooseflesh
refresh

Bangladesh
in the flesh

esident
hesitant
president
resident

61

esque
desk

burlesque
grotesque

picturesque

ess
Bess
bless
chess
dress
guess
less
mess
press
stress
Tess
yes

access
address
bench-press
caress
confess
depress
digress
distress
duress
excess
express
finesse
impress
Loch Ness
oppress
outguess
possess
profess
progress

recess
regress
repress
success
suppress
undress
unless

air express
fancy dress
full-court press
more or less
nonetheless
overdress
printing press
repossess
second-guess
s.o.s.

change of address
nevertheless
pony express

anybody's guess
freedom of the press
Gettysburg Address

essed as in blessed, see est

esser as in lesser, see essor

essful
stressful

distressful
successful

ession
freshen
session

aggression
concession
confession
depression
discretion
expression
impression
jam session
obsession
oppression
possession
procession
profession
progression
rap session
recession
refreshen
repression
succession
suppression

indiscretion
self-expression
summer session

essive
aggressive
excessive
expressive
impressive

obsessive
oppressive
possessive
progressive

essor

dresser
guesser
lesser
yes sir

aggressor
assessor
compressor
confessor
hairdresser
oppressor
possessor
processor
professor
successor

fancy dresser
food processor
predecessor
second-guesser
word processor

essy

dressy
Jessie
messy

est

best
blessed
breast
chest
crest
dressed

guessed
guest
jest
messed
nest
pest
pressed
quest
rest
stressed
test
vest
west
zest

addressed
arrest
bird nest
blood test
caressed
Celeste
confessed
conquest
contest
crow's nest
depressed
detest
digressed
distressed
expressed
finessed
fun fest
hope chest
impressed
invest

life vest
next best
obsessed
oppressed
outguessed
possessed
professed
progressed
protest
recessed
repressed
request
screen test
suggest
suppressed
undressed
Wild West

beauty rest
day of rest
decongest
false arrest
hornet's nest
last request
level best
manifest
overdressed
second best
treasure chest
unimpressed

bulletproof vest
medicine chest
permanent-pressed
under arrest

ester

Chester
Esther
fester

jester
Lester
pester
tester

ancestor
court jester
investor
protestor
semester

polyester

estion

question

congestion
digestion
suggestion

decongestion
indigestion
pop the question

out of the question

estor as in investor, see ester

et

bet
debt
fret
get
jet
met
net
pet
set
sweat

threat
vet
wet
whet
yet

abet
all set
all wet
brunette
cadet
cold sweat
coquette
Corvette
dragnet
dudette
duet
forget
Jeanette
jet set
no sweat
not yet
Paulette
quartet
regret
reset
sunset
Tibet
upset

alphabet
Antoinette
bassinet
bayonet
Bernadette
better yet
cigarette
clarinet
dripping wet
Juliet

majorette
minuet
out of debt
pirouette
safety net
silhouette
Soviet
suffragette
teacher's pet

mosquito net
national debt
Russian roulette

etal as in metal, see eddle

etch

etch
fetch
retch
sketch
stretch
wretch

homestretch

ete as in athlete, see eet

eter as in meter, see eeder

ether as in together, see eather

etic
athletic
cosmetic
frenetic
genetic
magnetic
pathetic
phonetic
poetic
synthetic

anesthetic
diabetic
dietetic
energetic
sympathetic

apologetic

ette as in brunette, see et

etter
better
cheddar
deader
debtor
letter
redder
shredder
sweater
wetter

fan letter
forgetter
go-getter
jet setter
love letter
newsletter

trendsetter
doubleheader
paper shredder

etti as in confetti, see etty

ettle as in kettle, see eddle

etto
ghetto
meadow

falsetto
Gepetto
libretto
stiletto

etty
Betty
Eddie
Freddie
heady
petty
ready
steady
sweaty
Teddy

already
confetti
go steady
machete
spaghetti
unsteady

rough and ready

eur as in chauffeur, see ure

evel
bevel
devil
level
revel

daredevil
dishevel

even
Devon
heaven
Kevin
seven

eleven
thank heaven

ever
clever
ever
lever
never
sever
Trevor

endeavor
forever
however
whatever
whenever
wherever
whichever
whoever

ew

blew
blue
boo
brew
chew
clue
crew
cue
dew
do
drew
due
ewe
few
flew
flu
glue
gnu
goo
grew
hue
knew
mew
moo
new
pew
pooh
rue
screw
shoe
slew
stew
sue
threw
through
to
too

true
two
view
who
woo
you
zoo

ado
ah-choo
anew
bamboo
boo-boo
boohoo
brand-new
breakthrough
canoe
cashew
choo-choo
construe
corkscrew
cuckoo
curfew
debut
dog-doo
drive-through
goo-goo
hairdo
horseshoe
how-to
into
IQ
kazoo
kung fu
miscue
misdo
muumuu
on cue
on view

outdo
outgrew
past due
Peru
PU
pursue
redo
renew
review
revue
Says who?
see-through
shampoo
snafu
subdue
taboo
tattoo
thank you
true blue
tutu
undo
unscrew
unto
untrue
voodoo
who's who
withdrew
world-view
yoo-hoo

avenue
ballyhoo
barbecue
bird's-eye view
black-and-blue
book review
buckaroo
bugaboo
caribou

cockatoo
countersue
curlicue
I love you
impromptu
interview
Irish stew
jujitsu
kangaroo
Malibu
misconstrue
navy blue
no can do
Oahu
overdo
overdue
peek-a-boo
point of view
postage due
quite a few
rendezvous
residue
revenue
stinkaroo
Super Glue
switcheroo
through and through
Timbuktu
toodle-oo
tried and true
two by two
Waterloo
well-to-do
whoop-de-do

catch-22
hullabaloo
out of the blue
red, white, and blue

skeleton crew
Winnie the Pooh

cock-a-doodle-doo
panoramic view

ewd as in shrewd,
see **ude**

ewed as in brewed,
see **ude**

ews as in chews,
see **use 2**

ewy
buoy
chewy
dewy
gooey
phooey
screwy

chop suey
mildewy

ex
checks
decks
ex
flecks
flex
hex
necks
pecks
sex
treks

vex
wrecks

affects
annex
apex
collects
complex
connects
corrects
defects
detects
directs
duplex
effects
ejects
elects
erects
expects
index
infects
injects
insects
inspects
Kleenex
neglects
objects
perfects
perplex
projects
prospects
protects
reflects
reflex
rejects
respects
selects
subjects
suspects

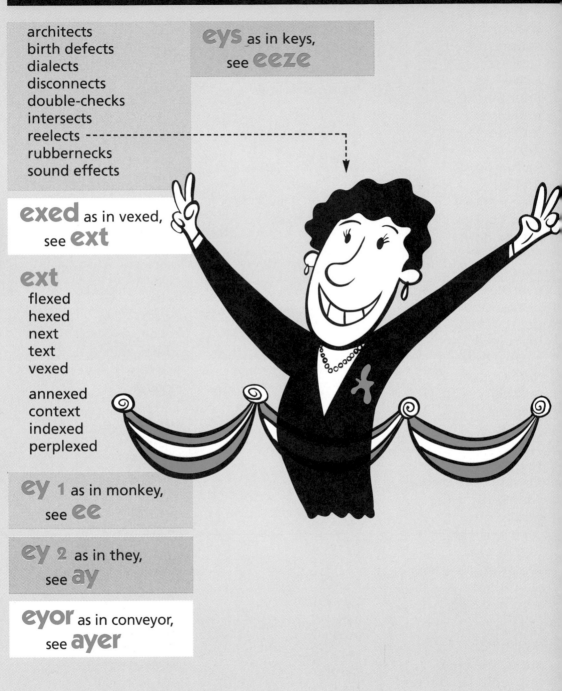

architects
birth defects
dialects
disconnects
double-checks
intersects
reelects --------------------------------
rubbernecks
sound effects

eys as in keys,
see **eeze**

exed as in vexed,
see **ext**

ext
flexed
hexed
next
text
vexed

annexed
context
indexed
perplexed

ey 1 as in monkey,
see **ee**

ey 2 as in they,
see **ay**

eyor as in conveyor,
see **ayer**

i as in alibi,
see **y**

iable

liable
pliable
viable

reliable

justifiable
undeniable
unreliable

ial as in trial,
see **ile** 1

iance

clients
giants
science

alliance
appliance
defiance
reliance

iant

Bryant
client
giant
pliant

defiant
reliant

self-reliant

ib

bib
crib
fib
glib
nib
rib

ad lib
prime rib
sparerib

women's lib

ibble

dribble
kibble
nibble
quibble
scribble
Sibyl

ibe

bribe
gibe
scribe
tribe

describe
imbibe
inscribe
prescribe
subscribe
transcribe

diatribe

ibit

ad-lib it
exhibit
inhibit

prohibit
flibbertigibbet

ic as in picnic,
see **ick**

ice 1

dice
ice
lice
mice
nice
price
rice
slice
spice
splice
twice
vice

advice
concise
device
entice
no dice
precise
sale price
suffice
think twice

merchandise
paradise
sacrifice
three blind mice

at any price
fool's paradise
legal advice
self-sacrifice
sugar and spice

ice 2 as in police, see ease 2

iced
diced
heist
iced
priced
sliced
spiced

enticed
high-priced
sufficed

overpriced
poltergeist
sacrificed

ich as in rich, see itch

icial
initial
judicial
official

artificial
beneficial
prejudicial
superficial
unofficial

ician as in musician, see ition

icient
deficient
efficient
omniscient
sufficient

inefficient
insufficient
self-sufficient

icious
vicious

ambitious
auspicious
delicious
fictitious
judicious
malicious
nutritious
suspicious

repetitious
superstitious

icit
kiss it
miss it

dismiss it
elicit
explicit
illicit
implicit
is this it?
solicit

icity
duplicity
ethnicity

publicity
simplicity
toxicity

authenticity
domesticity
eccentricity
elasticity
electricity - - - - - -

ick
brick
chick
click
flick
kick
lick
nick
pick
prick
quick
sick
slick
stick
thick
tick
trick

airsick
beatnik
broomstick
card trick
Chap Stick
chopstick
drumstick
handpick
heartsick
homesick
lipstick
lovesick

nitpick
picnic
seasick
sidekick
slapstick
St. Nick
toothpick
yardstick

candlestick
dirty trick
heretic
lunatic
Moby Dick
nervous tic

icked as in licked, see ict

icken
chicken
quicken
sicken
stricken
thicken

grief-stricken
spring chicken

panic-stricken
rubber chicken

icker
bicker
clicker
flicker
kicker
liquor
picker

quicker
sicker
slicker
sticker
thicker
ticker
wicker

nitpicker
picnicker

city slicker

icket
cricket
picket
thicket
ticket
wicket

ickle
fickle
nickel
pickle
sickle
tickle
trickle

bicycle
dill pickle
icicle
Popsicle
tricycle
vehicle

pumpernickel

hammer and sickle

ickly
prickly
quickly
sickly
thickly
tickly

icks
bricks
chicks
clicks
fix
flicks
kicks
licks
mix
nicks
nix
picks
pricks
six
sticks
ticks
tricks
wicks

cake mix
chopsticks
conflicts
drumsticks
evicts
lipsticks
nitpicks
picnics
pinpricks
predicts
quick fix
restricts
toothpicks

transfix

bag of tricks
contradicts
fiddlesticks
pick-up-sticks
politics
ton of bricks

icky

icky
Mickey
Nicky
picky
quickie
sticky
tricky
Vicki

icle as in vehicle,
see **ickle**

ics as in politics,
see **icks**

ict

clicked
flicked
kicked
licked
nicked
picked
pricked
slicked
strict
ticked
tricked

afflict
conflict
convict
evict
handpicked
inflict
nitpicked
picnicked
predict
restrict

contradict
derelict

iction

diction
fiction
friction

addiction
conviction
eviction
nonfiction
prediction
restriction

benediction
contradiction
drug addiction
jurisdiction
science fiction

ictor

stricter
tricked 'er
victor

constrictor
predictor

contradictor

icts as in conflicts,
see **icks**

icy

icy
pricey
spicy

nicey-nicey

id

bid
did
grid
hid
id
kid
lid
rid
Sid
skid
slid
squid

amid
eyelid
forbid
hybrid
Madrid
outbid
outdid
redid
whiz kid

arachnid
overdid
pyramid

idal as in tidal, see **idle**

iddy as in giddy, see **itty**

idden

bidden
hidden

bedridden
forbidden

overridden

idder as in bidder, see **itter**

iddle

brittle
diddle
fiddle
griddle
little
middle
piddle
riddle
twiddle
whittle

acquittal
belittle
committal
hospital
transmittal

Chicken Little
noncommittal
peanut brittle
second fiddle

little by little

ide

bride
chide
cried
died
dried
dyed
eyed
fried
glide
guide
hide
lied
pride
pried
ride
shied
side
sighed
slide
snide
spied
stride
tide
tied
tried
vied
wide

applied
aside
bedside
beside
bright-eyed
chloride

cockeyed
collide
confide
cross-eyed
decide
deep-fried
defied
denied
divide
fireside
implied
inside
joyride
landslide
misguide
outside
provide
relied
replied
reside
riptide
roadside
subside
supplied
tongue-tied
untied
worldwide

clarified
coincide
dignified
eagle-eyed
far and wide
glorified
horrified
horseback ride
justified
magnified
modified

73

multiplied
notified
occupied
pacified
petrified
qualified
satisfied
side by side
slip and slide
teary-eyed
terrified
verified

disqualified
dissatisfied
exemplified
here comes the bride
identified
insecticide
Jekyll and Hyde
personified
preoccupied
unsatisfied

ider

biter
brighter
cider
fighter
glider
lighter
rider
slighter
spider
tighter
whiter
wider
writer

crime-fighter

divider
firefighter
ghostwriter
hang glider
highlighter
insider
moonlighter
nail biter
outsider
provider
songwriter
typewriter

idge

bridge
fridge
ridge

abridge
drawbridge

idious

hideous
fastidious
insidious

idity

acidity
cupidity
humidity
morbidity
stupidity
timidity
validity

idle

bridal
bridle
idle

idol
tidal
title
vital

entitle
recital
subtitle

homicidal

idy

flighty
Friday
Heidi
ID
mighty
nightie
tidy

almighty
untidy

Aphrodite
high and mighty

ie as in pie, see y

iece as in piece, see ease 2

ied as in lied, see ide

ief
beef
brief
chief
grief
leaf
reef
thief

belief
corned beef
debrief
fire chief
good grief
motif
relief
roast beef

cloverleaf
disbelief
handkerchief

commander-in-chief

ield
field
healed
peeled
reeled
sealed
shield
yield

appealed
concealed
four-wheeled
high-heeled
mine field
revealed
windshield

ier as in pier, see eer

ies as in lies, see ize

iet
buy it
diet
eye it
quiet
riot
try it

iety
piety

anxiety
propriety
society
variety

notoriety

ieve as in grieve, see eave

iever as in believer, see eaver

ife
knife
life

strife
wife

housewife
jackknife
nightlife
wildlife

husband and wife
larger-than-life

iff
cliff
if
miff
sniff
stiff
tiff
whiff

midriff
scared stiff

iffed as in sniffed, see ift

iffy
iffy
jiffy
spiffy

ific
horrific
Pacific
prolific
specific
terrific

scientific

75

ift
drift
gift
lift
miffed
rift
shift
sift
sniffed
swift
thrift
whiffed

airlift
face-lift
makeshift
night shift
shoplift
ski lift
snowdrift
spendthrift
uplift

ifty
fifty
nifty
shifty
thrifty

ig
big
dig
fig
gig
jig
pig
rig
swig
twig

wig
bigwig
oil rig
shindig

guinea pig

thingamajig

igger
bigger
digger
rigor
snigger
trigger
vigor

ditchdigger
gold digger
hair trigger

iggle
giggle
jiggle
squiggle
wiggle

iggly
giggly
jiggly
squiggly
wiggly

igh as in high, see y

ighs as in sighs, see ize

ight
bite
blight
bright
cite
Dwight
fight
flight
fright
height
kite
knight
light
might
night
plight
quite
right
rite
sight
site
slight
spite
sprite
tight
trite
white
write

airtight
all-night
all right
birthright
bullfight
catfight
daylight
delight
excite
eyesight

finite
firelight
fistfight
flashlight
foresight
forthright
frostbite
gang fight
good night
green light
handwrite
headlight
highlight
hindsight
ignite
incite
indict
insight
invite
limelight
midnight
moonlight
night-light
not quite
outright
playwright
polite
prizefight
recite
red light
searchlight
skintight
snakebite
Snow White
spotlight
stage fright
starlight
stoplight
sunlight

termite
tonight
twilight
unite
upright
uptight
white knight

appetite
black and white
civil right
copyright
day and night
dynamite
fahrenheit
gesundheit
impolite
neon light
neophyte
out-of-sight
overbite
overnight
oversight
parasite
pillow fight
reunite
satellite
socialite

meteorite
opening night
out like a light

ighten
brighten
frighten
heighten
lighten
tighten

whiten

enlighten

ighter as in fighter,
see **ider**

ighty as in flighty,
see **idy**

ign as in sign,
see **ine**

igned as in signed,
see **ind** 1

igor as in vigor,
see **igger**

igue as in intrigue,
see **eague**

ike
bike
hike
like
mic
pike
psych
spike
strike
tyke

alike
dislike

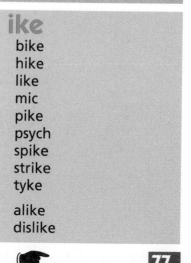

hitchhike
lifelike
unlike
warlike

childlike
hunger strike
ladylike
look-alike
motorbike

iker

biker
hiker
striker

hitchhiker

ild

child
dialed
filed
mild
piled
riled
smiled
styled
tiled
wild

brainchild
exiled
godchild
hogwild
misdialed
misfiled
moonchild
stepchild
stockpiled

ile 1

aisle
dial
file
I'll
isle
mile
Nile
pile
rile
smile
style
tile
trial
vile
while

argyle
awhile
exile
freestyle
high-style
life-style
meanwhile
nail file
profile
reptile
senile
stockpile
turnstile
woodpile
worthwhile

crocodile
domicile
family style
infantile
juvenile
out of style

rank and file
reconcile
single file

after a while
bibliophile
fingernail file
once in a while

ile 2 as in automobile, see eel

iled as in filed, see ild 1

ilian as in reptilian, see illion

ility

ability
agility
civility
facility
futility
hostility
humility
mobility
nobility
senility
stability
tranquillity
utility

capability
credibility
disability
durability

flexibility
gullibility
inability
liability
possibility
probability
sensibility
versatility

acceptability
adaptability
amiability
availability
compatibility
dependability
impossibility
responsibility

ilk
bilk
ilk
milk
silk

buttermilk
malted milk

ill
bill
chill
dill
drill
fill
frill
gill
grill
hill
ill
Jill
kill

mill
nil
Phil
pill
shrill
sill
skill
spill
still
thrill
till
trill
will

anthill
Brazil
downhill
dullsville
fire drill
freewill
fulfill
goodwill
ill will
instill
oil spill
refill
standstill
treadmill
until
uphill
vaudeville
windmill

chlorophyll
daffodil
dollar bill
game of skill
Jack and Jill
overkill
whippoorwill

windowsill

Buffalo Bill
Capitol Hill
king of the hill
run-of-the-mill

illa
villa

Attila
chinchilla
gorilla
guerilla
Manila
Priscilla
vanilla

ille as in bastille, see eel

illed
billed
build
chilled
drilled
filled
frilled
grilled
guild
killed
milled
skilled
spilled
stilled
thrilled
tilled
trilled
willed

79

fulfilled
rebuild
strong-willed
unskilled

overbuild
unfulfilled

iller

chiller
filler
killer
pillar
thriller

pain killer

caterpillar
chiller-diller

illion

billion
million
trillion
zillion

Brazilian
civilian
cotillion
pavilion
reptilian
Sicilian

illow

pillow
willow

Amarillo
armadillo
pussy willow
weeping willow

illy

Billy
chili
chilly
filly
frilly
hilly
lily
Millie
shrilly
silly

water lily
willy-nilly

ilt

built
guilt
hilt
jilt
kilt
lilt
quilt
spilt
stilt
tilt
wilt

im

brim
dim
grim
him
hymn
Jim
Kim
limb
prim
rim

skim
slim
swim
Tim
trim
whim

antonym
homonym
pseudonym
sink or swim
synonym

imble

cymbal
nimble
symbol
thimble

imbo

limbo

akimbo

ime

chime
climb
crime
dime
grime
I'm
lime
mime
prime
rhyme
slime
thyme
time

bedtime
bigtime

immer
dimmer
glimmer
grimmer
shimmer
simmer
slimmer
swimmer
trimmer

imp
blimp
chimp
crimp
imp
limp
primp
shrimp
skimp
wimp

imple
dimple
pimple
simple

impy
shrimpy
skimpy
wimpy

in
been
bin
chin
din
fin
grin

in
inn
kin
pin
shin
sin
skin
spin
thin
tin
twin
win

again
begin
Berlin
break-in
captain
cave-in
Corryn
drive-in
hairpin
has-been
pigskin
sheepskin
shoo-in
snakeskin
stand-in
tailspin
trash bin
unpin
within

bobby-pin
bowling pin
discipline
double chin
Gunga Din
mandolin
next of kin

daytime
enzyme
lifetime
meantime
nighttime
old-time
part-time
pastime
peacetime
prime time
showtime
small-time
sometime
springtime
sublime
wartime

anytime
curtain time
dinnertime
every time
Father Time
maritime
mountain climb
one more time
overtime
pantomime
party time
summertime

all in good time
nursery rhyme
one at a time
partners in crime

once in a lifetime
once upon a time

81

ina to ind

play to win
Rin Tin Tin
rolling pin
safety pin
thick and thin
violin

fraternal twin
guilty as sin
Rumpelstiltskin
self-discipline

Huckleberry Finn
identical twin
time and time again

ina 1 as in ballerina, see ena

ina 2
China
Dinah

angina

North Carolina
South Carolina

ince
blintze
chintz
hints
mince
mints
prince
prints
rinse
since
sprints

tints
wince

blueprints
convince
footprints
imprints
misprints

inch
cinch
clinch
finch
flinch
inch
lynch
pinch

inch by inch

inct
blinked
clinked
inked
kinked
linked
winked

distinct
extinct
hoodwinked
instinct
precinct
succinct

ind 1
bind
blind
dined
find

fined
grind
kind
lined
mind
mined
pined
rind
signed
whined
wind

assigned
behind
combined
confined
declined
defined
designed
entwined
headlined
outlined
refined
remind
resigned
snow-blind
streamlined
unkind
unwind

change of mind
colorblind
humankind
intertwined
lemon rind
mastermind
never mind
one-track mind
peace of mind
underlined

undermined
unrefined

boggle the mind
one of a kind

ind 2 as in wind,
see **inned**

indle
dwindle
kindle
spindle
swindle

ine 1
dine
fine
line
mine
nine
pine
shine
shrine
sign
spine
swine
twine
vine
whine
wine

airline
alpine
assign
baseline

beeline
benign
canine
chow line
clothesline
cloud nine
coal mine
coastline
combine
confine
cosign
deadline
decline
define
design
divine
Einstein
entwine
feline
goal line
gold mine
grapevine
guideline
hairline
headline
hemline
hot line
incline
lifeline
neckline
outline
outshine
peace sign
pipeline
punch line
recline
refine
resign
shoeshine

sideline
skyline
stop sign
streamline
sunshine

borderline
checkout line
clinging vine
danger sign
dollar sign
draw the line
drop a line
first in line
Frankenstein
intertwine
iodine
out of line
Palestine
picket line
porcupine
rain or shine
rise and shine
storyline
toe the line
traffic fine
underline
undermine
valentine
warning sign

ine 2 as in routine,
see **een**

ined as in dined,
see **ind 1**

iner

diner
miner
minor
shiner
whiner

airliner
coal miner
designer
eyeliner
headliner
jetliner
one-liner
recliner
shoeshiner

Asia Minor
forty-niner
hair designer

ing

bring
cling
ding
fling
king
ping
ring
sing
sling
spring
sting
string
swing
thing
wing
wring
zing

bee sting
Beijing
class ring
drawstring
earring
first-string
offspring
plaything
porch swing
shoestring
Sing Sing
something
wingding

anything
bathtub ring
boxing ring
diamond ring
ding-a-ling
everything
rite of spring
static cling
teething ring

puppet on a string

inge

binge
cringe
fringe
hinge
singe
tinge
twinge

infringe
syringe

inger 1

finger
linger
ringer
singer
stinger
zinger

bee stinger
folk singer
gunslinger
humdinger
mud slinger
wingdinger

inger 2

binger
ginger
injure

ingle

jingle
mingle
shingle
single
tingle

commingle
Kriss Kringle

ingo

bingo
dingo
gringo
lingo
Ringo

flamingo

ingy 1
clingy
dinghy
springy
zingy

ingy 2
dingy
fringy
stingy

ini
beanie
genie
Jeanie
meany
teeny
wienie

bikini
Houdini
linguine
martini
zucchini

eeny meeny
fettucine
teeny weeny
tortellini

inister
minister
sinister

administer
prime minister

inity
trinity

affinity
divinity
infinity
vicinity

femininity
masculinity

ink
blink
brink
clink
drink ----→
fink
ink
kink
link
mink
pink
rink
shrink
sink
slink
stink
think
wink
zinc

cuff link
hoodwink
hot pink
lip sync
rethink
soft drink

missing link
on the blink
pen and ink

rinky-dink
roller rink
tickled pink

inked as in blinked, see inct

inkle
crinkle
sprinkle
twinkle
wrinkle

periwinkle
Rip Van Winkle

inky
blinky
dinky
pinkie
slinky
stinky
Twinkie

Helsinki

rinky-dinky

inned
grinned
pinned
sinned
skinned
thinned
wind

downwind
tailwind
thick-skinned

whirlwind
woodwind

bag of wind
disciplined

inner

dinner
grinner
inner
sinner
spinner
thinner
winner

beginner
Berliner
prizewinner

inny

any
Ginny
many
mini
Minnie
ninny
skinny
tinny
whinny

New Guinea

ino 1

rhino

albino

ino 2

Reno

bambino

casino
Latino

Angeleno
cappuccino
Filipino
palomino

int

flint
glint
hint
lint
mint
print
splint
sprint
squint
stint
tint

blueprint
fine print
footprint
imprint
misprint
newsprint
shin splint
spearmint

fingerprint
peppermint
U.S. Mint

inter

printer
splinter
sprinter
winter

midwinter

ints as in hints, see ince

inus

dryness
Linus
minus
shyness
sinus
slyness
spryness

Your Highness

plus or minus

iny

shiny
spiny
tiny
whiny

ion

Brian
lion
Ryan

Hawaiian
Orion
O'Brien
sea lion

dandelion

ip

blip
chip
clip
dip
drip

flip
grip
gyp
hip
lip
nip
pip
quip
rip
ship
sip
skip
slip
snip
strip
tip
trip
whip
zip

bean dip
catnip
courtship
drag strip
equip
fat lip
field trip
friendship
guilt trip
hardship
hot tip
kinship
Q-Tip
round trip
spaceship
unzip

battleship
censorship
chips and dip

chocolate chip
comic strip
crack the whip
double-dip
ego trip
fellowship
fingertip
Gaza Strip
internship
leadership
membership
ownership
paper clip
penmanship
pirate ship
poker chip
salesmanship
scholarship
skinny-dip
sportsmanship
Sunset Strip

apprenticeship
bargaining chip
championship
citizenship
companionship
dictatorship
Freudian slip
good sportsmanship
guardianship
one-upmanship
postnasal drip
potato chip
stiff upper lip

ipe

gripe
hype
pipe
ripe
stripe
swipe
type
wipe

bagpipe
peace pipe
pinstripe
pitch pipe
sideswipe
tailpipe
unripe
windpipe

guttersnipe
overripe
prototype

media hype
stereotype

iper

diaper
griper
hyper
piper
sniper
viper
wiper

bagpiper
pied piper
sandpiper

ipped

chipped
clipped
crypt
dipped
dripped
flipped
gypped
nipped
quipped
ripped
script
shipped
sipped
skipped
slipped
snipped
stripped
tipped
tripped
whipped
zipped

equipped
postscript
tight-lipped
transcript

manuscript
nondescript

ipper

chipper
clipper
dipper
dripper
flipper
shipper
sipper
skipper
slipper
tipper
tripper
zipper

Big Dipper
glass slipper

ipple

cripple
ripple
triple

ippy

dippy
drippy
hippie
lippy
nippy
Skippy
snippy
yippee
zippy

Mississippi

ipsy

gypsy
tipsy

ipt as in script, see ipped

iption

conniption
description

Egyptian
inscription
prescription
subscription

ique as in unique, see eek

ir as in stir, see er

ird as in third, see erd

ire

choir
dire
fire
hire
sire
spire
squire
tire
wire

acquire
admire
afire
aspire
attire
backfire
barbed wire
bonfire
campfire
cease-fire
church choir
conspire

crossfire
desire
entire
expire
flat tire
haywire
hot-wire
inquire
inspire
live wire
on fire
perspire
require
retire
sapphire
satire
spitfire
surefire
transpire
umpire
vampire

ball of fire
overtire
rapid-fire

irk as in smirk,
see **erk**

irl as in twirl,
see **url**

irly as in swirly,
see **urly**

irm as in firm,
see **erm**

irred as in stirred,
see **erd**

irst
burst
cursed
first
nursed
thirst
worst

cloudburst
coerced
conversed
dispersed
feet-first
headfirst
immersed
knockwurst
outburst
rehearsed
reversed
sunburst
well-versed

die of thirst
ladies first
reimbursed
unrehearsed

irt as in skirt,
see **ert**

irth
birth
earth
girth
mirth
worth

childbirth
net worth
rebirth
self-worth
unearth

irty
dirty
flirty
Gertie
squirty
thirty

is 1 as in this,
see **iss**

is 2 as in his,
see **iz**

isco
Crisco
disco
Frisco

Nabisco

San Francisco

ise 1 as in paradise,
see **ice 1**

ise 2 as in rise, see ize

iser as in wiser, see izer

ish
dish
fish
squish
swish
wish

cold fish
death wish
goldfish

jellyfish

ision
vision

collision
decision
division
envision
incision
Parisian
precision
provision
revision

double vision
indecision
split decision
supervision
television
tunnel vision

landmark decision

isk
brisk
disc
disk
frisk
risk
whisk

high risk
slipped disk
tsk tsk

asterisk
floppy disk

isky
frisky
risky
whiskey

ism
prism
quiz 'em
schism

baptism
fascism
racism
realism
truism

activism
atheism
barbarism
chauvinism
communism

criticism
cynicism
egotism
heroism
hypnotism
idealism
journalism
magnetism
mannerism
mysticism
optimism
organism
pacifism
pessimism
plagiarism
skepticism
socialism
symbolism
terrorism
vandalism
witticism

antagonism
cannibalism
capitalism
commercialism
favoritism
patriotism
romanticism
volunteerism

colloquialism
industrialism
materialism
professionalism
sensationalism
spiritualism

individualism
vegetarianism

isor as in visor, see **izer**

isp
crisp
lisp
wisp

isper
crisper
lisper
whisper

iss
bliss
hiss
kiss --------
miss
sis
Swiss
this

amiss
dismiss
near miss

hit or miss

issed as in kissed, see **ist**

ission as in mission, see **ition**

issive
missive

admissive
permissive
submissive

issue
issue
kiss you
miss you
tissue

scar tissue

issy
hissy
kissy
missy
prissy
sissy

ist
cyst
fist
gist
hissed
kissed
list
missed
mist
twist
wrist

assist

blacklist
checklist
consist
dismissed
enlist
exist
gymnast
insist
persist
price list
resist
tongue twist

coexist
reminisced
shopping list

enthusiast

istance
distance

assistance
consistence
existence
insistence
long-distance
persistence
resistance

istence as in existence, see **istance**

ister
blister
Mister
sister
twister

91

stepsister
transistor

istic

mystic

artistic
holistic
linguistic
simplistic
statistic

altruistic
fatalistic
futuristic
optimistic
realistic

animalistic
antagonistic
characteristic
idealistic
opportunistic
ritualistic
unrealistic
vital statistic

istle

bristle
gristle
missile
thistle
whistle

dismissal

istory

blistery
history
mystery

it

bit
fit
flit
get
grit
hit
it
kit
knit
lit
mitt
pit
quit
sit
skit
slit
spit
split
wit
zit

acquit
admit
armpit
close-knit
cockpit
commit
forget
helmet
legit
mess kit
misfit
moonlit
nitwit
omit
outfit
outwit
permit

pinch-hit
smash hit
snake pit
submit
sunlit
switch-hit
tar pit
tight fit
tool kit
transmit
unfit

advocate
baby-sit
benefit
bit by bit
counterfeit
estimate
first aid kit
graduate
hypocrite
perfect fit
separate
throw a fit

banana split
bottomless pit
conniption fit
deliberate
lickety-split

ita

cheetah
pita
Rita

fajita
Juanita

señorita

Santa Anita

ital as in vital,
see **idle**

itch

ditch
glitch
hitch
itch
niche
pitch
rich
snitch
stitch
switch
twitch
which
witch

bewitch
enrich
light switch
unhitch

fever pitch
master switch
strike it rich

ite 1 as in bite,
see **ight**

ite 2 as in petite,
see **eet**

iter as in writer,
see **ider**

ith

myth
smith
with
blacksmith
gunsmith
herewith
locksmith

ither

dither
hither
slither
wither
zither

itic

critic

arthritic

analytic
movie critic
parasitic

itical

critical

political

analytical
hypocritical

ition

mission

addition
admission
ambition
audition
beautician

commission
condition
edition
ignition
magician
musician
nutrition
optician
permission
petition
physician
position
rendition
submission
suspicion
technician
tradition
transition
transmission
tuition

abolition
acquisition
air-condition
ammunition
apparition
coalition
competition
composition
definition
demolition
dietician
disposition
electrician
exhibition
expedition
imposition
inhibition
inquisition

intermission
intuition
malnutrition
obstetrician
politician
premonition
preposition
prohibition
proposition
recognition
repetition
superstition

decomposition
mathematician
out of commission
pediatrician

itious as in ambitious, see icious

itis

arthritis
bronchitis
delight us
despite us
excite us
gastritis
invite us

laryngitis
reunite us
tonsillitis

appendicitis

ito as in bandito, see edo

its

bits
blitz
fits
flits
gets
grits
hits
its
kits
knits
mitts
pits
quits
sits
skits
slits
spits
splits
spritz
wits
zits

admits
armpits
cockpits
commits
misfits
nitwits
outfits
outwits
permits
tar pits
tidbits
transmits

baby-sits
counterfeits
hypocrites

on the fritz
banana splits
hominy grits

ittal as in acquittal, see iddle

itten

bitten
kitten
mitten
smitten
written

frostbitten
Great Britain
handwritten
typewritten
unwritten

itter

bidder
bitter
critter
fritter
glitter
hitter
kidder
knitter
litter
quitter
sitter
spitter
titter
twitter

consider
low bidder
baby-sitter
kitty litter
reconsider

ittery

glittery
jittery
skittery

ittle as in little, see iddle

itty

biddy
bitty
city
ditty
flitty
giddy
gritty
kiddie
kitty
pity
pretty
witty

committee
self-pity

inner city
itty-bitty
nitty-gritty
Salt Lake City

itz as in blitz, see its

itzy

ditzy
glitzy
Mitzi
ritzy

itsy-bitsy

iva

Godiva
saliva

ival

rival

archrival
arrival
revival
survival

ive 1

dive
drive
five
hive
I've
jive
live
strive
thrive

alive
archive
arrive
beehive
connive
contrive
crash-dive
deprive

high dive
high five
nosedive
revive
skydive
survive
take five
test drive

deep-sea dive
nine-to-five

ive 2

give
live
sieve

forgive
outlive
relive

ivel

civil
drivel
shrivel
snivel
swivel

uncivil

iven

driven
given
striven

forgiven
God-given

power-driven

95

iver 1

diver
driver

cabdriver
conniver
screwdriver
skydiver
slave driver
survivor

racecar driver - - - - -

iver 2

giver
liver
quiver
river
shiver
sliver

chopped liver
deliver
downriver
forgive her

ivity

activity
captivity
festivity
nativity

creativity
objectivity
productivity
relativity
sensitivity

insensitivity
radioactivity

ix as in fix, see icks

iz

fizz
frizz
his
is
Liz
Ms.
quiz
'tis
whiz

as is
gee whiz
pop quiz
showbiz

izard

blizzard
gizzard
lizard
wizard

ize

buys
cries
dies
dries
dyes

eyes
flies
fries
guise
guys
highs
lies
pies
prize
rise
shies
sighs
size
skies
spies
thighs
ties
tries
vise
wise

advise
applies
arise
baptize
capsize
chastise
clockwise
comprise
defies
denies
despise
devise
disguise
door prize
drip-dries
first prize
franchise
French fries

hi-fis
high-rise
implies
king-size
Levi's
likewise
mud pies
neckties - - - - - - - →

outcries
pigsties
relies
replies
revise
snake eyes
sunrise
supplies
surprise
unties
unwise
wise guys

advertise
agonize
alibis
analyze
authorize
beautifies
booby prize
burglarize
butterflies
certifies
civilize
clarifies
colonize
compromise
criticize
dragonflies
dramatize
eagle eyes

emphasize
energize
enterprise
exercise
family ties
fantasize
fertilize
glorifies
goo-goo eyes
gratifies
harmonize
horrifies
hypnotize
idolize
improvise
jeopardize
justifies
legalize
lullabies
magnifies
memorize
mesmerize
mobilize
modernize
modifies
mortifies
multiplies
mystifies
neutralize
Nobel Prize
notifies
occupies
organize
ostracize
otherwise

pacifies
paralyze
pasteurize
patronize
penalize
plagiarize
publicize
qualifies
ratifies
realize
recognize
satirize
satisfies
scrutinize
sensitize
signifies
simplifies
socialize
specialize
specifies
stabilize
sterilize
stupefies
summarize
supervise
sympathize
take the prize
tantalize
televise
tenderize
terrifies
terrorize
theorize
tranquilize
traumatize
unifies
utilize
verbalize
verifies

victimize
vitalize
vocalize

alphabetize
antagonize
apologize
capitalize
categorize
characterize
commercialize
demoralize
demystifies
deodorize
disqualifies
dissatisfies
economize
exemplifies
familiarize
family ties

idealize
identifies
intensifies
little white lies
monopolize
nationalize
personifies
popularize
preoccupies
reorganize
revitalize
romanticize
solidifies
take by surprise
visualize

riser
visor
wiser

advisor
incisor

advertiser
atomizer
energizer
exerciser
fertilizer
improviser
organizer
supervisor
vaporizer

deodorizer

izer
geyser
miser

izz as in frizz,
see **iz**

izzard as in blizzard,
see **izard**

izzle
chisel
drizzle
fizzle
sizzle

izzy
busy
dizzy
fizzy
frizzy
is he?
tizzy

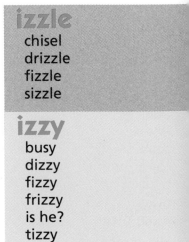

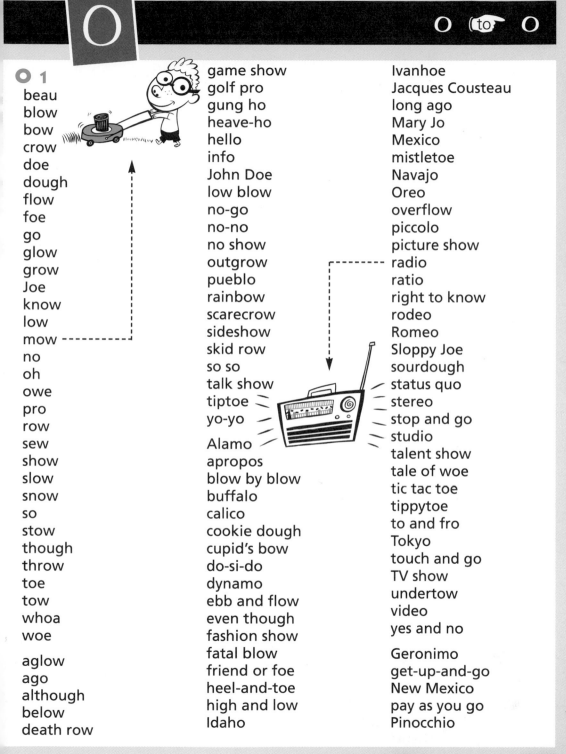

O 1

beau
blow
bow
crow
doe
dough
flow
foe
go
glow
grow
Joe
know
low
mow
no
oh
owe
pro
row
sew
show
slow
snow
so
stow
though
throw
toe
tow
whoa
woe

aglow
ago
although
below
death row

game show
golf pro
gung ho
heave-ho
hello
info
John Doe
low blow
no-go
no-no
no show
outgrow
pueblo
rainbow
scarecrow
sideshow
skid row
so so
talk show
tiptoe
yo-yo
Alamo
apropos
blow by blow
buffalo
calico
cookie dough
cupid's bow
do-si-do
dynamo
ebb and flow
even though
fashion show
fatal blow
friend or foe
heel-and-toe
high and low
Idaho

Ivanhoe
Jacques Cousteau
long ago
Mary Jo
Mexico
mistletoe
Navajo
Oreo
overflow
piccolo
picture show
radio
ratio
right to know
rodeo
Romeo
Sloppy Joe
sourdough
status quo
stereo
stop and go
studio
talent show
tale of woe
tic tac toe
tippytoe
to and fro
Tokyo
touch and go
TV show
undertow
video
yes and no

Geronimo
get-up-and-go
New Mexico
pay as you go
Pinocchio

pistachio
portfolio
ready, set, go

o 2 as in do,
see **ew**

oach
broach
coach
poach
roach

approach
cockroach
reproach
stagecoach

oad 1 as in toad,
see **ode**

oad 2 as in broad,
see **awed**

oaf
loaf
oaf

oak as in soak,
see **oke**

oaks as in cloaks,
see **okes**

oal as in coal,
see **ole**

oam as in foam,
see **ome** 1

oan as in loan,
see **one** 1

oar as in soar,
see **ore**

oard as in board,
see **ord** 1

oarder as in boarder,
see **order**

oared as in roared,
see **ord** 1

oarse as in coarse,
see **orse**

oast as in coast,
see **ost** 1

oat as in coat,
see **ote**

oax as in coax,
see **okes**

ob
blob
bob
daub
glob
gob
job
knob
lob
mob
rob
slob - - - ->
snob
sob
swab
throb

con job
corncob
doorknob
heartthrob
hobnob
snow job

cotton swab
inside job
shish kebab

corn on the cob
thingamabob

obber
clobber
robber
slobber
sobber

grave-robber
macabre

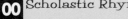

obble

bauble
bobble
gobble
hobble
squabble
wobble

obbler

cobbler
gobbler
hobbler
squabbler
wobbler

cherry cobbler

obby

Bobby
hobby
knobby
lobby
snobby

obe

globe
Job
lobe
probe
robe

bathrobe
disrobe
earlobe
space probe
wardrobe

oble

global
Mobil
mobile
noble

Chernobyl
immobile

ocal

focal
local
vocal
yokel

bifocal

ocious

atrocious
ferocious
precocious

supercalifragilistic-
expialidotious

ocity

atrocity
ferocity
monstrosity
velocity

animosity
curiosity
generosity
reciprocity

ock

Bach
block
chalk

clock
crock
doc
dock
flock
frock
gawk
hawk
Jacques
jock
knock
lock
mock
rock
shock
smock
sock
squawk
stock
talk
walk
wok

back talk
Bangkok
beanstalk
boardwalk
cell block
crosswalk
deadlock
fast-talk
girl talk
gridlock
hard rock
headlock
Hitchcock
jaywalk
jive talk
knock knock

ocker to oddle

livestock
Mohawk
o'clock
outtalk
padlock
peacock
pep talk
punk rock
roadblock
shamrock
shell shock
Sherlock
sidewalk
sleepwalk
small talk
space walk
sunblock
sweet talk
ticktock
unlock
woodblock

aftershock
alarm clock
auction block
baby talk
butcher block
chopping block
cuckoo clock
culture shock
double talk
laughingstock
mental block
nature walk
out of stock
poppycock
round-the-clock
stumbling block
tomahawk

"What's up, Doc?"
writer's block

ocker
blocker
knocker
locker
rocker
shocker
soccer
talker
walker

fast talker
footlocker
jaywalker
night stalker
sleepwalker

ocket
docket
locket
pocket
rocket
socket

light socket
pickpocket
skyrocket

Davy Crockett

ocks as in rocks, see **ox**

ockey as in hockey, see **awky**

ocky as in rocky, see **awky**

oco
cocoa
loco

ocracy
autocracy
bureaucracy
democracy
hypocrisy

aristocracy

od as in nod, see **awed**

oda as in soda, see **ota**

oddle
bottle
coddle
dawdle
model
throttle
toddle
waddle

Aristotle

ode

bowed
code
crowed
flowed
glowed
goad
load
mode
mowed
ode
owed
road
rode
rowed
showed
slowed
snowed
stowed
strode
toad
towed

abode
carload
crossroad
decode
dress code
erode
explode
freeload
implode
Morse Code
railroad
tiptoed
truckload
unload
workload
zip code

à la mode
electrode
episode
hit the road
overflowed
overload
penal code
pigeon-toed

area code

odge

dodge
lodge

dislodge
hodgepodge

odious

odious

commodious
melodious

ody

Audi
bawdy
body
Dotty
gaudy
haughty
knotty
naughty
potty
Saudi
Scottie
shoddy
snotty
spotty

embody
homebody
karate
nobody
somebody

antibody
anybody
busybody
student body

everybody
heavenly body

oe 1 as in doe, see o

oe 2 as in shoe, see ew

oes 1 as in shoes, see use

oes 2 as in goes, see ose 2

off

coif
cough
off
scoff
trough

blast off
brush-off

103

cutoff
kickoff
liftoff
payoff
play-off
rip-off
show-off
trade-off
well-off

on and off
stroganoff

often

coffin
often
soften

og

bog
clog
dog
flog
fog
frog
grog
hog
jog
log

bulldog
bullfrog
groundhog
hounddog
leapfrog
prologue
road hog
ship's log
top dog

watchdog

catalog
chili dog
dialogue
monologue
synagogue
travelogue
underdog

oggle

boggle
goggle
joggle
ogle

boondoggle

oggy

doggie
foggy
froggy
groggy
smoggy
soggy

ogical

logical

illogical

astrological
biological
chronological
geological
mythological
psychological

ography

biography
demography
geography
photography

bibliography
choreography
oceanography

autobiography

ogue 1

brogue
rogue
vogue

ogue 2 as in

dialogue,
see og

oic

stoic

heroic

oice

choice
Joyce
voice

first choice
no choice
one voice
rejoice
Rolls-Royce
turquoise

oid

Floyd
Freud
Lloyd
toyed
void

annoyed
avoid
destroyed
devoid
employed
enjoyed
tabloid

asteroid
celluloid
null and void
overjoyed
paranoid
Polaroid
self-employed
unemployed

oil

boil
broil
coil
foil
loyal
oil
royal
soil
spoil
toil

disloyal
gargoyle
hard-boil
recoil

tinfoil
turmoil

oin

coin
groin
join
loin

Des Moines
purloin
rejoin
sirloin

flip a coin
tenderloin

oing as in going, see owing

oint

joint
point

appoint
ballpoint
checkpoint
high point
pinpoint
viewpoint
West Point

disappoint
focal point
needlepoint
out of joint
starting point

oir as in memoir, see ar

oise as in noise, see oys

oke

broke
choke
Coke
croak
folk
joke
oak
poke
smoke
soak
spoke
stoke
stroke
woke
yolk

awoke
cowpoke
dead broke
egg yolk
heatstroke
kinfolk
provoke
slowpoke
sunstroke

artichoke
cloud of smoke
Diet Coke
go for broke
holy smoke

okey-doke
poison oak

oken

broken
oaken
spoken
token

awoken
heartbroken
Hoboken
housebroken
love token
misspoken
outspoken
plainspoken
soft-spoken
unbroken
unspoken

oker

broker
choker
joker
poker
smoker

pawnbroker
provoker
stockbroker

mediocre

okes

chokes
cloaks
coax
Cokes
croaks
folks

hoax
jokes
oaks
pokes
smokes
spokes
stokes
strokes
yolks

provokes

artichokes
Diet Cokes

ol 1 as in alcohol, see all

ol 2 as in control, see ole

ola

cola
Lola

Crayola
Loyola
payola
viola

ayatollah
Coca-Cola
gladiola
Pepsi-Cola

olar

bowler
molar
polar
roller
solar
stroller

controller
high roller
patroller
steamroller

old

bold
bowled
cold
doled
fold
gold
hold
mold
old
polled
rolled
scold
sold
strolled
told

age-old
behold
billfold
blindfold
cajoled
catch cold
choke hold
consoled
controlled
enfold

enrolled
extolled
foothold
household
ice-cold
out cold
paroled
patrolled
retold
steamrolled
stronghold
threshold
toehold
unfold
untold
withhold

common cold
days of old
good as gold
heart of gold
hot and cold
pigeonholed
pot of gold
rock-and-rolled
self-controlled
solid gold
stranglehold
uncontrolled

out in the cold

older

bolder
boulder
colder
older
shoulder
smolder

cold shoulder
pot holder
shareholder

ole

bowl
coal
dole
foal
goal
hole
Joel
knoll
Lowell
mole
pole
poll
role
roll
scroll
sole
soul
stole
stroll
toll
troll
whole

cajole
charcoal
console
control
Creole
drum roll
egg roll
enroll
extol
fishbowl
flagpole

foxhole
keyhole
loophole
manhole
mudhole
North Pole
parole
patrol
payroll
peephole
porthole
pothole
Rose Bowl
steamroll
tadpole
unroll

buttonhole
camisole
casserole
cruise control
cubbyhole
fishing pole
heart and soul
Old King Cole
pigeonhole
rock and roll
self-control
starring role
sugar bowl
swimming hole
toilet bowl
Tootsie Roll
totem pole

ace in the hole
body and soul
Hollywood Bowl
out of control
remote control

oled as in cajoled, see **old**

olen
colon
Nolan
stolen
swollen

semicolon

olic
colic
frolic

hydraulic
symbolic

chocoholic
diabolic
foodaholic
fun and frolic
sleepaholic
workaholic

olish
polish
smallish
tallish

abolish
demolish

apple-polish
spit-and-polish

olk as in yolk, see **oke**

olks as in folks, see **okes**

oll 1 as in roll, see **ole**

oll 2 as in doll, see **all**

ollar as in dollar, see **aller**

oller as in roller, see **olar**

olley as in trolley, see **olly**

ollow as in follow, see **allow 2**

olly
Ali
collie
crawly
dolly
folly
golly
holly
jolly
Molly
Polly
trolley

volley
Wally

by golly
finale
Svengali
tamale

creepy-crawly
grand finale
hot tamale
melancholy

olo
polo
solo

ologist
biologist
ecologist
geologist
psychologist
zoologist

archaeologist
dermatologist
sociologist

ology
anthology
apology
astrology
biology
chronology
ecology
geology
mythology
pathology
psychology

technology
zoology

archaeology
criminology
dermatology
sociology
terminology

meteorology

olster
bolster
holster
oldster
pollster

olt
bolt
colt
dolt
jolt

deadbolt
revolt

lightning bolt

olve
solve

dissolve
evolve
involve
resolve
revolve

oly
goalie
holey
holy

slowly
solely
wholly

parolee
unholy

guacamole
ravioli
roly-poly

om
balm
bomb
calm
Guam
mom
palm
prom
psalm
qualm
tom

A-bomb
dive-bomb
embalm
fire bomb
pompom
sitcom
time bomb
tom-tom
wigwam

intercom
peeping Tom
supermom
Vietnam

oma
coma

aroma
diploma

Oklahoma

omb 1 as in comb, see ome 1

omb 2 as in tomb, see oom

ome 1
chrome
comb
dome
foam
gnome
home
poem
roam
Rome

Stockholm
syndrome

Astrodome
broken home
foster home
home sweet home
honeycomb
metronome
mobile home
palindrome
shaving foam
Superdome

ome 2 as in come,
see **um**

ometer
barometer
kilometer
odometer
speedometer
thermometer

omic
comic

atomic

astronomic
economic
stand-up comic

omination
domination
nomination

abomination
denomination

ommy
mommy
swami
Tommy

pastrami
tsunami

origami

omp
chomp
clomp

romp
stomp
swamp
tromp
whomp

on 1 as in con,
see **awn**

on 2 as in ton,
see **un**

ona
Jonah
Mona

kimono

Arizona
Barcelona

oncho
honcho
poncho

ond
blond
bond
conned
dawned
donned
fawned
fond
pawned
pond
wand
yawned

beyond
doggoned
fishpond
James Bond
respond

correspond
magic wand
vagabond

onder
blonder
condor
fonder
launder
ponder
squander
wander
yonder

onds as in bonds,
see **ons**

one 1
blown
bone
clone
cone
drone
flown
groan
grown
hone
Joan
known
loan
lone
moan

own
phone
prone
sewn
shone
shown
stone
throne
thrown
tone
zone

alone
backbone
birthstone
car phone
cologne
condone
cyclone
dethrone
dial tone
disown
end zone
full-blown
full-grown
grindstone
headphone
headstone
homegrown
hormone
jawbone
milestone
outshone
ozone
pay phone
pinecone
postpone
Ramon
rhinestone
sno-cone

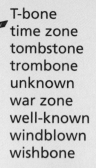

T-bone
time zone
tombstone
trombone
unknown
war zone
well-known
windblown
wishbone

baritone
buffer zone
chaperon
cobblestone
combat zone
crazy bone
doggie bone
funny bone
ice cream cone
microphone
moan and groan
monotone
overgrown
rolling stone
saxophone
stepping-stone
telephone
twilight zone
xylophone
Yellowstone

accident-prone

one 2 as in gone,
see **awn**

one 3 as in done,
see **un**

one 4 as in
minestrone,
see **ony**

oney as in money,
see **unny**

ong
dong
gong
long
song
strong
thong
throng
wrong

along
belong
ding-dong
folk song
headlong
headstrong
Hong Kong
King Kong
lifelong
love song
oblong
Ping-Pong
prolong
sarong
so long
swan song

all along
dinner gong
get along
hop-a-long

right or wrong
sing-along
tagalong

oni as in macaroni, see **ony**

onia
Sonia

ammonia
begonia
Bologna
pneumonia

onial
colonial

ceremonial
matrimonial
testimonial

onic
chronic
phonic
sonic
tonic

bionic
demonic
harmonic
ironic
moronic
Platonic
symphonic
catatonic
electronic
Panasonic

supersonic
telephonic

stereophonic

onica
Hanukkah
harmonica
Veronica

Santa Monica

onical
chronicle
conical
monocle

ironical

onish
admonish
astonish

onk
bonk
honk
konk
zonk

only
lonely
only

one and only
sad and lonely

onna
Donna
Ghana
gonna
sauna
wanna

Chicana
iguana
mañana
piranha

prima donna
Tijuana

Americana
flora and fauna

onned as in conned, see **ond**

onomy
astronomy
autonomy
economy

onor
goner
honor
yawner

dishonor

ons

blondes
bonds
bronze
cons
dawns
dons
fawns
Hans
lawns
pawns
ponds
swans
wands
yawns

batons
ex-cons
icons
long johns
morons
neutrons
pecans
pythons
responds

Amazons
corresponds
leprechauns
marathons
paragons
pros and cons
vagabonds

ont as in front, see unt

onto

pronto
Tonto

Toronto

ony

bony
crony
phony
pony
Sony
stony
Tony

baloney
Shoshone

abalone
alimony
ceremony
macaroni
matrimony
minestrone
pepperoni
rigatoni
sanctimony
testimony

phony-baloney

oo as in zoo, see ew

ooch

mooch
pooch
smooch

ood 1 as in food, see ude

ood 2 as in blood, see ud

ood 3

could
good
hood
should
stood
wood
would

childhood
deadwood
driftwood
falsehood
no-good
redwood
sainthood

brotherhood
fatherhood
Hollywood
likelihood
livelihood
motherhood
neighborhood
pretty good
Robin Hood
sisterhood
understood

misunderstood
Red Riding Hood
so far so good

finger-licking good

113

oodle
brutal
doodle
feudal
futile
noodle
poodle
strudel

apple strudel
Yankee Doodle

oody
beauty
bootie
booty
cootie
cutie
duty
fruity
Judy
moody
snooty
Trudy

off duty

bathing beauty
double-duty
heavy duty
Howdy Doody
Sleeping Beauty
tutti-frutti

ooed as in shampooed, see ude

ooey as in gooey, see ewy

oof 1
goof
poof
proof
roof
spoof

aloof
childproof
fireproof
foolproof
soundproof

oof 2
hoof
roof
woof

oofy
goofy
poofy
spoofy

ook 1 as in spook, see uke

ook 2
book
brook
cook
crook
hook
look
nook

rook
shook
took

checkbook
fishhook
handbook
mistook
notebook
outlook
scrapbook
textbook
unhook

Captain Cook
comic book
dirty look
donnybrook
overlook

gobbledygook

ookie
bookie
cookie
hooky
rookie

ool
cool
drool
fool
fuel
ghoul
mule
pool
rule
school
spool
stool

tool
yule

barstool
car pool
cesspool
gag rule
high school
home rule
mob rule
module
preschool
tidepool
toadstool
whirlpool

April fool
as a rule
golden rule
Liverpool
miniscule
molecule
overrule
ridicule
Sunday School
supercool
swimming pool
nobody's fool
nursery school

majority rule

ooler

cooler
crueler
drooler
jeweler
ruler

car pooler
preschooler

oom

bloom
boom
broom
doom
fume
gloom
groom
loom
plume
room
tomb
whom
womb
zoom

assume
bathroom
bridegroom
classroom
consume
costume
courtroom
entomb
exhume
heirloom
homeroom
leg room
mushroom
perfume
presume
rest room

baby boom
bride and groom
elbow room
gloom and doom
locker room
love in bloom

powder room
smoke-filled room
sonic boom

oomer as in

groomer,
see **umor**

oomy

gloomy
roomy

perfumy

oon

croon
dune
goon
June
loon
moon
noon
prune
soon
spoon
strewn
swoon
tune

baboon
balloon
bassoon
buffoon
cartoon
cocoon
commune
fine tune
full moon

harpoon
high noon
immune
lagoon
lampoon
maroon
monsoon
Neptune
platoon
pontoon
raccoon
Rangoon
saloon
spittoon
too soon
twelve noon
tycoon
typhoon

afternoon
Cameroon
Daniel Boone
honeymoon
loony tune
macaroon
opportune
out of tune
pretty soon
trial balloon

hot-air balloon
man in the moon

ooner

crooner
lunar
schooner
sooner
tuner

honeymooner

oop

bloop
coop
coupe
droop
dupe
goop
group
hoop
loop
poop
scoop
sloop
snoop
soup
stoop
swoop
troop
troupe
whoop

in-group
peer group
regroup
scout troop

alley oop
chicken soup
hula hoop

inside scoop
nincompoop
pressure group

ooper

blooper
drooper
pooper
scooper
snooper
stupor
super
trooper
trouper

state trooper

paratrooper
party pooper
pooper-scooper
super-duper

oopy

droopy
goopy
snoopy
soupy
whoopee

oor 1 as in poor, see ure

oor 2 as in door, see ore

oos as in tattoos, see use 2

oose 1 as in choose,
see **use** 2

oose 2 as in moose,
see **use** 1

oost as in roost,
see **uced**

ooster
booster
rooster

oot 1 as in hoot,
see **ute**

oot 2
foot
put
root
soot

afoot
barefoot
Big Foot
hotfoot
input
kaput
output
shotput

pussyfoot
tenderfoot
underfoot

ooter as in scooter,
see **uter**

ooth
booth
couth
Ruth
sleuth
tooth
truth
youth

Babe Ruth
half-truth
phone booth
sweet tooth
uncouth
untruth

kissing booth
naked truth
snaggletooth
voting booth

fountain of youth
moment of truth

ootie as in cootie,
see **oody**

ooty as is snooty,
see **oody**

ooze as in snooze,
see **use** 2

op
bop
chop
clop
cop
crop
drop
flop
hop
lop
mop
plop
pop
prop
shop
slop
stop
swap
top

Aesop
bebop
bellhop
big top
blacktop
box top
bus stop
cough drop
doorstop
eavesdrop
flattop
flip-flop
gumdrop
hilltop
hip hop
kerplop
name-drop
nonstop
pawnshop

117

pit stop
pork chop
raindrop
rooftop
shortstop
sock hop
teardrop
tiptop
treetop
truck stop
workshop

barbershop
belly flop
body shop
coffee shop
curly top
lemon drop
lollipop
mom and pop
mountaintop
party-hop
traffic-stop
window shop

cream of the crop
karate chop

ope
cope
dope
grope
hope
lope
mope
nope
pope
rope
scope
slope

soap
taupe

elope
jump rope
no hope
tightrope
towrope

antelope
bar of soap
cantaloupe
envelope
horoscope
microscope
periscope
stethoscope
telescope

opey
dopey
Hopi
mopey
soapy

opia
utopia

cornucopia
Ethiopia

opic
topic
tropic

subtopic

microscopic
telescopic

opper
chopper

copper
dropper
pauper
popper
proper
shopper
stopper
topper
whopper

clodhopper
eavesdropper
eyedropper
eye-popper
grasshopper
heartstopper
improper
name-dropper
sharecropper
show-stopper
woodchopper

teenybopper
window-shopper

oppy
choppy
copy
floppy
poppy
sloppy

jalopy
serape

carbon copy

option
option

adoption

opy as in copy, see oppy

or as is for, see ore

ora

aura
Dora
Nora

angora
fedora
menorah
señora

oral

choral
coral
floral
laurel
moral
oral
quarrel

amoral
immoral
pastoral

orce as in force, see orse

orch

porch
scorch
torch

ord 1

board
bored
chord
cord
floored
Ford
gourd
hoard
lord
poured
roared
scored
snored
soared
stored
sword
ward
warred

abhorred
aboard
adored
afford
award
backboard
billboard
blackboard
cardboard
chalkboard
dashboard
discord
explored
fjord
ignored
keyboard
landlord
outscored
record

restored
reward
rip cord
scoreboard
skateboard
slumlord
surfboard
toward
washboard

all aboard
boogieboard
checkerboard
diving board
drawing board
harpsichord
overboard
room and board
smorgasbord
sounding board
spinal chord
tape-record
unexplored

across the board
bulletin board
stiff as a board

ord 2 as in word, see erd

order

boarder
border
courter
hoarder
mortar
order
porter

quarter
shorter

cavorter
court order
exporter
gag order
importer
recorder
reporter
supporter
transporter

flight recorder
law and order
made-to-order
out of order
tape recorder

ore

boar
bore
chore
core
corps
door
drawer
floor
for
four
gore
lore
more
nor
oar
or
poor
pore
pour
roar

snore
soar
score
shore
sore
store
swore
tore
war
wore
your

abhor
adore
ashore
before
cold sore
cold war
condor
decor
downpour
drugstore
encore
explore
eyesore
folklore
galore
hard-core
hoped-for
ignore
indoor
mentor
next-door
no more
outdoor
outscore
Peace Corps
postwar
rapport
restore

seashore
señor
ten-four
therefore
trapdoor
uproar

all ashore
antiwar
anymore
apple core
Baltimore
blood and gore
carnivore
civil war
corridor
dinosaur
door-to-door
Ecuador
evermore
furthermore
Marine Corps
matador
metaphor
nevermore
por favor
reservoir
rich or poor
saddle sore
ship-to-shore
Singapore
sophomore
Theodore
troubadour
tug of war
two-by-four
underscore

forevermore
titanosaur

ored as in bored, see **ord** 1

orge
forge
George
gorge

engorge

Valley Forge

orial
oriole

censorial
memorial
pictorial
tutorial

dictatorial
editorial
territorial

oric
caloric
euphoric
historic

prehistoric
sophomoric

orify
glorify
horrify

orious
glorious

laborious

notorious
uproarious
victorious

ority
authority
majority
minority
priority
seniority
sorority

inferiority
moral majority
silent majority
superiority

orium
emporium

auditorium
crematorium
moratorium

ork 1
cork
dork
fork
pork
stork

New York
pitchfork

ork 2 as in work, see **erk**

orm 1
dorm
form
norm
storm
swarm
warm

barnstorm
brainstorm
conform
deform
duststorm
free-form
inform
lukewarm
perform
platform
reform
snowstorm
transform

co-ed dorm
misinform
thunderstorm
uniform

orm 2 as in worm, see **erm**

ormal
formal
normal

abnormal
informal

semiformal

121

ormer
former
warmer

barnstormer
benchwarmer
chairwarmer
conformer
informer
performer
reformer
transformer

orn
born
corn
horn
morn
mourn
scorn
sworn
thorn
torn
warn
worn

acorn
adorn
airborne
bullhorn
first-born
foghorn
forewarn
forlorn
greenhorn
inborn
lovelorn
newborn
outworn

popcorn
reborn
shoehorn
timeworn
unborn
well-worn

Capricorn
ear of corn
foreign-born
Matterhorn
native-born
unicorn
weatherworn

orning
morning
mourning
warning

flood warning
good morning

tornado warning

orse
coarse
course
force
hoarse
horse
source

air force
brute force
clotheshorse
crash course
dark horse
divorce
endorse
enforce

golf course
main course
of course
racehorse
remorse
resource
task force
work force

charley horse
driving force
reinforce
rocking horse
show of force

collision course
matter of course
obstacle course

ort
court
fort
forte
port
quart
short
snort
sort
sport
thwart
wart

airport
bad sport
cavort
cohort
contort
deport
distort
escort

export
good sport
import
Newport
night court
passport
report
resort
seaport
spoilsport
support
transport

child support
heliport
last resort
Supreme Court
tennis court
traffic court
worrywart

orter as in shorter, see order

orth
fourth
north

come forth

back and forth
July Fourth

so on and so forth

ortify
fortify
mortify

ortion
portion

contortion
distortion
proportion

orty
forty
shorty
sporty
warty

ory
glory
gory
Laurie
quarry
story

love story
Old Glory
rock quarry

allegory
bedtime story
category
hunky-dory
laboratory
lavatory
mandatory
morning glory
purgatory
territory

conservatory
derogatory
explanatory
obligatory
observatory
reformatory

os 1 as in cosmos, see ose 1

os 2 as in videos, see ose 2

osal
disposal
proposal

ose 1
close
dose
gross

cosmos
engross
Laos
morose
up close
verbose

adios
comatose
diagnose
grandiose

ose 2
beaux
blows
bows
chose
close
clothes
crows
doze
flows
foes

froze
glows
goes
grows
hose
knows
lows
mows
nose
owes
pose
pros
prose
rose
rows
sews
shows
slows
snows
those
throws
toes
tows
woes

bozos
bulldoze
dispose
enclose
expose
fire hose
impose
low blows
no-nos
no-shows
oppose
propose
pug nose
rainbows

scarecrows
sideshows
suppose
tiptoes
yo-yos

buffaloes
bungalows
Cheerios
come to blows
decompose
dominoes
dynamos
Eskimos
heaven knows
nose-to-nose
Oreos
overflows
panty hose
radios
rodeos
runny nose
stereos
twinkle toes
videos

anything goes
open and close
overexpose

osh
gosh
josh
nosh
posh
quash
slosh
squash
wash

brainwash
carwash
hogwash
mouthwash
my gosh
whitewash

osion
corrosion
erosion
explosion
implosion

osity as in curiosity, see ocity

osive
corrosive
erosive
explosive

oss 1 as in gross, see ose 1

oss 2
boss
cross
floss
gloss
loss
moss
Ross
sauce
toss

across

crisscross
hot sauce ---->
lip gloss
Red Cross
ring toss
soy sauce

applesauce
at a loss
dental floss
double-cross
hearing loss

memory loss
profit and loss
sign of the cross

ost 1
boast
coast
ghost
grossed
host
most
post
roast
toast -----------

almost
bedpost
engrossed
goalpost
guidepost
outgrossed
outpost
pot roast
signpost
topmost
utmost

coast-to-coast
diagnosed
hitching post
innermost
parcel post
trading post
whipping post

tossed

crisscrossed
defrost
exhaust
low-cost

double-crossed
holocaust

at any cost

oster
foster
roster

defroster
impostor

osure
closure

composure
enclosure
exposure

osy
cozy
mosey
nosy
Rosie
rosy

ossed 1 as in
grossed,
see **ost** 1

ossed as in bossed,
see **ost** 2

ossum
awesome
blossom
possum

opossum
play possum

ossy
Aussie
bossy
glossy
mossy
posse
saucy

ost 2
bossed
cost
crossed
flossed
frost
glossed
lost

ot
blot
bought
brought
caught
clot
cot
dot

fought
got
hot
jot
knot
lot
not
ought
plot
pot
rot
Scot
shot
slot
snot
sought
spot
squat
swat
taught
taut
thought
tot
trot
what
yacht

big shot
blind spot
bloodshot
boycott
cannot
cheap shot
crackpot
distraught
dogtrot
flowerpot
forgot
gunshot

hot shot
inkblot
jackpot
long shot
mascot
mug shot
red-hot
robot
self-taught
slingshot
snapshot
somewhat
so what?
store-bought
teapot
tight spot
whatnot

afterthought
apricot
astronaut
beauty spot
boiling hot
booster shot
Camelot
coffee-pot
diddly-squat
food for thought
hit the spot
hot to trot
Lancelot
melting pot
not so hot
on the dot
on the spot
parking lot
polka dot
thanks a lot
tie the knot

forget-me-not
like it or not

ota

quota
soda

iota
pagoda
ricotta
Toyota

Minnesota
North Dakota
South Dakota

otch

blotch
botch
notch
Scotch
swatch
watch

birdwatch
hopscotch
stopwatch
topnotch
weight-watch
wristwatch

ote

bloat
boat
coat
dote
float
gloat
goat

moat
note
oat
quote
throat
tote
vote
wrote

afloat
cutthroat
devote
dreamboat
footnote
keynote
lifeboat
love note
misquote
outvote
promote
raincoat
remote
rewrote
rowboat
scapegoat
sore throat
steamboat
turncoat

anecdote
antidote
miss the boat
overcoat
petticoat
right to vote
rock the boat
root beer float
sugarcoat

one man, one vote

oth 1

both
growth
oath

regrowth

overgrowth
under oath

oth 2

broth
cloth
froth
moth
sloth

chicken broth
three-toed sloth

other

brother
mother
other
smother

another
each other
godmother
grandmother
none other
Oh, brother!
stepmother

one another

fairy godmother

otic

aquatic
chaotic
exotic

hypnotic
melodic
narcotic
neurotic
psychotic

idiotic
patriotic

antibiotic

otion

lotion
motion
notion
ocean
potion

commotion
devotion
emotion
love potion
promotion
slow motion

locomotion
magic potion

otional

devotional
emotional
promotional

unemotional

otten

cotton
gotten
rotten

forgotten
spoiled rotten

127

otter

broader
daughter
fodder
hotter
odder
otter
plotter
potter
prodder
slaughter
tauter
totter
trotter
water

bathwater
dishwater
floodwater
fly swatter
globetrotter
hot rodder
manslaughter
step-daughter

alma mater
bread and water
holy water
teeter-totter
underwater
walk on water

ottery

lottery
pottery
watery

ottle as in bottle, see oddle

otto

auto
grotto
lotto
motto

otty as in knotty, see ody

ou as in you, see ew

ouble

bubble
double
rubble
stubble
trouble

car trouble
see double
soap bubble

double trouble
on the double

ouch

couch
crouch
grouch
ouch
pouch
slouch
vouch

oud

bowed
cloud
crowd
loud
plowed
proud
shroud
vowed
wowed

allowed
aloud
in-crowd
kowtowed
meowed
outloud
rain cloud
war cloud

bushy-browed
overcrowd
thundercloud

ouder as in louder, see owder

ough 1 as in rough, see uff

ough 2 as in cough, see off

ough 3 as in
through,
see **ew**

ough 4 as in dough,
see **o**

ougher as in
tougher,
see **uffer**

ought as in bought,
see **ot**

ould as in would,
see **ood 3**

oulder as in boulder,
see **older**

ounce
bounce
counts
flounce
mounts
ounce
pounce
trounce

accounts
amounts
announce
discounts
pronounce

renounce
bank accounts
mispronounce
ounce for ounce

ound
bound
browned
clowned
crowned
downed
drowned
found
frowned
ground
hound
mound
pound
round
sound
wound

abound
aground
around
astound
background
bloodhound ----
campground
chowhound
compound
dog pound
dumbfound
earthbound
foreground
greyhound
inbound
newfound
outbound

playground
profound
rebound
renowned
snowbound
spellbound
surround
year-round

all around
battleground
fool around
homeward bound
honorbound
lost and found
musclebound
neutral ground
outward bound
pitcher's mound
round and round
runaround
solid ground
underground

merry-go-round
up and around

happy hunting ground

ount
count
mount

account
amount
discount
head count

bank account
paramount
tantamount

129

ounts to out

ounts as in accounts, see ounce

oup as in soup, see oop

our 1
cower
flour
flower
hour
our
power
scour
shower
sour
tower

devour
empower
horsepower
lunch hour
Mayflower
noon hour
rain shower
rush hour
wallflower
wildflower
willpower

cauliflower
dinner hour
Eiffel Tower
overpower
superpower
sweet and sour
veto power

ivory tower

our 2 as in tour, see ure

our 3 as in four, see ore

oured as in devoured, see owered

ourn as in adjourn, see urn

ourse as in course, see orse

ouse
blouse
douse
house
louse
mouse
spouse

bird house
church mouse
clubhouse
courthouse
doghouse
firehouse
full house
lighthouse
madhouse
outhouse
penthouse

powerhouse
roughhouse
warehouse
White House

cat and mouse
haunted house
house-to-house
Mickey Mouse
on the house

oust
doused
joust
oust
roust

out
bout
clout
doubt
drought
out
pout
rout
route
scout
shout
snout
spout
sprout
stout
trout

about
blackout
blowout
Boy Scout
campout
cookout

devout
dropout
dugout
fade-out
fallout
far out
Girl Scout
handout
hangout
holdout
knockout
lookout
no doubt
pass out
psych-out
sauerkraut
shoot-out
sold-out
stakeout
standout
take-out
throughout
tryout
without
workout

beyond doubt
Brussels sprout
do without
down and out
falling-out
go without
in and out
inside out
knockabout
odd man out
roundabout
runabout
talent scout

day in, day out
knock-down-drag-out
over and out
up and about

outer as in stouter, see owder

outh 1

mouth
south

big mouth
Deep South
loudmouth

blabbermouth
hand-to-mouth
word of mouth

outh 2 as in youth, see ooth

ove 1

clove
cove
dove
drove
grove
mauve
stove
wove

alcove
by jove

ove 2

dove
glove
love
of
shove

above
self-love
sort of

boxing glove
puppy love
turtledove

brotherly love
labor of love
tunnel of love

none of the above

ove 3

groove
move
prove
you've

approve
disprove
false move
improve
remove

disapprove
on the move

over

clover
over
rover

bowl over

changeover
hangover
Land Rover
layover
leftover
once-over
pushover
sleep over
spillover
turnover
warmed-over

Cliffs of Dover
four-leaf clover

OW 1

bough
bow
brow
chow
cow
how
now
ow
plow
pow
row
sow
vow
wow

allow
bowwow
eyebrow
know-how
kowtow
luau
meow
Moscow
powwow

snowplow
somehow

anyhow
cat's meow
here and now
holy cow
solemn vow
take a bow

OW 2 as in blow, see O 1

owder

chowder
doubter
louder
pouter
powder
prouder
shouter
stouter

clam chowder
gun powder

owed 1 as in snowed, see ode

owed 2 as in vowed, see oud

owel as in towel, see owl

ower as in power, see our 1

owered

coward
cowered
flowered
Howard
powered
scoured
showered
soured
towered

devoured
empowered

overpowered

owing

blowing
crowing
flowing
glowing
going
growing
knowing
mowing
rowing - - - - - - -
sewing
showing
snowing
throwing
towing

all-knowing
churchgoing
free-flowing
mind-blowing
ongoing
outgoing
tiptoeing

easygoing
overflowing
partygoing

owl

bowel
foul
growl
howl
owl
prowl
scowl
towel
vowel

on the prowl
wise old owl

owledge

college
knowledge

acknowledge

own 1 as in flown,
see one 1

own 2

brown
clown
crown
down

drown
frown
gown
noun
town

ballgown
breakdown
countdown
crackdown
crosstown
downtown
face-down
ghost town
hoedown
hometown
knockdown
letdown
lowdown
meltdown
nightgown
pronoun
put-down
renown
slowdown
small-town
splashdown
sundown
touchdown

broken-down
cap and gown
Chinatown
circus clown ----
hand-me-down
out-of-town
trickle-down
up and down
upside down
wedding gown

owned as in

drowned,
see ound

ows as in blows,
see ose 2

owy

blowy
Chloe
doughy
Joey
showy
snowy

ox

blocks
box
clocks
docks
flocks
fox
gawks
hawks
jocks
knocks
locks
mocks
ox
pox
rocks
shocks
smocks

socks
sox
squawks
stocks
talks
walks
woks

cashbox
crosswalks
deadlocks
detox
Fort Knox
jaywalks
knee socks
lunchbox
mailbox
Mohawks
outfox
peacocks
Reeboks
roadblocks
sandbox
shamrocks
sleepwalks
soap box
sweat socks
ticktocks
toy box
unlocks
Xerox

aftershocks
chatterbox
chickenpox
Goldilocks
music box
orthodox
paradox
shadowbox

stumbling blocks
tomahawks

jack-in-the-box
Pandora's box
unorthodox

oxy
boxy
foxy
proxy

oy
boy
buoy
coy
joy
ploy
Roy
soy
toy
Troy

ahoy
annoy
destroy
employ
enjoy
killjoy
life buoy
oh boy

corduroy
Illinois
overjoy
pride and joy
real McCoy

oyal as in royal, see oil

oyed as in employed, see oid

oys
boys
joys
noise
ploys
poise
toys

annoys
cowboys
decoys
destroys
enjoys
killjoys
turquoise

Tinkertoys
traffic noise

oze as in doze, see ose 2

ozen
chosen
frozen - - - - - - -

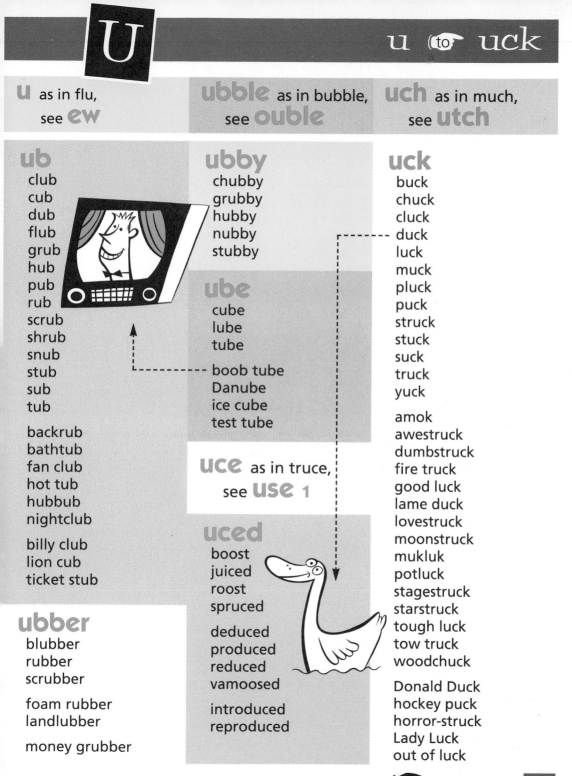

u as in flu,
see **ew**

ubble as in bubble,
see **ouble**

uch as in much,
see **utch**

ub

club
cub
dub
flub
grub
hub
pub
rub
scrub
shrub
snub
stub
sub
tub

backrub
bathtub
fan club
hot tub
hubbub
nightclub

billy club
lion cub
ticket stub

ubber

blubber
rubber
scrubber

foam rubber
landlubber

money grubber

ubby

chubby
grubby
hubby
nubby
stubby

ube

cube
lube
tube

boob tube
Danube
ice cube
test tube

uce as in truce,
see **use** 1

uced

boost
juiced
roost
spruced

deduced
produced
reduced
vamoosed

introduced
reproduced

uck

buck
chuck
cluck
duck
luck
muck
pluck
puck
struck
stuck
suck
truck
yuck

amok
awestruck
dumbstruck
fire truck
good luck
lame duck
lovestruck
moonstruck
mukluk
potluck
stagestruck
starstruck
tough luck
tow truck
woodchuck

Donald Duck
hockey puck
horror-struck
Lady Luck
out of luck

pass the buck
sitting duck
thunderstruck

beginner's luck

ucked as in plucked, see uct

ucker
clucker
pucker
sucker
trucker

bloodsucker

uckle
buckle
chuckle
knuckle

pinochle
swashbuckle
white-knuckle

honeysuckle

ucks
bucks
clucks
crux
ducks
flux
plucks
pucks
shucks
sucks
trucks

tux
aw, shucks
deluxe
dump trucks

ucky
Chuckie
ducky
lucky
mucky
plucky
yucky

Kentucky
unlucky

rubber ducky

happy-go-lucky

uct
bucked
chucked
clucked
ducked
duct
plucked
sucked
trucked
tucked

abduct
conduct
construct
deduct
destruct
instruct
obstruct
tear duct

aqueduct
reconstruct
self-destruct

uction
suction

abduction
construction
deduction
destruction
instruction
obstruction
production
reduction

introduction
reconstruction
reproduction

uctive
constructive
destructive
instructive
productive

reproductive
self-destructive
unproductive

counterproductive

uctor
abductor
conductor
instructor

ud

blood
bud
crud
dud
flood
mud
scud
spud
thud

blue blood
flash flood
Milk Dud
rosebud
taste bud

creeping crud
flesh and blood

stick in the mud

uda

Judah
Buddha

Bermuda

barracuda

udder as in rudder, see utter

uddle

cuddle - - - - - - - - - - - - - - - - - >
huddle
muddle
puddle
scuttle

shuttle
subtle

befuddle
mud puddle
space shuttle

uddy

bloody
buddy
cruddy
muddy
nutty
putty
study

good buddy
peanutty

fuddy-duddy
nature study
Silly Putty
understudy

ude

booed
brewed
brood
chewed
crewed
crude

cued
dude
feud
food
glued
hued
mewed
mood
mooed
nude
poohed
prude
rude
rued
shrewd
spewed
stewed
sued
viewed
wooed

allude
boo-hooed
conclude
construed
delude
dog food
elude
exclude
exude
fast food
include
intrude
protrude
pursued
renewed
reviewed
Saint Jude
seafood

seclude
shampooed
soul food
subdued
tattooed
unglued

altitude
aptitude
attitude
baby food
ballyhooed
barbecued
family feud
gratitude
interlude
interviewed
in the mood
latitude
longitude
misconstrued
multitude
rendezvoused
solitude

udent
prudent
student

udge
budge
drudge
fudge
grudge
judge
nudge
sludge
smudge

trudge
hot fudge
misjudge
prejudge

ue as in blue,
see **ew**

ued as in glued,
see **ude**

uel
cruel
dual
duel
fuel
gruel
jewel

renewal

ues as in blues,
see **use** 2

uff
bluff
buff
cuff
fluff
gruff
huff
muff
puff
rough
scruff

scuff
snuff
stuff
tough

cream puff
enough
handcuff
kid stuff
rebuff

blindman's bluff
fair enough
huff and puff
overstuff
powder puff
rough and tough
sure enough

uffer
bluffer
buffer
gruffer
rougher
suffer
tougher

stocking stuffer

uffle
duffel
muffle
ruffle
scuffle
shuffle
snuffle
truffle

dust ruffle

uffy
fluffy
huffy
puffy
stuffy
toughie

ug
bug
chug
drug
dug
glug
hug
jug
lug
mug
plug
pug
rug
shrug
slug
smug
snug
thug
tug
ugh

bear hug
bedbug
beer mug
earplug
fireplug
humbug
unplug

chugalug
doodlebug

jitterbug
ladybug
litterbug
wonder drug

uge
huge
rouge
Scrooge
stooge

deluge
refuge

Baton Rouge
subterfuge

uggle
juggle
smuggle
snuggle
struggle

uggler
juggler
smuggler
snuggler
struggler

uild as in build, see illed

uise as in bruise, see use 2

uiser as in cruiser, see user

uit as in suit, see ute

uke
duke
fluke
kook
Luke
nuke
puke
spook

rebuke

antinuke

goobledygook

ule as in rule, see ool

ulge
bulge

divulge
indulge

overindulge

ulk
bulk
hulk
skulk
sulk

ull 1

cull
dull
gull
hull
lull
null
skull

annul
numskull
sea gull

ull 2

bull
full
pull
wool

chock-full
pit bull
push-pull
steel wool

Istanbul
Sitting Bull

ully

bully
fully
pulley
woolly

wild and woolly

ulp

gulp
pulp

ulsive

compulsive
impulsive
repulsive

ult

cult

adult
consult
exult
insult
occult
result
tumult

catapult
difficult
young adult

ulture

culture
vulture

agriculture
counterculture
horticulture

uly

coolly
cruelly
drooly
newly
stoolie
truly

unruly

um

bum
chum
come
crumb
drum
dumb
from
glum
gum
hum
mum
numb
plum
rum
scum
slum
some
strum
sum
thumb
yum

beach bum
become
eardrum
green thumb
ho-hum
humdrum
outcome
succumb
Tom Thumb
yum-yum

bubble gum
chewing gum
cookie crumb
deaf and dumb
overcome

rule of thumb

chrysanthemum
fee-fie-fo-fum

umb as in crumb,
see **um**

umber 1
lumber
number
slumber

cucumber
outnumber

umber 2 as in plumber,
see **ummer**

umble
crumble
fumble
grumble
humble
jumble
mumble
rumble
stumble - - - - - - - - -
tumble

rough-and-tumble

umbling
bumbling
fumbling
grumbling
humbling
jumbling
mumbling
rumbling
stumbling
tumbling

ume as in assume,
see **oom**

umer as in consumer,
see **umor**

ummer
bummer
drummer
dumber
hummer
plumber
strummer
summer

latecomer
midsummer
newcomer
nose-thumber

up-and-comer

Indian summer

ummy
chummy
crummy
dummy
gummy
mummy
rummy
scummy
tummy
yummy

gin rummy

umor
bloomer
groomer
humor
rumor
tumor

consumer
costumer
good humor
late bloomer

baby boomer

umorous
humorous
numerous

ump
bump
chump
clump
dump
grump
hump

umpkin to unch

jump
lump
plump
pump
rump
slump
stump
thump
trump
ump

broad jump
goose bump
ski jump
speed bump
trash dump
tree stump

city dump
stomach pump
sugar lump
triple jump

umpkin
bumpkin
pumpkin

umption
gumption

assumption
consumption
presumption

umpy
bumpy
clumpy
dumpy
frumpy

jumpy
lumpy
stumpy

un
bun
done
fun
gun
hon
Hun
none
nun
one
pun
run
shun
son
spun
stun
sun
ton
won

all done
begun
blowgun
dog run
grandson
hired gun
home run
homespun
no one
outdone
outrun
redone
rerun
shotgun

someone
top gun
trial run
undone
well done

Air Force One
all or none
anyone
everyone
hit-and-run
hole in one
honeybun
hot dog bun
jump the gun
native son
9-1-1
number one
one by one
overdone
underdone

fun in the sun
hamburger bun
over and done
prodigal son

Attila the Hun

unch
brunch
bunch
crunch
hunch
lunch
munch
punch
scrunch

fruit punch

school lunch
whole bunch

honeybunch
out to lunch
pleased as punch

unction
function
junction

conjunction
dysfunction
malfunction

und
fund
gunned
punned
shunned
stunned
sunned

refund
trust fund

cummerbund

under
blunder
plunder
thunder
under
wonder

boy wonder
down under
no wonder

blood and thunder
loot and plunder

une as in tune, see oon

ung
clung
flung
hung
lung
rung
sprung
stung
sung
swung
tongue
wrung
young

among
far-flung
forked tongue
high-strung
unsung

egg foo yung
iron lung
mother tongue

slip of the tongue

unge
lunge
plunge
sponge

unger
hunger
younger

fishmonger
warmonger

rumormonger

ungle
bungle
jungle

concrete jungle

union
union

communion
reunion

unity
unity

community
immunity
impunity

opportunity

equal opportunity

diplomatic immunity

unk
bunk
chunk
clunk
drunk
dunk
flunk
funk

143

hunk
junk
monk
plunk
punk
shrunk
skunk
slunk
spunk
stunk
sunk
trunk

chipmunk
kerplunk
preshrunk
slam dunk

unken
drunken
Duncan
shrunken
sunken

unker
bunker
clunker
drunker
hunker
punker

slam-dunker

Archie Bunker

unky
chunky
clunky
funky

junky
monkey
punky
spunky

grease monkey

junk-food junky

unned as in punned, see und

unnel
funnel
tunnel

unner
gunner
punner
runner
stunner

front-runner
roadrunner
tail gunner

unny
bunny
funny
honey
money
runny
sonny
sunny

Bugs Bunny
hush money

Easter bunny
even money

unt
blunt
brunt
bunt
front
grunt
hunt
punt
runt
stunt

confront
forefront
homefront
manhunt
witch hunt

elephant
treasure hunt

unter
hunter
punter

headhunter
manhunter

unts
bunts
dunce
fronts
grunts
hunts
months
once
punts
runts
stunts

at once
witch hunts

all at once

up
cup
pup
up

backup
blowup
breakup
buildup
checkup
close-up
crackup
cutup
dress up
foul-up
grown-up
hang-up
hiccup
lineup
makeup
mix-up
pickup
roundup
setup
shut up
stickup
teacup
throw up
toss-up
touch-up
washed-up

all shook up
buckle up

buttercup
coffee cup
cover-up
cuddle up
giddy-up
paper cup
pick-me-up
runner-up
7-up

uper as in super, see ooper

upid
cupid
stupid

upiter
Jupiter
stupider

uple
pupil
scruple

quadruple

upped as in hiccupped, see upt

upper
supper

hiccupper

picker-upper

uppy
guppy
puppy
yuppie

upt
cupped
upped

abrupt
bankrupt
corrupt
disrupt
erupt
hiccupped

interrupt

uption
corruption
disruption
eruption

interruption

ur as in fur, see er

urable
curable
durable

endurable
incurable
securable

145

ural

mural
plural
rural

intramural

urance

assurance
endurance
insurance

reassurance
self-assurance

urb

blurb
curb
herb
verb

adverb
disturb
news blurb
perturb
proverb
suburb
superb

do not disturb

urch

birch
church
lurch
perch
search

research
soul-search

urder as in murder, see erter

urdle

curdle
fertile
girdle
hurdle
hurtle
turtle

urdy

birdy
nerdy
sturdy
wordy

ure

boor
cure
lure
poor
pure
sure
tour
your
you're

amour
assure
brochure
chauffeur
contour
demure
detour
endure
ensure

fer sure
impure
insure
liqueur
masseur
mature
obscure
secure
unsure
velour

amateur
aperture
connoisseur
curvature
immature
insecure
manicure
overture
pedicure
premature
reassure
saboteur

urf

serf
Smurf
surf
turf

urge as in surge, see erge

urgency

urgency

emergency
insurgency

urgent as in
insurgent,
see **ergent**

urious
curious
furious

injurious
luxurious

urity
purity
surety

impurity
maturity
obscurity
security

immaturity
insecurity

urk as in lurk,
see **erk**

url
curl
earl
girl
hurl
pearl
squirrel
swirl
twirl
whirl

awhirl

dream girl
unfurl

cover girl

mother of pearl

urly
burly
curly
early
pearly
Shirley
surly
swirly
twirly

hurly-burly

urn
burn
churn
earn
fern
learn
stern
turn
urn
yearn

adjourn
concern
downturn
heartburn
intern
Jules Verne
nocturne
return
slow burn
sojourn

sunburn
upturn
U-turn

live and learn
out of turn
overturn
tax return
toss and turn

urp
burp
chirp
slurp

syrup
usurp

Wyatt Earp

urr as in blur,
see **er**

urred as in occurred,
see **erd**

urry
blurry
curry
flurry
furry
hurry
scurry
worry

Missouri

not to worry

urse as in nurse,
see **erse**

ursed as in nursed,
see **irst**

urst as in burst,
see **irst**

urt as in blurt,
see **ert**

urtle as in turtle,
see **urdle**

ury
fury
jury

grand jury
Missouri

us
bus
cuss
fuss
muss
plus
pus
thus
us

discuss
nonplus
school bus

gloomy Gus
make a fuss

no fuss, no muss

usable
bruisable
usable

excusable
reusable
unusable

inexcusable

use 1
Bruce
deuce
goose
juice
loose
moose
mousse
noose
spruce
truce
use
Zeus

abuse
caboose
chartreuse
deduce
excuse
footloose
hang loose
induce
masseuse
misuse
mongoose

no use
papoose
produce
recluse
reduce
refuse
vamoose

child abuse
Dr. Seuss
hangman's noose
introduce
Mother Goose
no excuse
on the loose
out of use
reproduce
silly goose
what's the use?

chocolate mousse

use 2
blues
boos
bruise
chews
choose
clues
cruise
dues
fuse
glues
hues
lose
mews
moos
muse
news

ooze
ruse
screws
shoes ---------
snooze
stews
sues
use
views
whose
zoos

abuse
accuse
amuse
bad news
boo-boos
boohoos
canoes
cashews
confuse
construes
corkscrews
cuckoos
curfews
defuse
effuse
enthuse
excuse
gumshoes
infuse
kazoos
miscues
misuse
muumuus
peruse
pursues
refuse
reviews

shampoos
short fuse
subdues
taboos
tattoos

avenues
baby shoes
barbecues ------
blow a fuse
born to lose
buckaroos
high-heeled shoes
interviews
kangaroos
pick and choose
revenues
win or lose

rhythm and blues

user
bruiser
chooser
cruiser
loser
muser
snoozer

user

abuser
accuser
bad loser
nonuser

child abuser
two-time loser

ush 1
blush
brush
crush
flush
gush
hush
lush
mush
plush
rush
shush
slush

bum's rush
cheek blush
gold rush
hairbrush
hush-hush
toothbrush

ush 2
bush
push
whoosh

ambush
rosebush

ushy
bushy
cushy
gushy
pushy

usion
fusion

collusion
conclusion
confusion
delusion
exclusion
illusion
inclusion
intrusion
protrusion
seclusion
transfusion

blood transfusion
disillusion

optical illusion

usive
abusive
conclusive
conducive
elusive
exclusive
illusive
intrusive
obtrusive
reclusive
seclusive

inconclusive
unobtrusive

usk
brusque
dusk
husk
musk
tusk

uss 1
puss
schuss

octopus --------
Oedipus
platypus
sourpuss

uss 2 as in fuss,
see **us**

ussed as in
discussed,
see **ust**

ussion
Russian

concussion
discussion
percussion

repercussion

ust
bussed
bust
crust
cussed

dust
fussed
gust
just
mussed
must
rust
thrust
trust

adjust
brain trust
coal dust
combust
crop dust
discussed
disgust
distrust
drug bust
entrust
gold dust
mistrust
nonplussed
pie crust
robust
sawdust
stardust
tongue-thrust
unjust

bite the dust
wanderlust

usted
busted
dusted
rusted
trusted

disgusted
mistrusted

uster

cluster
duster
fluster
luster
muster

blockbuster
crimebuster
lackluster

filibuster

ustle

bustle
hustle
muscle
mussel
Russell
rustle
tussle

hustle and bustle

usty

crusty
dusty
gusty
musty
rusty
trustee

ut 1

but
butt
cut
glut
gut
hut

jut
mutt
nut
putt
rut
shut
smut
strut
what

catgut
chestnut
clear-cut
haircut
King Tut
precut
rebut
shortcut
somewhat
so what
uncut

coconut
halibut
in a rut
Lilliput
scuttlebutt
undercut
uppercut

cigarette butt
emerald cut
open and shut

ut 2 as in put, see oot 2

utch

clutch
crutch
Dutch
hutch
much
such
touch

not much
retouch
soft touch

final touch
Midas touch
overmuch
pretty much
rabbit hutch
such and such

ute

beaut
boot
brute
Butte
chute
coot
cute
flute
fruit
hoot
loot
lute
moot
mute

151

newt
root
route
scoot
shoot
snoot
suit
toot

acute
astute
Beirut
commute
compute
deaf mute
dilute
dispute
en route
grapefruit
lawsuit
minute
outshoot
pollute
pursuit
recruit
refute
repute
salute
space suit
square root
tribute
uproot
zoot suit

absolute
attribute
birthday suit
constitute
destitute

execute
hot pursuit
ill repute
institute
monkey suit
overshoot
parachute
persecute
prosecute
resolute
substitute
troubleshoot

electrocute
forbidden fruit

Trivial Pursuit

uter

cuter
looter
neuter
pewter
rooter
scooter
shooter
suitor
tutor

commuter
computer
peashooter
polluter
recruiter
sharpshooter

motor scooter
persecutor
prosecutor
troubleshooter

uth as in truth, see **ooth**

ution

pollution
solution

absolution
air pollution
constitution
contribution
destitution
dissolution
distribution
evolution
execution
institution
persecution
prosecution
resolution
retribution
revolution
substitution

electrocution

utor as in tutor, see **uter**

utt as in mutt, see **ut** 1

utter

butter
clutter
cutter

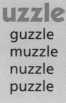
flutter
gutter
mutter
putter
rudder
shudder
shutter
sputter
stutter
udder
utter

rain gutter
woodcutter

bread and butter
cookie cutter
paper cutter
peanut butter - - - - - - - -

uys as in buys,
see **ize**

uzz
buzz
does
fuzz
was

abuzz

uzzle
guzzle
muzzle
nuzzle
puzzle

uttle as in scuttle,
see **uddle**

utty as in nutty,
see **uddy**

uture
future
moocher
suture

ux as in flux,
see **ucks**

uy as in guy,
see **y**

PEANUT BUTTER

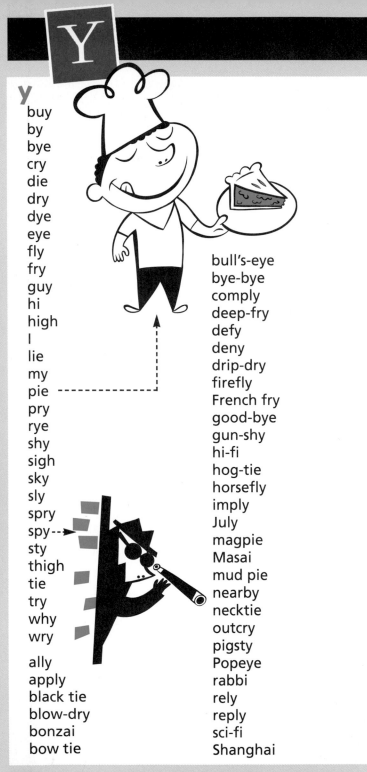

y

buy
by
bye
cry
die
dry
dye
eye
fly
fry
guy
hi
high
I
lie
my
pie
pry
rye
shy
sigh
sky
sly
spry
spy
sty
thigh
tie
try
why
wry

ally
apply
black tie
blow-dry
bonzai
bow tie

bull's-eye
bye-bye
comply
deep-fry
defy
deny
drip-dry
firefly
French fry
good-bye
gun-shy
hi-fi
hog-tie
horsefly
imply
July
magpie
Masai
mud pie
nearby
necktie
outcry
pigsty
Popeye
rabbi
rely
reply
sci-fi
Shanghai

shut-eye
sky-high
small fry
standby
supply
tongue-tie
untie
war cry
wise guy

alibi
amplify
apple pie
battle cry
beautify
beddy-bye
butterfly
camera-shy
certify
clarify
classify
crucify
cutie pie
dignify
do or die
dragonfly
evil eye
eye to eye
falsify
FBI
fortify
glorify
gratify
high and dry
horrify
hushaby
justify
lullaby
magnify

modify
mortify
multiply
mummify
mystify
notify
nullify
occupy
pacify
Paraguay
passerby
petrify
pizza pie
private eye
purify
qualify
ratify
rectify
rockaby
samurai
satisfy
signify
simplify
specify
stupefy
terrify
testify
tsetse fly
underlie
unify
Uruguay
verify
you and I

demystify
disqualify
dissatisfy
electrify
Eskimo Pie

exemplify
Fourth of July
identify
intensify
little white lie
personify
preoccupy
solidify

ycle as in bicycle,
see ickle

ye as in bye,
see y

yle as in style,
see ile 1

ym as in synonym,
see im

yme as in rhyme,
see ime

ype as in type,
see ipe

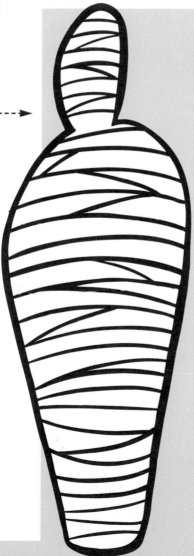

Index

ahead/**ed**
ahoy/**oy**
aid/**ade 1**
aide/**ade 1**
ail/**ale 1**
aim/**aim**
air/**air**
airborne/**orn**
aircraft/**aft**
airfare/**air**
airlift/**ift**
airline/**ine 1**
airliner/**iner**
airmail/**ale 1**
airplane/**ain**
airport/**ort**
airsick/**ick**
airtight/**ight**
airy/**ary**
aisle/**ile 1**
ajar/**ar**
akimbo/**imbo**
Al/**al**
Alabama/**ama 2**
alabaster/**aster**
Alamo/**o**
alarm/**arm 1**
albino/**ino 1**
Albuquerque/**erky**
Alcatraz/**azz**
alcohol/**all**
alcove/**ove 1**
ale/**ale 1**
alert/**ert**
Algeria/**eria**
Ali/**olly**
alibi/**y**
alibis/**ize**
alienate/**ate**
alike/**ike**
alimony/**ony**
alive/**ive 1**
all/**all**
allege/**edge**
allegory/**ory**
alleviate/**ate**
alley/**alley**
alliance/**iance**
alligator/**ader**

allocate/**ate**
allow/**ow 1**
allowed/**oud**
allude/**ude**
ally/**y**
alma mater/**otter**
almanac/**ack**
almighty/**idy**
almost/**ost 1**
aloe/**allow 1**
alone/**one 1**
along/**ong**
aloof/**oof 1**
aloud/**oud**
alphabet/**et**
alphabetize/**ize**
alpine/**ine 1**
already/**etty**
altar/**alter**
alter/**alter**
although/**o**
altitude/**ude**
altogether/**eather**
altruistic/**istic**
always/**aze**
am/**am**
A.M./**em**
Amarillo/**illow**
amass/**ass**
amassed/**ast**
amateur/**ure**
amaze/**aze**
Amazon/**awn**
Amazons/**ons**
ambition/**ition**
ambitious/**icious**
ambush/**ush 2**
amen/**en**
amend/**end**
Americana/**onna**
amiability/**ility**
amid/**id**
amiss/**iss**
ammonia/**onia**
ammunition/**ition**
amnesiac/**ack**
amok/**uck**
among/**ung**
amoral/**oral**

amount/**ount**
amounts/**ounce**
amour/**ure**
amp/**amp**
amplify/**y**
amputate/**ate**
Amsterdam/**am**
amuse/**use 2**
an/**an**
anagram/**am**
analytic/**itic**
analytical/**itical**
analyze/**ize**
ancestor/**ester**
and/**and**
Androcles/**eeze**
anecdote/**ote**
anesthetic/**etic**
anew/**ew**
Angeleno/**ino 2**
angina/**ina 2**
angora/**ora**
animalistic/**istic**
animate/**ate**
animation/**ation**
animator/**ader**
animosity/**ocity**
Anna/**ana 1**
Anne/**an**
annex/**ex**
annexed/**ext**
Annie/**anny**
annihilate/**ate**
announce/**ounce**
annoy/**oy**
annoyed/**oid**
annoys/**oys**
annul/**ull 1**
another/**other**
ant/**ant 1**
antagonism/**ism**
antagonistic/**istic**
antagonize/**ize**
anteater/**eeder**
antelope/**ope**
anthill/**ill**
anthology/**ology**
antibiotic/**otic**
antibody/**ody**

antic/**antic**
anticipate/**ate**
anticipation/**ation**
antidote/**ote**
antifreeze/**eeze**
antinuke/**uke**
antique/**eek**
antiwar/**ore**
Antoine/**awn**
Antoinette/**et**
antonym/**im**
ants/**ance**
anxiety/**iety**
any/**enny, inny**
anybody/**ody**
anyhow/**ow 1**
anymore/**ore**
anyone/**un**
anyplace/**ace**
anything/**ing**
anytime/**ime**
anywhere/**air**
Apache/**atchy**
apart/**art 1**
ape/**ape**
aperture/**ure**
apex/**ex**
Aphrodite/**idy**
apiece/**ease 2**
Apollo/**allow 2**
apologetic/**etic**
apologize/**ize**
apology/**ology**
appall/**all**
appalled/**alled**
apparent/**arent**
apparition/**ition**
appeal/**eel**
appealed/**ield**
appear/**eer**
appendicitis/**itis**
appetite/**ight**
applaud/**awed**
applause/**ause**
apple/**apple**
applecart/**art 1**
applesauce/**oss 2**
appliance/**iance**
application/**ation**

applied/**ide**
applies/**ize**
apply/**y**
appoint/**oint**
appreciate/**ate**
appreciation/**ation**
apprehend/**end**
apprehension/**ention**
apprehensive/**ensive**
apprenticeship/**ip**
approach/**oach**
approve/**ove 3**
apricot/**ot**
apropos/**o**
aptitude/**ude**
Aquarius/**arious**
aquatic/**otic**
aqueduct/**uct**
arachnid/**id**
arbitrary/**ary**
arc/**ark**
arcade/**ade 1**
arch/**arch**
archaeologist/**ologist**
archaeology/**ology**
Archie Bunker/**unker**
architect/**ect**
architects/**ex**
archive/**ive 1**
archrival/**ival**
ardor/**arter**
are/**ar**
area/**area**
arena/**ena**
arf/**arf 1**
Argentina/**ena**
argyle/**ile 1**
arise/**ize**
aristocracy/**ocracy**
aristocrat/**at 1**
aristocratic/**atic**
Aristotle/**oddle**
Arizona/**ona**
ark/**ark**
Arkansas/**aw**
arm/**arm 1**
armada/**ada**
armadillo/**illow**
armband/**and**

armpit/**it**
armpits/**its**
aroma/**oma**
aromatic/**atic**
around/**ound**
arrange/**ange**
arrest/**est**
arrival/**ival**
arrive/**ive 1**
arrow/**arrow**
arrowhead/**ed**
art/**art 1**
arthritic/**itic**
arthritis/**itis**
artichoke/**oke**
artichokes/**okes**
artifact/**act**
artifacts/**ax**
artificial/**icial**
artistic/**istic**
arty/**ardy**
as/**azz**
ascend/**end**
ascertain/**ain**
ash/**ash 1**
ashore/**ore**
Asian/**asion**
Asiatic/**atic**
aside/**ide**
ask/**ask**
asleep/**eep**
asphalt/**alt**
asphyxiate/**ate**
aspire/**ire**
ass/**ass**
assassinate/**ate**
assassination/**ation**
assassinator/**ader**
assault/**alt**
assaulter/**alter**
assaults/**alts**
assemble/**emble**
assert/**ert**
assessor/**essor**
assign/**ine 1**
assigned/**ind 1**
assist/**ist**
assistance/**istance**
associate/**ate**

assume/**oom**
assumption/**umption**
assurance/**urance**
assure/**ure**
asterisk/**isk**
asteroid/**oid**
asthmatic/**atic**
astir/**er**
astonish/**onish**
astound/**ound**
Astrodome/**ome 1**
astrological/**ogical**
astrology/**ology**
astronaut/**ot**
astronomic/**omic**
astronomy/**onomy**
astute/**ute**
at/**at 1**
ate/**ate**
atheism/**ism**
athlete/**eet**
athletic/**etic**
Atlantic/**antic**
atmosphere/**eer**
atomic/**omic**
atomizer/**izer**
atrocious/**ocious**
atrocity/**ocity**
attach/**atch 1**
attack/**ack**
attacked/**act**
attacks/**ax**
attempt/**empt**
attend/**end**
attention/**ention**
attentive/**entive**
attic/**atic**
Attila/**illa**
attire/**ire**
attitude/**ude**
attract/**act**
attraction/**action**
attractive/**active**
attracts/**ax**
attribute/**ute**
auctioneer/**eer**
audacious/**acious**
audacity/**acity**
Audi/**ody**

audition/**ition**
auditorium/**orium**
Audubon/**awn**
aunt/**ant 1, aunt**
aunts/**ance**
aura/**ora**
auspicious/**icious**
Aussie/**ossy**
authenticity/**icity**
authority/**ority**
authorize/**ize**
auto/**otto**
autobiography/
    ography
autocracy/**ocracy**
autocratic/**atic**
autograph/**aff**
autographed/**aft**
automatic/**atic**
automobile/**eel**
autonomy/**onomy**
availability/**ility**
Avalon/**awn**
avant-garde/**ard 1**
avenue/**ew**
avenues/**use 2**
aversion/**ersion**
avert/**ert**
Avery/**avery**
aviary/**ary**
aviation/**ation**
aviator/**ader**
avoid/**oid**
await/**ate**
awake/**ake**
award/**ord 1**
aware/**air**
away/**ay**
awe/**aw**
awed/**awed**
awesome/**ossum**
awestruck/**uck**
awful/**awful**
awhile/**ile 1**
awhirl/**url**
awoke/**oke**
awoken/**oken**
ax/**ax**
ayatollah/**ola**

Aztec/eck

B

babble/abble
Babe Ruth/ooth
baboon/oon
baby/aby
baby-faced/aste
Babylon/awn
baby-sat/at 1
baby-sit/it
baby-sits/its
baby-sitter/itter
Bach/ock
back/ack
backache/ake
backboard/ord 1
backbone/one 1
backed/act
backfire/ire
background/ound
backhand/and
backlash/ash 1
backpack/ack
backpacked/act
backpedal/eddle
backrub/ub
backs/ax
backseat/eet
backslap/ap
backstab/ab 1
backstabber/abber
backstage/age 1
backtrack/ack
backup/up
backward/erd
backyard/ard 1
bacteria/eria
Bactine/een
bad/ad 1
bag/ag
baggy/aggy
bagpipe/ipe
bagpiper/iper
bail/ale 1
bait/ate
bake/ake
bald/alled

balderdash/ash 1
Bali/alley
ball/all
ballerina/ena
ballet/ay
ballets/aze
ballgown/own 2
balloon/oon
ballpark/ark
ballpoint/oint
ballyhoo/ew
ballyhooed/ude
balm/alm, om
baloney/ony
Baltimore/ore
bambino/ino 2
bamboo/ew
ban/an
banana/ana 1
band/and
Band-Aid/ade 1
bandanna/ana 1
bandito/edo
bandleader/eeder
bandmaster/aster
bandstand/and
bang/ang
Bangkok/ock
Bangladesh/esh
bank/ank
bankrupt/upt
banned/and
banner/anner
baptism/ism
baptize/ize
bar/ar
barbarism/ism
barbarity/arity
barbecue/ew
barbecued/ude
barbecues/use 2
barbershop/op
Barcelona/ona
bard/ard 1
bare/air
barefoot/oot 2
barer/arer
barf/arf 1
barge/arge

baritone/one 1
bark/ark
barn/arn
barnstorm/orm 1
barnstormer/ormer
barnyard/ard 1
barometer/ometer
baron/aron
barracuda/uda
barrage/age
barred/ard
barren/aron
barricade/ade 1
Barry/ary
barstool/ool
bartender/ender
barter/arter 1
base/ace
baseball/all
baseline/ine 1
bash/ash 1
basin/ason
bask/ask
basket/asket
basketball/all
bass/ace, ass
bassinet/et
bassoon/oon
baste/aste
bastille/eel
bat/at 1
batch/atch 1
bath/ath
bathrobe/obe
bathroom/oom
bathtub/ub
bathwater/otter
Batman/an
baton/awn
Baton Rouge/uge
batons/ons
batter/atter
battery/attery
battle/attle
battleground/ound
battleship/ip
batty/atty
bauble/obble
Bavaria/area

bawdy/ody
bawl/all
bawled/alled
bay/ay
bayonet/et
bays/aze
bazaar/ar
be/ee
beach/each
bead/eed
beady/eedy
beagle/egal
beak/eek
beaker/eaker
beam/eem
bean/een
beanbag/ag
beanie/ini
beanstalk/ock
bear/air
bearish/erish
beast/east
beat/eet
beaten/eaten
beater/eeder
beatnik/ick
beau/o
beaut/ute
beautician/ition
beautifies/ize
beautify/y
beauty/oody
beaver/eaver
beaux/ose 2
bebop/op
became/aim
because/ause
become/um
bed/ed
bedbug/ug
bedpost/ost 1
bedridden/idden
bedside/ide
bedtime/ime
bee/ee
beef/ief
beefsteak/ake
beehive/ive 1
beeline/ine 1

been/**in**
beep/**eep**
beeper/**eeper**
beer/**eer**
bees/**eeze**
beet/**eet**
beetle/**eedle**
before/**ore**
beforehand/**and**
befuddle/**uddle**
beg/**eg**
began/**an**
begin/**in**
beginner/**inner**
begonia/**onia**
begun/**un**
behalf/**aff**
behave/**ave**
behead/**ed**
beheld/**eld**
behind/**ind 1**
behold/**old**
Beijing/**ing**
Beirut/**ute**
belch/**elch**
belief/**ief**
believe/**eave**
believer/**eaver**
belittle/**iddle**
bell/**ell**
belle/**ell**
bellhop/**op**
bellow/**ellow**
belly/**elly**
bellyache/**ake**
belong/**ong**
below/**o**
belt/**elt**
Ben/**en**
bench/**ench**
bend/**end**
beneath/**eath 2**
benediction/**iction**
beneficial/**icial**
benefit/**it**
Ben Hur/**er**
benign/**ine 1**
Benito/**edo**
Benny/**enny**

bent/**ent**
bequeath/**eath 2**
Berlin/**in**
Berliner/**inner**
Bermuda/**uda**
Bernadette/**et**
Bernard/**ard 1**
berry/**ary**
berserk/**erk**
Bert/**ert**
beside/**ide**
Bess/**ess**
best/**est**
bet/**et**
betrayed/**ade 1**
betrayer/**ayer**
betrays/**aze**
better/**etter**
Betty/**etty**
between/**een**
bevel/**evel**
beware/**air**
bewitch/**itch**
beyond/**ond**
bib/**ib**
bibliography/
    ography
bibliophile/**ile 1**
bicep/**ep**
bicker/**icker**
bicycle/**ickle**
bid/**id**
bidden/**idden**
bidder/**itter**
biddy/**itty**
bifocal/**ocal**
big/**ig**
Big Bird/**erd**
Big Foot/**oot 2**
bigger/**igger**
bigtime/**ime**
bigwig/**ig**
bike/**ike**
biker/**iker**
bikini/**ini**
bilk/**ilk**
bill/**ill**
billboard/**ord 1**
billed/**illed**

billfold/**old**
billion/**illion**
billionaire/**air**
Billy/**illy**
bin/**in**
bind/**ind 1**
binge/**inge**
binger/**inger 2**
bingo/**ingo**
biography/**ography**
biological/**ogical**
biologist/**ologist**
biology/**ology**
bionic/**onic**
biped/**ed**
birch/**urch**
bird/**erd**
birdbath/**ath**
birdbrain/**ain**
birdcall/**all**
birdwatch/**otch**
birdy/**urdy**
Birmingham/**am**
birth/**irth**
birthday/**ay**
birthdays/**aze**
birthmark/**ark**
birthplace/**ace**
birthrate/**ate**
birthright/**ight**
birthstone/**one 1**
bit/**it**
bite/**ight**
biter/**ider**
bits/**its**
bitten/**itten**
bitter/**itter**
bittersweet/**eet**
bitty/**itty**
bizarre/**ar**
blab/**ab 1**
blabber/**abber**
blabbermouth/
    outh 1
blabby/**abby**
black/**ack**
blackball/**all**
blackballed/**alled**
blackbird/**erd**

blackboard/**ord 1**
blackjack/**ack**
blacklist/**ist**
blackmail/**ale 1**
blackout/**out**
blacksmith/**ith**
blacktop/**op**
bladder/**atter**
blade/**ade 1**
blah/**aw**
Blake/**ake**
blame/**aim**
bland/**and**
blank/**ank**
blanky/**anky**
blare/**air**
blast/**ast**
blaster/**aster**
blaze/**aze**
blazon/**azon**
bleach/**each**
bleacher/**eacher**
bleak/**eek**
bleat/**eet**
bled/**ed**
bleed/**eed**
bleeder/**eeder**
bleep/**eep**
blend/**end**
blender/**ender**
bless/**ess**
blessed/**est**
blew/**ew**
blight/**ight**
blimp/**imp**
blind/**ind 1**
blindfold/**old**
blink/**ink**
blinked/**inct**
blinky/**inky**
blintze/**ince**
blip/**ip**
bliss/**iss**
blister/**ister**
blistery/**istory**
blitz/**its**
blitzkrieg/**eague**
blizzard/**izard**
bloat/**ote**

blob/**ob**
block/**ock**
blockade/**ade 1**
blockbuster/**uster**
blocker/**ocker**
blockhead/**ed**
blocks/**ox**
blond/**ond**
blonder/**onder**
blondes/**ons**
blood/**ud**
bloodhound/**ound**
bloodshed/**ed**
bloodshot/**ot**
bloodstain/**ain**
bloodstream/**eem**
bloodsucker/**ucker**
bloody/**uddy**
bloomer/**umor**
bloop/**oop**
blooper/**ooper**
blossom/**ossum**
blot/**ot**
blotch/**otch**
blouse/**ouse**
blow/**o**
blowgun/**un**
blowhard/**ard 1**
blowing/**owing**
blown/**one 1**
blowout/**out**
blows/**ose 2**
blowup/**up**
blowy/**owy**
blubber/**ubber**
blue/**ew**
bluejay/**ay**
bluejays/**aze**
blueprint/**int**
blueprints/**ince**
blues/**use 2**
bluff/**uff**
bluffer/**uffer**
blunder/**under**
blunt/**unt**
blur/**er**
blurb/**urb**
blurred/**erd**
blurry/**urry**

blurt/**ert**
blush/**ush 1**
boar/**ore**
board/**ord 1**
boarder/**order**
boardwalk/**ock**
boast/**ost 1**
boat/**ote**
bob/**ob**
bobble/**obble**
Bobby/**obby**
bobsled/**ed**
body/**ody**
bodyguard/**ard 1**
bog/**og**
boggle/**oggle**
boil/**oil**
bold/**old**
bolder/**older**
bolero/**arrow**
Bologna/**onia**
bolster/**olster**
bolt/**olt**
bomb/**om**
bombard/**ard 1**
bombast/**ast**
bombastic/**astic**
bombshell/**ell**
bon-bon/**awn**
bond/**ond**
Bond, James/**ond**
bonds/**ons**
bone/**one 1**
bonehead/**ed**
bonfire/**ire**
bonk/**onk**
bonny/**awny**
bon voyage/**age 2**
bony/**ony**
bonzai/**y**
boo/**ew**
booed/**ude**
boogieboard/**ord 1**
boo-hooed/**ude**
boo-hoos/**use 2**
book/**ook 2**
bookcase/**ace**
bookie/**ookie**
bookmark/**ark**

bookmobile/**eel**
bookshelf/**elf**
bookworm/**erm**
boom/**oom**
boomerang/**ang**
boondoggle/**oggle**
Boone, Daniel/**oon**
boor/**ure**
boos/**use 2**
boost/**uced**
booster/**ooster**
boot/**ute**
booth/**ooth**
bootie/**oody**
booty/**oody**
bop/**op**
Bo Peep/**eep**
border/**order**
borderline/**ine 1**
bore/**ore**
bored/**ord 1**
born/**orn**
boss/**oss 2**
bossed/**ost 2**
bossy/**ossy**
botch/**otch**
both/**oth**
bother/**ather**
bottle/**oddle**
bottlecap/**ap**
bottlefed/**ed**
bottleneck/**eck**
bouffant/**aunt**
bough/**ow 1**
bought/**ot**
boulder/**older**
boulevard/**ard 1**
bounce/**ounce**
bound/**ound**
bouquet/**ay**
bouquets/**aze**
bout/**out**
boutique/**eek**
bow/**o, ow 1**
bowed/**ode, oud**
bowel/**owl**
bowl/**ole**
bowled/**old**
bowler/**olar**

bows/**ose 2**
bowwow/**ow 1**
box/**ox**
boxcar/**ar**
boxy/**oxy**
boy/**oy**
boycott/**ot**
boyfriend/**end**
boys/**oys**
bozos/**ose 2**
brace/**ace**
braced/**aste**
brag/**ag**
braid/**ade 1**
Braille/**ale 1**
brain/**ain**
brainchild/**ild**
brainstorm/**orm 1**
brainwash/**osh**
brainwave/**ave**
brake/**ake**
bran/**an**
brand/**and**
brand-new/**ew**
brash/**ash 1**
brass/**ass**
brassy/**assy**
brat/**at 1**
bratty/**atty**
brave/**ave**
braver/**aver**
bravery/**avery**
brawl/**all**
brawled/**alled**
brawler/**aller**
brawny/**awny**
bray/**ay**
brazen/**azon**
Brazil/**ill**
Brazilian/**illion**
bread/**ed**
break/**ake**
breakdown/**own 2**
breakthrough/**ew**
breakup/**up**
breast/**est**
breath/**eath 1**
breathe/**eethe**
bred/**ed**

breed/**eed**
breeze/**eeze**
breezy/**easy**
brew/**ew**
brewed/**ude**
Brian/**ion**
bribe/**ibe**
brick/**ick**
bricks/**icks**
bridal/**idle**
bride/**ide**
bridegroom/**oom**
bridesmaid/**ade 1**
bridge/**idge**
bridle/**idle**
brief/**ief**
briefcase/**ace**
bright/**ight**
brighten/**ighten**
brighter/**ider**
brim/**im**
bring/**ing**
brink/**ink**
brisk/**isk**
bristle/**istle**
brittle/**iddle**
broach/**oach**
broad/**awed**
broadcast/**ast**
broadcaster/**aster**
broader/**otter**
brochure/**ure**
brogue/**ogue 1**
broil/**oil**
broke/**oke**
broken/**oken**
broker/**oker**
bronchitis/**itis**
bronze/**ons**
brood/**ude**
brook/**ook 2**
broom/**oom**
broomstick/**ick**
broth/**oth 2**
brother/**other**
brotherhood/**ood 3**
brought/**ot**
brow/**ow 1**
browbeat/**eet**

browbeaten/**eaten**
brown/**own 2**
browned/**ound**
Bruce/**use 1**
bruisable/**usable**
bruise/**use 2**
bruiser/**user**
brunch/**unch**
brunette/**et**
brunt/**unt**
brush/**ush 1**
brush-off/**off**
brusque/**usk**
brutal/**oodle**
brutality/**ality 1**
brute/**ute**
Bryant/**iant**
bubble/**ouble**
buccaneer/**eer**
buck/**uck**
buckaroo/**ew 2**
buckaroos/**use**
bucked/**uct**
buckle/**uckle**
bucks/**ucks**
bud/**ud**
Buddha/**uda**
buddy/**uddy**
budge/**udge**
buff/**uff**
buffalo/**o**
Buffalo Bill/**ill**
buffaloes/**ose 2**
buffer/**uffer**
buffoon/**oon**
bug/**ug**
bugaboo/**ew**
build/**illed**
buildup/**up**
built/**ilt**
Bulgaria/**area**
bulge/**ulge**
bulk/**ulk**
bull/**ull 2**
bulldog/**og**
bulldoze/**ose 2**
bullfight/**ight**
bullfrog/**og**
bullhorn/**orn**

bullpen/**en**
bully/**ully**
bum/**um**
bumblebee/**ee**
bumblebees/**eeze**
bumbling/**umbling**
bummer/**ummer**
bump/**ump**
bumpkin/**umpkin**
bumpy/**umpy**
bun/**un**
bunch/**unch**
bungalows/**ose 2**
bungle/**ungle**
bunk/**unk**
bunkbed/**ed**
bunker/**unker**
Bunker, Archie/**unker**
bunny/**unny**
bunt/**unt**
bunts/**unts**
buoy/**ewy, oy**
bureaucracy/**ocracy**
bureaucrat/**at 1**
bureaucratic/**atic**
burglarize/**ize**
burlap/**ap**
burlesque/**esque**
burly/**urly**
burn/**urn**
burp/**urp**
burr/**er**
burrito/**edo**
burst/**irst**
bury/**ary**
bus/**us**
bush/**ush 2**
bushy/**ushy**
bussed/**ust**
bust/**ust**
busted/**usted**
bustle/**ustle**
busy/**izzy**
busybody/**ody**
but/**ut 1**
butt/**ut 1**
Butte/**ute**
butter/**utter**
butterball/**all**

buttercup/**up**
butterflies/**ize**
butterfly/**y**
buttermilk/**ilk**
buttonhole/**ole**
buy/**y**
buys/**ize**
buzz/**uzz**
buzzword/**erd**
by/**y**
bye/**y**
bypass/**ass**

C

cab/**ab 1**
caballero/**arrow**
cabby/**abby**
cabdriver/**iver 1**
cable/**able**
caboose/**use 1**
cache/**ash 1**
cackle/**ackle**
cad/**ad 1**
caddie/**atty**
cadet/**et**
Cadillac/**ack**
Cadillacs/**ax**
Caesar/**eezer**
cafe/**ay**
cafes/**aze**
cafeteria/**eria**
caffeine/**een**
cage/**age 1**
cajole/**ole**
cajoled/**old**
cake/**ake**
calamari/**arry 2**
calculate/**ate**
calculation/**ation**
calculator/**ader**
calf/**aff**
calico/**o**
call/**all**
called/**alled**
caller/**aller**
calm/**alm, om**
caloric/**oric**
Camaro/**arrow**

came/**aim**
camelback/**ack**
Camelot/**ot**
Cameroon/**oon**
camisole/**ole**
camouflage/**age 2**
camp/**amp**
campaign/**ain**
camper/**amper**
campfire/**ire**
campground/**ound**
can/**an**
canal/**al**
canary/**ary**
cancan/**an**
cancellation/**ation**
candidate/**ate**
candlestick/**ick**
cane/**ain**
canine/**ine 1**
canned/**and**
cannibalism/**ism**
cannonball/**all**
cannot/**ot**
canoe/**ew**
canoes/**use 2**
can't/**ant 1**
cantaloupe/**ope**
canteen/**een**
cantina/**ena**
cap/**ap**
capability/**ility**
capacity/**acity**
cape/**ape**
Cape Cod/**awed**
capitalism/**ism**
capitalize/**ize**
cappuccino/**ino 2**
caprice/**ease 2**
Capricorn/**orn**
capsize/**ize**
captain/**in**
captivate/**ate**
captivity/**ivity**
car/**ar**
carat/**arrot**
caravan/**an**
carbohydrate/**ate**
card/**ard 1**

cardboard/**ord 1**
care/**air**
career/**eer**
carefree/**ee**
caress/**ess**
caressed/**est**
caribou/**ew**
carload/**ode**
carnivore/**ore**
carousel/**ell**
Carrie/**ary**
carrot/**arrot**
carry/**ary**
cart/**art 1**
cartoon/**oon**
cartwheel/**eel**
carve/**arve**
carwash/**osh**
case/**ace**
Casey/**acy**
cash/**ash 1**
cashbox/**ox**
cashew/**ew**
cashews/**use 2**
cashier/**eer**
cashmere/**eer**
casino/**ino 2**
cask/**ask**
casket/**asket**
casserole/**ole**
cast/**ast**
caste/**ast**
cat/**at 1**
catalog/**og**
catalytic/**itic**
catamaran/**an**
catapult/**ult**
catatonic/**onic**
catch/**atch 1**
catch-22/**ew**
catchy/**atchy**
categorize/**ize**
category/**ory**
cater/**ader**
caterpillar/**iller**
caterwaul/**all**
catfight/**ight**
catgut/**ut 1**
catnap/**ap**

catnip/**ip**
cattle/**attle**
catty/**atty**
Caucasian/**asion**
caught/**ot**
cauliflower/**our 1**
cause/**ause**
cavalcade/**ade 1**
cavalier/**eer**
cave/**ave**
caveman/**an 1**
caviar/**ar**
cavity/**avity**
cavort/**ort**
cavorter/**order**
cease/**ease 2**
ceased/**east**
cease-fire/**ire**
cedar/**eeder**
celebrate/**ate**
celebration/**ation**
Celeste/**est**
cell/**ell**
cellar/**eller**
cellmate/**ate**
cello/**ellow**
cellophane/**ain**
celluloid/**oid**
Celt/**elt**
cement/**ent**
cemetery/**ary**
censorial/**orial**
censorship/**ip**
censure/**enture**
cent/**ent**
center/**enter**
centerpiece/**ease 2**
centigrade/**ade 1**
centimeter/**eeder**
centipede/**eed**
cents/**ense**
ceremonial/**onial**
ceremony/**ony**
certifies/**ize**
certify/**y**
cesspool/**ool**
Cézanne/**awn**
Chad/**ad 1**
chain/**ain**

chair/**air**
chalk/**ock**
chalkboard/**ord 1**
champ/**amp**
champagne/**ain**
championship/**ip**
chance/**ance**
chandelier/**eer**
change/**ange**
changeover/**over**
chant/**ant 1**
chants/**ance**
chaotic/**otic**
chap/**ap**
chapel/**apple**
chaperon/**one 1**
characteristic/**istic**
characterize/**ize**
charade/**ade 1**
charcoal/**ole**
charge/**arge**
charismatic/**atic**
charity/**arity**
charm/**arm 1**
charred/**ard 1**
chart/**art 1**
charter/**arter**
chartreuse/**use 1**
chase/**ace**
chased/**aste**
chasm/**asm**
chassis/**assy**
chaste/**aste**
chasten/**ason**
chastise/**ize**
chat/**at 1**
chatter/**atter**
chatterbox/**ox**
chatty/**atty**
chauffeur/**ure**
chauvinism/**ism**
cheap/**eep**
cheaper/**eeper**
cheapskate/**ate**
cheat/**eet**
cheater/**eeder**
check/**eck**
checkbook/**ook 2**
checked/**ect**

checkerboard/**ord 1**
checkered/**ecord**
checklist/**ist**
checkmate/**ate**
checkpoint/**oint**
checks/**ex**
checkup/**up**
cheddar/**etter**
cheek/**eek**
cheer/**eer**
cheerful/**earful**
Cheerios/**ose 2**
cheerleader/**eeder**
cheery/**eery**
cheese/**eeze**
cheesecake/**ake**
cheesy/**easy**
cheetah/**ita**
chef/**ef**
chenille/**eel**
cherish/**erish**
Chernobyl/**oble**
cherry/**ary**
Chesapeake/**eek**
chess/**ess**
chest/**est**
Chester/**ester**
chestnut/**ut 1**
chew/**ew**
chewed/**ude**
chews/**use 2**
chewy/**ewy**
Cheyenne/**en**
Chicana/**onna**
chick/**ick**
chickadees/**eeze**
chicken/**icken**
chickenpox/**ox**
chicks/**icks**
chide/**ide**
chief/**ief**
chiffon/**awn**
child/**ild**
childbirth/**irth**
childhood/**ood 3**
childlike/**ike**
childproof/**oof 1**
chili/**illy**
chill/**ill**

chilled/**illed**
chiller/**iller**
chilly/**illy**
chime/**ime**
chimp/**imp**
chimpanzee/**ee**
chimpanzees/**eeze**
chin/**in**
China/**ina 2**
Chinatown/**own 2**
chinchilla/**illa**
Chinese/**eeze**
chintz/**ince**
chip/**ip**
chipmunk/**unk**
chipped/**ipped**
chipper/**ipper**
chirp/**urp**
chisel/**izzle**
chitchat/**at 1**
Chloe/**owy**
chloride/**ide**
chlorine/**een**
chlorophyll/**ill**
chocoholic/**olic**
choice/**oice**
choir/**ire**
choke/**oke**
choker/**oker**
chokes/**okes**
cholesterol/**all**
chomp/**omp**
choose/**use 2**
chooser/**user**
chop/**op**
Chopin/**an**
chopper/**opper**
choppy/**oppy**
chopstick/**ick**
chopsticks/**icks**
chop suey/**ewy**
choral/**oral**
chorale/**al**
chord/**ord**
chore/**ore**
choreography/
    ography
chose/**ose 2**
chosen/**ozen**

chow/**ow 1**
chowder/**owder**
chowhound/**ound**
chow mein/**ain**
Christina/**ena**
chrome/**ome 1**
chronic/**onic**
chronicle/**onical**
chronological/**ogical**
chronology/**ology**
chrysanthemum/**um**
chubby/**ubby**
chuck/**uck**
chucked/**uct**
Chuckie/**ucky**
chuckle/**uckle**
chug/**ug**
chugalug/**ug**
chum/**um**
chummy/**ummy**
chump/**ump**
chunk/**unk**
chunky/**unky**
church/**urch**
churchgoing/**owing**
churn/**urn**
chute/**ute**
cicada/**ada**
cider/**ider**
cigar/**ar**
cigarette/**et**
cinch/**inch**
Cincinnati/**atty**
Cinderella/**ella**
cinerama/
    ama 1, ama 2
circulate/**ate**
circulation/**ation**
circumstance/**ance**
citation/**ation**
cite/**ight**
citizenship/**ip**
city/**itty**
civil/**ivel**
civilian/**illion**
civility/**ility**
civilization/**ation**
civilize/**ize**
clad/**ad 1**

claim/**aim**
clam/**am**
clambake/**ake**
clammy/**ammy**
clamp/**amp**
clan/**an**
clang/**ang**
clank/**ank**
clanky/**anky**
clap/**ap**
Clara/**ara**
clarified/**ide**
clarifies/**ize**
clarify/**y**
clarinet/**et**
Clarisse/**ease 2**
clarity/**arity**
Clark/**ark**
clash/**ash 1**
clasp/**asp**
class/**ass**
classify/**y**
classmate/**ate**
classroom/**oom**
classy/**assy**
clatter/**atter**
Claude/**awed**
clause/**ause**
claw/**aw**
clawed/**awed**
claws/**ause**
clay/**ay**
clean/**een**
clear/**eer**
clearer/**earer**
cleaver/**eaver**
clef/**ef**
clench/**ench**
clerk/**erk**
clever/**ever**
click/**ick**
clicked/**ict**
clicker/**icker**
clicks/**icks**
client/**iant**
clientele/**ell**
clients/**iance**
cliff/**iff**
Cliffs of Dover/**over**

climax/**ax**	clunk/**unk**	collar/**aller**	communication/**ation**
climb/**ime**	clunker/**unker**	colleague/**eague**	communion/**union**
clinch/**inch**	clunky/**unky**	collect/**ect**	communism/**ism**
cling/**ing**	cluster/**uster**	collection/**ection**	community/**unity**
clingy/**ingy** 1	clutch/**utch**	collector/**ector**	commute/**ute**
clink/**ink**	clutter/**utter**	collects/**ex**	commuter/**uter**
clinked/**inct**	coach/**oach**	Colleen/**een**	compact/**act**
clip/**ip**	coal/**ole**	college/**owledge**	companionship/**ip**
clipped/**ipped**	coalition/**ition**	collegian/**egion**	compare/**air**
clipper/**ipper**	coarse/**orse**	collide/**ide**	compatibility/**ility**
cloaks/**okes**	coast/**ost** 1	collie/**olly**	compel/**ell**
clobber/**obber**	coastline/**ine** 1	collision/**ision**	compelled/**eld**
clock/**ock**	coat/**ote**	colloquialism/**ism**	compete/**eet**
clocks/**ox**	coax/**okes**	collusion/**usion**	competition/**ition**
clockwise/**ize**	cobbler/**obbler**	cologne/**one** 1	complain/**ain**
clockwork/**erk**	cobblestone/**one** 1	colon/**olen**	complete/**eet**
clod/**awed**	Cochise/**ease** 1	colonel/**ernal**	complex/**ex**
clodhopper/**opper**	cockatoo/**ew**	colonial/**onial**	complexion/**ection**
clog/**og**	cockeyed/**ide**	colonize/**ize**	complicate/**ate**
clomp/**omp**	cockpit/**it**	colorblind/**ind** 1	complication/**ation**
clone/**one** 1	cockpits/**its**	colt/**olt**	compliment/**ent**
clop/**op**	cockroach/**oach**	coma/**oma**	compliments/**ense**
close/**ose** 1, ose 2	cocktail/**ale** 1	comatose/**ose** 1	comply/**y**
closure/**osure**	cocky/**awky**	comb/**ome** 1	composition/**ition**
clot/**ot**	cocoa/**oco**	combat/**at** 1	composure/**osure**
cloth/**oth** 2	coconut/**ut** 1	combination/**ation**	compound/**ound**
clothes/**ose** 2	cocoon/**oon**	combine/**ine** 1	comprehend/**end**
clotheshorse/**orse**	coddle/**oddle**	combined/**ind** 1	comprehension/
clothesline/**ine** 1	code/**ode**	combust/**ust**	**ention**
cloud/**oud**	coed/**ed**	come/**um**	comprehensive/
cloudburst/**irst**	coerce/**erse**	comedic/**edic**	**ensive**
clout/**out**	coerced/**irst**	comic/**omic**	compressor/**essor**
clove/**ove** 1	coercion/**ersion**	comma/**ama** 1	comprise/**ize**
clover/**over**	coexist/**ist**	command/**and**	compromise/**ize**
cloverleaf/**ief**	coffeepot/**ot**	commence/**ense**	compulsive/**ulsive**
clown/**own** 2	cohort/**ort**	commentary/**ary**	compute/**ute**
clowned/**ound**	coif/**off**	commerce/**erse**	computer/**uter**
club/**ub**	coil/**oil**	commercialism/**ism**	comrade/**ad** 1
clubhouse/**ouse**	coin/**oin**	commercialize/**ize**	con/**awn**
Club Med/**ed**	coincide/**ide**	commingle/**ingle**	conceal/**eel**
cluck/**uck**	coincidental/**ental**	commission/**ition**	concealed/**ield**
clucked/**uct**	Coke/**oke**	commit/**it**	concede/**eed**
clucker/**ucker**	Cokes/**okes**	commits/**its**	conceit/**eet**
clucks/**ucks**	cola/**ola**	committal/**iddle**	conceive/**eave**
clue/**ew**	cold/**old**	committee/**itty**	concentrate/**ate**
clues/**use** 2	colder/**older**	commodious/**odious**	concentration/**ation**
clump/**ump**	Colgate/**ate**	commotion/**otion**	concept/**ept**
clumpy/**umpy**	colic/**olic**	commune/**oon**	conception/**eption**
clung/**ung**	collage/**age** 2	communicate/**ate**	concern/**urn**

concession/**ession**
conch/**aunch**
concise/**ice 1**
conclude/**ude**
conclusion/**usion**
conclusive/**usive**
concrete/**eet**
concur/**er**
concurred/**erd**
concussion/**ussion**
condemn/**em**
condense/**ense**
condition/**ition**
condone/**one 1**
condor/**onder, ore**
conducive/**usive**
conduct/**uct**
conductor/**uctor**
cone/**one 1**
confer/**er**
conferred/**erd**
confess/**ess**
confessed/**est**
confession/**ession**
confessor/**essor**
confetti/**etty**
confidante/**aunt**
confide/**ide**
confidential/**ential**
confidentiality/
   ality 1
confine/**ine 1**
confined/**ind 1**
confirm/**erm**
confirmation/**ation**
confiscate/**ate**
conflict/**ict**
conflicts/**icks**
conform/**orm 1**
conformer/**ormer**
confront/**unt**
confuse/**use 2**
confusion/**usion**
congeal/**eel**
congeniality/**ality 1**
congestion/**estion**
congratulate/**ate**
congregation/**ation**
conical/**onical**

conjunction/**unction**
connect/**ect**
connection/**ection**
connector/**ector**
connects/**ex**
conned/**ond**
Connie/**awny**
conniption/**iption**
connive/**ive 1**
conniver/**iver 1**
connoisseur/**ure**
conquest/**est**
cons/**ons**
consent/**ent**
consequence/**ense**
consequently/**ently**
conservatory/**ory**
conserve/**erve**
consider/**itter**
consideration/**ation**
cosign/**ine 1**
consist/**ist**
consistence/**istance**
consolation/**ation**
console/**ole**
consoled/**old**
conspire/**ire**
constitute/**ute**
constitution/**ution**
constitutionality/
   ality 1
constrictor/**ictor**
construct/**uct**
construction/**uction**
constructive/**uctive**
construe/**ew**
construed/**ude**
construes/**use 2**
consult/**ult**
consume/**oom**
consumer/**umor**
consumption/
   umption
contacts/**ax**
contagious/**ageous**
contain/**ain**
contaminate/**ate**
contemplate/**ate**
contemporary/**ary**

contempt/**empt**
contender/**ender**
content/**ent**
contently/**ently**
contest/**est**
context/**ext**
continental/**ental**
contort/**ort**
contortion/**ortion**
contour/**ure**
contraband/**and**
contract/**act**
contraction/**action**
contradict/**ict**
contradiction/**iction**
contradictor/**ictor**
contradicts/**icks**
contrary/**ary**
contrast/**ast**
contribution/**ution**
contrive/**ive 1**
control/**ole**
controlled/**old**
controller/**olar**
convalescent/**escent**
convene/**een**
convention/**ention**
converge/**erge**
conversation/**ation**
converse/**erse**
conversed/**irst**
conversion/**ersion**
convert/**ert**
converter/**erter**
conveyor/**ayer**
convict/**ict**
conviction/**iction**
convince/**ince**
cook/**ook 2**
cookie/**ookie**
cookout/**out**
cool/**ool**
cooler/**ooler**
coolly/**uly**
coop/**oop**
cooperate/**ate**
cooperation/**ation**
coordinate/**ate**
coordination/**ation**

coordinator/**ader**
coot/**ute**
cootie/**oody**
cop/**op**
cope/**ope**
copper/**opper**
copy/**oppy**
copyright/**ight**
coquette/**et**
coral/**oral**
cord/**ord 1**
corduroy/**oy**
core/**ore**
cork/**ork 1**
corkscrew/**ew**
corkscrews/**use 2**
corn/**orn**
corncob/**ob**
cornucopia/**opia**
corporation/**ation**
corps/**ore**
corral/**al**
correct/**ect**
correction/**ection**
corrects/**ex**
correspond/**ond**
corresponds/**ons**
corridor/**ore**
corrosion/**osion**
corrosive/**osive**
corrupt/**upt**
corruption/**uption**
Corryn/**in**
corsage/**age 2**
Corvette/**et**
cosmetic/**etic**
cosmos/**ose 1**
cost/**ost 2**
costar/**ar**
costarred/**ard 1**
costume/**oom**
costumer/**umor**
cot/**ot**
cotillion/**illion**
cotton/**otten**
cottontail/**ale 1**
couch/**ouch**
cough/**off**
could/**ood 3**

count/ount
countdown/own 2
counterculture/
    ulture
counterfeit/it
counterfeits/its
counterpart/art 1
counterproductive/
    uctive
countersue/ew
counts/ounce
coupe/oop
coupon/awn
courageous/ageous
course/orse
court/ort
courter/order
courthouse/ouse
courtroom/oom
courtship/ip
Cousteau, Jacques/o
couth/ooth
cove/ove 1
covert/ert
cow/ow 1
coward/owered
cowboys/oys
cower/our 1
cowered/owered
cowhand/and
cowpoke/oke
coy/oy
cozy/osy
CPR/ar
crab/ab 1
crabby/abby
crack/ack
crackdown/own 2
cracked/act
crackerjack/ack
crackle/ackle
crackpot/ot
cracks/ax
crackup/up
craft/aft
crafty/afty
cram/am
cramp/amp
crane/ain

crank/ank
cranky/anky
crash/ash 1
crass/ass
crate/ate
crater/ader
crave/ave
crawl/all
crawled/alled
crawly/olly
Crayola/ola
craze/aze
crazy/azy
creak/eek
creaky/eaky
cream/eem
creamy/eamy
crease/ease 2
creased/east
create/ate
creation/ation 1
creativity/ivity
creator/ader
creature/eacher
credential/ential
credibility/ility
creed/eed
creek/eek
creep/eep
creeper/eeper
creepy/eepy
crematorium/orium
Creole/ole
crept/ept
crescent/escent
crest/est
cretin/eaten
crew/ew
crewed/ude
crib/ib
cricket/icket
cried/ide
cries/ize
crime/ime
criminology/ology
crimp/imp
cringe/inge
crinkle/inkle
cripple/ipple

Crisco/isco
crisp/isp
crisper/isper
crisscross/oss 2
crisscrossed/ost 2
critic/itic
critical/itical
criticism/ism
criticize/ize
critique/eek
critter/itter
croak/oke
croaks/okes
crock/ock
Crockett, Davy/ocket
crocodile/ile 1
crony/ony
crook/ook 2
croon/oon
crooner/ooner
crop/op
croquet/ay
cross/oss 2
crossed/ost 2
crossfire/ire
crossroad/ode
crosstown/own 2
crosswalk/ock
crosswalks/ox
crossword/erd
crouch/ouch
crow/o
crowd/oud
crowed/ode
crowing/owing
crown/own 2
crowned/ound
crows/ose 2
crucify/y
crud/ud
cruddy/uddy
crude/ude
cruel/uel
crueler/ooler
cruelly/uly
cruise/use 2
cruiser/user
crumb/um
crumble/umble

crummy/ummy
crunch/unch
crusade/ade 1
crusader/ader
crush/ush 1
crust/ust
crusty/usty
crutch/utch
crux/ucks
cry/y
crypt/ipped
cub/ub
cubbyhole/ole
cube/ube
cuckoo/ew
cuckoos/use 2
cucumber/umber 1
cuddle/uddle
cue/ew
cued/ude
cuff/uff
cuisine/een
cul-de-sac/ack
culinary/ary
cull/ull 1
cult/ult
cultivate/ate
culture/ulture
cummerbund/und
cup/up
cupcake/ake
cupid/upid
cupidity/idity
cupped/upt
curable/urable
curb/urb
curdle/urdle
cure/ure
curfew/ew 2
curfews/use
curiosity/ocity
curious/urious
curl/url
curlicue/ew
curly/urly
curry/urry
curse/erse
cursed/irst
curt/ert

curtail/**ale 1**
curvacious/**acious**
curvature/**ure**
curve/**erve**
cushy/**ushy**
cuss/**us**
cussed/**ust**
customary/**ary**
cut/**ut 1**
cute/**ute**
cuter/**uter**
cutie/**oody**
cutoff/**off**
cutter/**utter**
cutthroat/**ote**
cutup/**up**
cyclone/**one 1**
cymbal/**imble**
cynicism/**ism**
cyst/**ist**
czar/**ar**
Czech/**eck**

D

dab/**ab 1**
dabble/**abble**
dad/**ad 1**
daddy/**atty**
daffodil/**ill**
daily/**aily**
dairy/**ary**
daisy/**azy**
dally/**alley**
Dalmatian/**ation**
dam/**am**
damp/**amp**
damper/**amper**
dance/**ance**
dandelion/**ion**
dang/**ang**
Daniel Boone/**oon**
dank/**ank**
Danny/**anny**
Danube/**ube**
dare/**air**
daredevil/**evel**
dark/**ark**
Darlene/**een**

darn/**arn**
dart/**art 1**
dash/**ash 1**
dashboard/**ord 1**
date/**ate**
daub/**ob**
daughter/**otter**
daunt/**aunt**
Davy Crockett/**ocket**
dawdle/**oddle**
dawn/**awn**
dawned/**ond**
dawns/**ons**
day/**ay**
daybreak/**ake**
daydream/**eem**
daylight/**ight**
days/**aze**
daytime/**ime**
daze/**aze**
dead/**ed**
deadbeat/**eet**
deadbolt/**olt**
deader/**etter**
deadline/**ine 1**
deadlock/**ock**
deadlocks/**ox**
deadpan/**an**
deadwood/**ood 3**
deaf/**ef**
deal/**eel**
dealt/**elt**
dean/**een**
dear/**eer**
Dear Abby/**abby**
dearer/**earer**
dearie/**eery**
death/**eath 1**
deathbed/**ed**
Death Valley/**alley**
debacle/**ackle**
debate/**ate**
debater/**ader**
debonair/**air**
debrief/**ief**
debt/**et**
debtor/**etter**
debut/**ew**
debutante/**aunt**

decade/**ade 1**
decaf/**aff**
decal/**al**
decathlon/**awn**
decay/**ay**
decayed/**ade 1**
decays/**aze**
decease/**ease 2**
deceased/**east**
deceit/**eet**
deceive/**eave**
December/**ember**
deception/**eption**
decide/**ide**
decision/**ision**
deck/**eck**
decked/**ect**
decks/**ex**
declaration/**ation**
declare/**air**
decline/**ine 1**
declined/**ind 1**
decode/**ode**
decompose/**ose 2**
decomposition/**ition**
decongest/**est**
decongestion/**estion**
decor/**ore**
decorate/**ate**
decoration/**ation**
decorator/**ader**
decoys/**oys**
decrease/**ease 2**
decreased/**east**
dedicate/
   ate, edicate
dedication/**ation**
deduce/**use 1**
deduced/**uced**
deduct/**uct**
deduction/**uction**
deed/**eed**
deem/**eem**
deep/**eep**
deeper/**eeper**
deep-fried/**ide**
deer/**eer**
deface/**ace**
defaced/**aste**

defame/**aim**
default/**alt**
defaults/**alts**
defeat/**eet**
defect/**ect**
defective/**ective**
defector/**ector**
defects/**ex**
defend/**end**
defender/**ender**
defense/**ense**
defensive/**ensive**
defer/**er**
deferential/**ential**
deferred/**erd**
defiance/**iance**
defiant/**iant**
deficient/**icient**
defied/**ide**
defies/**ize**
define/**ine 1**
defined/**ind 1**
definition/**ition**
deflate/**ate**
deform/**orm 1**
defrost/**ost 2**
defroster/**oster**
deft/**eft**
defuse/**use 2**
defy/**y**
degree/**ee**
degrees/**eeze**
dehydration/**ation**
dejection/**ection**
Delaware/**air**
delay/**ay 1**
delayed/**ade**
delays/**aze**
delegate/**ate**
delete/**eet**
deli/**elly**
deliberate/**ate, it**
delicious/**icious**
delight/**ight**
delirious/**erious**
deliver/**iver 2**
Della/**ella**
delude/**ude**
deluge/**uge**

delusion/**usion**
deluxe/**ucks**
delve/**elve**
demand/**and**
demerit/**arrot**
democracy/**ocracy**
democrat/**at 1**
democratic/**atic**
demography/
    ography
demolish/**olish**
demolition/**ition**
demonic/**onic**
demonstrate/**ate**
demonstration/**ation**
demonstrator/**ader**
demoralize/**ize**
demur/**er**
demure/**ure**
demystifies/**ize**
demystify/**y**
den/**en**
denied/**ide**
denies/**ize**
Denmark/**ark**
Denny/**enny**
denomination/
    omination
dense/**ense**
density/**ensity**
dent/**ent**
dental/**ental**
dents/**ense**
denture/**enture**
deny/**y**
deodorize/**ize**
deodorizer/**izer**
depart/**art 1**
departmental/**ental**
depend/**end**
dependability/**ility**
deport/**ort**
depravity/**avity**
depress/**ess**
depressed/**est**
depression/**ession**
deprive/**ive 1**
derail/**ale 1**
derelict/**ict**

dermatologist/
    ologist
dermatology/**ology**
derogatory/**ory**
descend/**end**
descent/**ent**
describe/**ibe**
description/**iption**
desert/**ert**
deserter/**erter**
deserve/**erve**
design/**ine 1**
designed/**ind 1**
designer/**iner**
desire/**ire**
desk/**esque**
Des Moines/**oin**
despair/**air**
desperation/**ation**
despise/**ize**
dessert/**ert**
destination/**ation**
destitute/**ute**
destitution/**ution**
destroy/**oy**
destroyed/**oid**
destroys/**oys**
destruct/**uct**
destruction/**uction**
destructive/**uctive**
detach/**atch 1**
detail/**ale 1**
detect/**ect**
detective/**ective**
detector/**ector**
detects/**ex**
detention/**ention**
deter/**er**
detergent/**ergent**
determination/**ation**
deterred/**erd**
detest/**est**
dethrone/**one 1**
detonate/**ate**
detonator/**ader**
detour/**ure**
detox/**ox**
detrimental/**ental**
deuce/**use 1**

devastate/**ate**
devastation/**ation**
deviate/**ate**
device/**ice**
devil/**evel**
devise/**ize 1**
devoid/**oid**
Devon/**even**
devote/**ote**
devotion/**otion**
devotional/**otional**
devour/**our 1**
devoured/**owered**
devout/**out**
dew/**ew**
dewy/**ewy**
dexterity/**arity**
diabetic/**etic**
diabolic/**olic**
diagnose/**ose 1**
diagnosed/**ost 1**
diagram/**am**
dial/**ile 1**
dialects/**ex**
dialed/**ild**
dialogue/**og**
Diana/**ana 1**
diaper/**iper**
diatribe/**ibe**
dice/**ice 1**
diced/**iced**
dictation/**ation**
dictator/**ader**
dictatorial/**orial**
dictatorship/**ip**
diction/**iction**
dictionary/**ary**
did/**id**
diddle/**iddle**
die/**y**
died/**ide**
diehard/**ard 1**
dies/**ize**
diet/**iet**
dietary/**ary**
Diet Coke/**oke**
Diet Cokes/**okes**
dietetic/**etic**
dietician/**ition**

difficult/**ult**
dig/**ig**
digestion/**estion**
digger/**igger**
dignified/**ide**
dignify/**y**
dignitary/**ary**
digress/**ess**
digressed/**est**
dilettante/**aunt**
dill/**ill**
dilute/**ute**
dim/**im**
dime/**ime**
dimension/**ention**
dimmer/**immer**
dimple/**imple**
din/**in**
Din, Gunga/**in**
Dinah/**ina 2**
dine/**ine 1**
dined/**ind 1**
diner/**iner**
dinero/**arrow**
ding/**ing**
ding-a-ling/**ing**
dingbat/**at 1**
dinghy/**ingy 1**
dingo/**ingo**
dingy/**ingy 2**
dinky/**inky**
dinner/**inner**
dinnertime/**ime**
dinosaur/**ore**
dip/**ip**
diphtheria/**eria**
diploma/**oma**
diplomat/**at 1**
diplomatic/**atic**
dipped/**ipped**
dipper/**ipper**
dippy/**ippy**
dire/**ire**
direct/**ect**
direction/**ection**
director/**ector**
directs/**ex**
dirt/**ert**
dirty/**irty**

disability/ility
disable/able
disagree/ee
disagreed/eed
disagrees/eeze
disappear/eer
disappoint/oint
disapprove/ove 3
disarm/arm 1
disaster/aster
disband/and
disbar/ar
disbelief/ief
disc/isk
discard/ard 1
discharge/arge
disciplinary/ary
discipline/in
disciplined/inned
disco/isco
disconnect/ect
disconnects/ex
discontent/ent
discord/ord 1
discotheque/eck
discount/ount
discounts/ounce
discreet/eet
discrete/eet
discretion/ession
discriminate/ate
discrimination/ation
discuss/us
discussed/ust
discussion/ussion
disdain/ain
disease/eeze
disembark/ark
disenchants/ance
disfavor/aver
disgrace/ace
disgraced/aste
disguise/ize
disgust/ust
disgusted/usted
dish/ish
dishevel/evel
dishonor/onor
dishpan/an

dishrag/ag
dishwater/otter
disillusion/usion
disinfect/ect
disinherit/arrot
disk/isk
dislike/ike
dislocate/ate
dislodge/odge
disloyal/oil
dismiss/iss
dismissal/istle
dismissed/ist
Disneyland/and
disobey/ay
disobeyed/ade 1
disobeys/aze
disown/one 1
disparity/arity
dispatch/atch 1
dispense/ense
disperse/erse
dispersed/irst
displaced/aste
display/ay
displayed/ade 1
displays/aze
displease/eeze
displeasure/easure
disposal/osal
dispose/ose 2
disposition/ition
disprove/ove 3
dispute/ute
disqualified/ide
disqualifies/ize
disqualify/y
disregard/ard 1
disrespect/ect
disrobe/obe
disrupt/upt
disruption/uption
dissatisfaction/action
dissatisfied/ide
dissatisfies/ize
dissatisfy/y
dissect/ect
dissension/ention
dissent/ent

dissenter/enter
dissolution/ution
dissolve/olve
distance/istance
distaste/aste
distinct/inct
distort/ort
distortion/ortion
distract/act
distraction/action
distracts/ax
distraught/ot
distress/ess
distressed/est
distressful/essful
distribution/ution
distrust/ust
disturb/urb
ditch/itch
ditchdigger/igger
dither/ither
ditty/itty
ditzy/itzy
dive/ive 1
diver/iver 1
diverge/erge
divergent/ergent
diverse/erse
diversion/ersion
diversity/ersity
divert/ert
divide/ide
dividend/end
divider/ider
divine/ine 1
divinity/inity
division/ision
divorce/orse
divulge/ulge
Dixieland/and
dizzy/izzy
do/ew
doc/ock
dock/ock
docket/ocket
docks/ox
Dr. Seuss/use 1
dodge/odge
doe/o

Doe, John/o
does/uzz
dog/og
dog-doo/ew
doggie/oggy
doggone/awn
doggoned/ond
doghouse/ouse
dogtrot/ot
dole/ole
doled/old
doll/all
dollar/aller
dolly/olly
dolt/olt
domain/ain
dome/ome 1
domesticity/icity
domicile/ile 1
dominate/ate
domination/
    omination
dominoes/ose 2
don/awn
Donald Duck/uck
donate/ate
donation/ation
done/un
dong/ong
Don Juan/awn
Donna/onna
donned/ond
donnybrook/ook 2
dons/ons
doodad/ad 1
doodle/oodle
doodlebug/ug
Doody, Howdy/oody
doom/oom
door/ore
doorbell/ell
doorknob/ob
doormat/at 1
doorstep/ep
doorstop/op
dope/ope
dopey/opey
Dora/ora
dork/ork 1

dorm/orm 1
dose/ose 1
dot/ot
dote/ote
Dotty/ody
double/ouble
double-check/eck
double-checked/ect
doubleheader/etter
doubt/out
doubter/owder
dough/o
doughy/owy
douse/ouse
doused/oust
dove/ove 1, ove 2
dovetail/ale 1
down/own 2
downcast/ast
downed/ound
downfall/all
downhill/ill
downpour/ore
downrange/ange
downriver/iver 2
downstream/eem
downtown/own 2
downturn/urn
downwind/inned
doze/ose 1
drab/ab 1
drabber/abber
drabby/abby
draft/aft
drafter/after
drafty/afty
drag/ag
draggy/aggy
dragnet/et
dragonflies/ize
dragonfly/y
drain/ain
drama/ama 1
dramatic/atic
dramatize/ize
drank/ank
drape/ape
drastic/astic
draw/aw

drawback/ack
drawbacks/ax
drawbridge/idge
drawer/ore
drawl/all
drawled/alled
drawn/awn
drawstring/ing
dread/ed
dream/eem
dreamboat/ote
dreamland/and
dreamt/empt
dreamy/eamy
dreary/eery
dredge/edge
drench/ench
dress/ess
dressed/est
dresser/essor
dressy/essy
drew/ew
dribble/ibble
dried/ide
dries/ize
drift/ift
driftwood/ood 3
drill/ill
drilled/illed
drink/ink
drip/ip
dripped/ipped
dripper/ipper
drippy/ippy
drive/ive 1
drivel/ivel
driven/iven
driver/iver 1
drizzle/izzle
dromedary/ary
drone/one 1
drool/ool
drooler/ooler
drooly/uly
droop/oop
drooper/ooper
droopy/oopy
drop/op
dropout/out

dropper/opper
drought/out
drove/ove 1
drown/own 2
drowned/ound
drudge/udge
drug/ug
drugstore/ore
drum/um
drummer/ummer
drumstick/ick
drumsticks/icks
drunk/unk
drunken/unken
drunker/unker
dry/y
dryness/inus
dual/uel
dub/ub
duck/uck
Duck, Donald/uck
ducked/uct
ducks/ucks
ducky/ucky
duct/uct
dud/ud
dude/ude
dudette/et
due/ew
duel/uel
dues/use 2
duet/et
duffel/uffle
dug/ug
dugout/out
duke/uke
dull/ull 1
dullsville/ill
dumb/um
dumbbell/ell
dumber/ummer
dumbfound/ound
dumbstruck/uck
dummy/ummy
dump/ump
dumpy/umpy
Duncan/unken
dunce/unts
dune/oon

dungarees/eeze
dunk/unk
dupe/oop
duplex/ex
duplicate/ate
duplication/ation
duplicator/ader
duplicity/icity
durability/ility
durable/urable
duration/ation
duress/ess
dusk/usk
dust/ust
dusted/usted
duster/uster
dustpan/an
duststorm/orm
dusty/usty
Dutch/utch
duty/oody
dwarf/arf 2
dwell/ell
dweller/eller
Dwight/ight
dwindle/indle
dye/y
dyed/ide
dyes/ize
dynamite/ight
dynamo/o
dynamos/ose 2
dysfunction/unction

E

each/each
eager/eager
eagle/egal
ear/eer
earache/ake
eardrum/um
earful/earful
earl/url
earlobe/obe
early/urly
earmark/ark
earn/urn
Earp, Wyatt/urp

earplug/**ug**
earring/**ing**
earth/**irth**
earthbound/**ound**
earthquake/**ake**
earthworm/**erm**
earwax/**ax**
ease/**eeze**
east/**east**
easy/**easy**
easygoing/**owing**
eat/**eet**
eaten/**eaten**
eater/**eeder**
eavesdrop/**op**
eavesdropper/**opper**
eccentricity/**icity**
ecclesiastic/**astic**
ecologist/**ologist**
ecology/**ology**
economic/**omic**
economize/**ize**
economy/**onomy**
ecstatic/**atic**
Ecuador/**ore**
Ed/**ed**
Eddie/**etty**
edge/**edge**
edition/**ition**
editorial/**orial**
educate/**ate**
educator/**ader**
eel/**eel**
eerie/**eery**
effect/**ect**
effective/**ective**
effects/**ex**
effervescent/**escent**
efficient/**icient**
effuse/**use 2**
egad/**ad 1**
egg/**eg**
egghead/**ed**
eggplant/**ant 1**
eggshell/**ell**
egotism/**ism**
Egyptian/**iption**
Eiffel Tower/**our 1**
eight/**ate**

eighteen/**een**
eighty/**ady**
Einstein/**ine 1**
eject/**ect**
ejection/**ection**
ejects/**ex**
elaborate/**ate**
Elaine/**ain**
elastic/**astic**
elasticity/**icity**
elate/**ate**
elation/**ation**
elect/**ect**
election/**ection**
elective/**ective**
electrician/**ition**
electricity/**icity**
electrify/**y**
electrocute/**ute**
electrocution/**ution**
electrode/**ode**
electronic/**onic**
elects/**ex**
elemental/**ental**
elephant/**unt**
elevate/**ate**
elevation/**ation**
elevator/**ader**
eleven/**even**
elf/**elf**
elicit/**icit**
eliminate/**ate**
elimination/**ation**
elite/**eet**
Elizabeth/**eath 1**
Ella/**ella**
elope/**ope**
elsewhere/**air**
elude/**ude**
elusive/**usive**
emancipate/**ate**
embalm/**alm, om**
ember/**ember**
emblazon/**azon**
embody/**ody**
embrace/**ace**
embraced/**aste**
emcee/**ee**
emerge/**erge**

emergency/**urgency**
emergent/**ergent**
emigrate/**ate**
emotion/**otion**
emotional/**otional**
emperor/**er**
emphasize/**ize**
employ/**oy**
employed/**oid**
employee/**ee**
emporium/**orium**
empower/**our 1**
empowered/**owered**
enable/**able**
enact/**act**
enchant/**ant 1**
enchants/**ance**
enchilada/**ada**
enclose/**ose 2**
enclosure/**osure**
encore/**ore**
end/**end**
endeavor/**ever**
endorse/**orse**
endurable/**urable**
endurance/**urance**
endure/**ure**
energetic/**etic**
energize/**ize**
energizer/**izer**
enfold/**old**
enforce/**orse**
engage/**age 1**
engineer/**eer**
engorge/**orge**
engrave/**ave**
engross/**ose 1**
engrossed/**ost 1**
enhance/**ance**
enjoy/**oy**
enjoyed/**oid**
enjoys/**oys**
enlarge/**arge**
enlighten/**ighten**
enlist/**ist**
enmesh/**esh**
enough/**uff**
enrage/**age 1**
enrich/**itch**

enroll/**ole**
enrolled/**old**
ensure/**ure**
enter/**enter**
enterprise/**ize**
entertain/**ain**
enthrall/**all**
enthralled/**alled**
enthuse/**use 2**
enthusiasm/**asm**
enthusiast/**ast, ist**
enthusiastic/**astic**
entice/**ice 1**
enticed/**iced**
entire/**ire**
entitle/**idle**
entomb/**oom**
entourage/**age 2**
entrance/**ance**
entreaty/**eedy**
entrust/**ust**
entwine/**ine 1**
entwined/**ind 1**
envelope/**ope**
environmental/**ental**
envision/**ision**
enzyme/**ime**
episode/**ode**
equality/**ality 2**
equate/**ate**
equation/**asion**
equator/**ader**
equip/**ip**
equipped/**ipped**
erase/**ace**
erased/**aste**
erect/**ect**
erects/**ex**
erode/**ode**
erosion/**osion**
erosive/**osive**
err/**er**
erratic/**atic**
erred/**erd**
error/**arer**
erupt/**upt**
eruption/**uption**
escalate/**ate**
escalator/**ader**

escapade/**ade 1**
escape/**ape**
escort/**ort**
Eskimo Pie/**y**
Eskimos/**ose 2**
espionage/**age 2**
essay/**ay**
essays/**aze**
essential/**ential**
estate/**ate, it**
esteem/**eem**
Esther/**ester**
estimate/**ate, it**
etch/**etch**
eternal/**ernal**
Ethiopia/**opia**
ethnicity/**icity**
Eugene/**een**
euphoric/**oric**
Eurasian/**asion**
evacuate/**ate**
evaluate/**ate**
evaluation/**ation**
evaporate/**ate**
evasion/**asion**
eve/**eave**
event/**ent**
ever/**ever**
evergreen/**een**
evermore/**ore**
everybody/**ody**
everyday/**ay**
everyone/**un**
everyplace/**ace**
everything/**ing**
everywhere/**air**
evict/**ict**
eviction/**iction**
evicts/**icks**
evidence/**ense**
evident/**ent**
evidently/**ently**
evolution/**ution**
evolve/**olve**
we/**ew**
x/**ex**
xact/**act**
xaggerate/**ate**
xaggerator/**ader**

exalt/**alt**
exam/**am**
exasperate/**ate**
exasperation/**ation**
excavate/**ate**
exceed/**eed**
excel/**ell**
excelled/**eld**
except/**ept**
exception/**eption**
excess/**ess**
excessive/**essive**
exchange/**ange**
excite/**ight**
exclaim/**aim**
exclude/**ude**
exclusion/**usion**
exclusive/**usive**
ex-con/**awn**
ex-cons/**ons**
excrete/**eet**
excursion/**ersion**
excusable/**usable**
excuse/**use 1, use 2**
execute/**ute**
execution/**ution**
exemplified/**ide**
exemplifies/**ize**
exemplify/**y**
exempt/**empt**
exercise/**ize**
exerciser/**izer**
exert/**ert**
exhale/**ale 1**
exhaust/**ost 2**
exhibit/**ibit**
exhibition/**ition**
exhilarate/**ate**
exhume/**oom**
exile/**ile 1**
exiled/**ild**
exist/**ist**
existence/**istance**
exotic/**otic**
expand/**and**
expanse/**ance**
expect/**ect**
expectation/**ation**
expects/**ex**

expedition/**ition**
expel/**ell**
expelled/**eld**
expense/**ense**
expensive/**ensive**
experiment/**ent**
experimental/**ental**
expire/**ire**
explain/**ain**
explanation/**ation**
explanatory/**ory**
explicit/**icit**
explode/**ode**
exploration/**ation**
explore/**ore**
explored/**ord 1**
explosion/**osion**
explosive/**osive**
export/**ort**
exporter/**order**
expose/**ose 2**
exposure/**osure**
express/**ess**
expressed/**est**
expression/**ession**
expressive/**essive**
extend/**end**
extension/**ention**
extensive/**ensive**
extent/**ent**
exterminate/**ate**
extermination/**ation**
exterminator/**ader**
external/**ernal**
extinct/**inct**
extol/**ole**
extolled/**old**
extract/**act**
extraction/**action**
extraordinary/**ary**
extreme/**eem**
extrovert/**ert**
exude/**ude**
exult/**ult**
eye/**y**
eyeball/**all**
eyebrow/**ow 1**
eyed/**ide**
eyedropper/**opper**

eyelash/**ash 1**
eyelid/**id**
eyeliner/**iner**
eyes/**ize**
eyesight/**ight**
eyesore/**ore**

F

fab/**ab 1**
fable/**able**
fabrication/**ation**
facade/**awed**
face/**ace**
faced/**aste**
facial/**acial**
facilitator/**ader**
facility/**ility**
fact/**act**
faction/**action**
facts/**ax**
fad/**ad 1**
faddy/**addy**
fade/**ade 1**
fahrenheit/**ight**
fail/**ale 1**
fair/**air**
fairer/**arer**
fairy/**ary**
fairyland/**and**
fajita/**ita**
fake/**ake**
falafel/**awful**
fall/**all**
fallout/**out**
falsehood/**ood 3**
falsetto/**etto**
falsify/**y**
falter/**alter**
fame/**aim**
familiarity/**arity**
familiarize/**ize**
fan/**an**
fanatic/**atic**
fanfare/**air**
fang/**ang**
fanned/**and**
fantasize/**ize**
fantastic/**astic**

fantasyland/**and**
far/**ar**
faraway/**ay**
fare/**air**
farewell/**ell**
farm/**arm 1**
fascinate/**ate**
fascination/**ation**
fascism/**ism**
fast/**ast**
faster/**aster**
fastidious/**idious**
fat/**at 1**
fatalistic/**istic**
fatality/**ality 1**
fate/**ate**
father/**ather 2**
fatherhood/**ood 3**
fatigue/**eague**
fatten/**atin**
fatter/**atter**
fatty/**atty**
fault/**alt**
faults/**alts**
favor/**aver**
favoritism/**ism**
fawn/**awn**
fawned/**ond**
fawns/**ons**
fax/**ax**
faze/**aze**
FBI/**y**
fear/**eer**
fearful/**earful**
feast/**east**
feat/**eet**
feather/**eather**
featherbrain/**ain**
feature/**eacher**
February/**ary**
fed/**ed**
fedora/**ora**
fee/**ee**
feed/**eed**
feedback/**ack**
feeder/**eeder**
feel/**eel**
fees/**eeze**
feet/**eet**

feline/**ine 1**
fell/**ell**
fella/**ella**
feller/**eller**
fellow/**ellow**
fellowship/**ip**
felt/**elt**
female/**ale 1**
femininity/**inity**
fence/**ense**
fender/**ender**
fern/**urn**
ferocious/**ocious**
ferocity/**ocity**
Ferrari/**arry 2**
ferret/**arrot**
ferry/**ary**
fertile/**urdle**
fertilize/**ize**
fertilizer/**izer**
fester/**ester**
festivity/**ivity**
fetch/**etch**
fettucine/**ini**
feud/**ude**
feudal/**oodle**
fever/**eaver**
few/**ew**
fiasco/**asco**
fib/**ib**
fickle/**ickle**
fiction/**iction**
fictitious/**icious**
fiddle/**iddle**
fiddlesticks/**icks**
field/**ield**
fifteen/**een**
fifty/**ifty**
fig/**ig**
fight/**ight**
fighter/**ider**
figurehead/**ed**
file/**ile 1**
filed/**ild**
filibuster/**uster**
Filipino/**ino 2**
fill/**ill**
filled/**illed**
filler/**iller**

filly/**illy**
fin/**in**
finale/**olly**
finality/**ality 1**
finance/**ance**
finch/**inch**
find/**ind 1**
fine/**ine 1**
fined/**ind 1**
finesse/**ess**
finessed/**est**
finger/**inger 1**
fingernail/**ale 1**
fingerprint/**int**
fingertip/**ip**
finite/**ight**
fink/**ink**
fir/**er**
fire/**ire**
firearm/**arm 1**
firefighter/**ider**
firefly/**y**
firehouse/**ouse**
firelight/**ight**
fireplace/**ace**
fireplug/**ug**
fireproof/**oof 1**
fireside/**ide**
firetrap/**ap**
firm/**erm**
first/**irst**
firsthand/**and**
fish/**ish**
fishbowl/**ole**
fishhook/**ook 2**
fishmonger/**unger**
fishpond/**ond**
fist/**ist**
fistfight/**ight**
fit/**it**
fits/**its**
five/**ive 1**
fix/**icks**
fixation/**ation**
fizz/**iz**
fizzle/**izzle**
fizzy/**izzy**
fjord/**ord 1**
flab/**ab 1**

flabbergast/**ast**
flabby/**abby**
flack/**ack**
flag/**ag**
flagpole/**ole**
flair/**air**
flake/**ake**
flame/**aim**
flamingo/**ingo**
flap/**ap**
flapjack/**ack**
flare/**air**
flash/**ash 1**
flashback/**ack**
flashlight/**ight**
flashy/**ashy**
flask/**ask**
flat/**at 1**
flatten/**atin**
flatter/**atter**
flattery/**attery**
flattop/**op**
flaunt/**aunt**
flavor/**aver**
flaw/**aw**
flawed/**awed**
flaws/**ause**
flea/**ee**
fleas/**eeze**
fleck/**eck**
flecked/**ect**
flecks/**ex**
fled/**ed**
flee/**ee**
fleece/**ease 2**
flees/**eeze**
fleet/**eet**
flesh/**esh**
flew/**ew**
flex/**ex**
flexed/**ext**
flexibility/**ility**
flibbertigibbet/**ibbit**
flick/**ick**
flicked/**ict**
flicker/**icker**
flicks/**icks**
flies/**ize**
flight/**ight**

flighty/idy
flinch/inch
fling/ing
flint/int
flip/ip
flipped/ipped
flipper/ipper
flirt/ert
flirtation/ation
flirtatious/acious
flirty/irty
flit/it
flits/its
flitty/itty
float/ote
flock/ock
flocks/ox
flog/og
flood/ud
floodwater/otter
floor/ore
floored/ord 1
flop/op
floppy/oppy
floral/oral
floss/oss 2
flossed/ost 2
flounce/ounce
flour/our 1
flow/o
flowed/ode
flower/our 1
flowered/owered
flowerpot/ot
flowing/owing
flown/one 1
flows/ose 2
Floyd/oid
flu/ew
flub/ub
fluctuate/ate
fluff/uff
fluffy/uffy
fluke/uke
flung/ung
flunk/unk
fluorescent/escent
flurry/urry
flush/ush 1

fluster/uster
flute/ute
flutter/utter
flux/ucks
fly/y
FM/em
foal/ole
foam/ome 1
focal/ocal
fodder/otter
foe/o
foes/ose 2
fog/og
foggy/oggy
foghorn/orn
foil/oil
fold/old
folk/oke
folklore/ore
folks/okes
follow/allow 2
folly/olly
fond/ond
fonder/onder
food/ude
foodaholic/olic
fool/ool
foolhardy/ardy
foolproof/oof 1
foot/oot 2
football/all
foothold/old
footlocker/ocker
footloose/use 1
footmark/ark
footnote/ote
footprint/int
footprints/ince
footwork/erk
for/ore
forbid/id
forbidden/idden
force/orse
Ford/ord 1
forecast/ast
forecaster/aster
forefront/unt
foreground/ound
forehead/ed

foresees/eeze
foresight/ight
forever/ever
forevermore/ore
forewarn/orn
forgave/ave
forge/orge
forget/et, it
forgetter/etter
forgive/ive 2
forgiven/iven
forgot/ot
forgotten/otten
fork/ork 1
forlorn/orn
form/orm 1
formal/ormal
formality/ality 1
format/at 1
formation/ation
former/ormer
formulate/ate
fort/ort
forte/ort
forthright/ight
fortify/ortify, y
fortune-teller/eller
forty/orty
forty-niner/iner
forward/erd
foster/oster
fought/ot
foul/owl
found/ound
foundation/ation
four/ore
fourteen/een
fourth/orth
four-wheeled/ield
fox/ox
foxhole/ole
foxy/oxy
fraction/action
fragmentary/ary
frail/ale 1
frame/aim
framework/erk
Fran/an
France/ance

franchise/ize
frank/ank
Frankenstein/ine 1
Frankfurt/ert
frankfurter/erter
Frankie/anky
frantic/antic
fraternal/ernal
fraud/awed
fray/ay
frayed/ade 1
freak/eek
freaky/eaky
freckle/eckle
Freddie/etty
free/ee
freed/eed
free-lance/ance
freeload/ode
freely/eally
frees/eeze
freestyle/ile 1
freewill/ill
freeze/eeze
freezer/eezer
freight/ate
freighter/ader
French/ench
frenetic/etic
frequent/ent
fresh/esh
freshen/ession
fret/et
Freud/oid
friction/iction
Friday/idy
fridge/idge
fried/ide
friend/end
friendship/ip
fries/ize
fright/ight
frighten/ighten
frill/ill
frilled/illed
frilly/illy
fringe/inge
fringy/ingy 2
Frisco/isco

frisk/**isk**
frisky/**isky**
Frito/**edo**
fritter/**itter**
frivolity/**ality 2**
frizz/**iz**
frizzy/**izzy**
frock/**ock**
frog/**og**
froggy/**oggy**
frolic/**olic**
from/**um**
front/**unt**
frontier/**eer**
fronts/**once**
frost/**ost 2**
frostbite/**ight**
frostbitten/**itten**
froth/**oth 2**
frown/**own 2**
frowned/**ound**
froze/**ose 2**
frozen/**ozen**
fruit/**ute**
fruitcake/**ake**
fruity/**oody**
frumpy/**umpy**
frustrate/**ate**
frustration/**ation**
fry/**y**
fuddy-duddy/**uddy**
fudge/**udge**
fuel/**uel**
fulfill/**ill**
fulfilled/**illed**
full/**ull 2**
fullback/**ack**
fully/**ully**
fumble/**umble**
fumbling/**umbling**
fume/**oom**
fumigate/**ate**
fun/**un**
function/**unction**
fund/**und**
fundamental/**ental**
funk/**unk**
funky/**unky**
funnel/**unnel**

funny/**unny**
fur/**er**
furious/**urious**
furry/**urry**
furthermore/**ore**
fury/**ury**
fuse/**use 2**
fusion/**usion**
fuss/**us**
fussed/**ust**
futile/**oodle**
futility/**ility**
future/**uture**
futuristic/**istic**
fuzz/**uzz**

G

gab/**ab 1**
gabber/**abber**
gabby/**abby**
gag/**ag**
ga-ga/**aw**
gaily/**aily**
gain/**ain**
gait/**ate**
gal/**al**
Galahad/**ad 1**
gale/**ale 1**
gall/**all**
gallbladder/**atter**
galley/**alley**
gallivant/**ant 1**
galore/**ore**
game/**aim**
gang/**ang**
gangplank/**ank**
gangway/**ay**
gap/**ap**
gape/**ape**
garage/**age 2**
gargoyle/**oil**
garish/**erish**
garter/**arter 1**
Gary/**ary**
gas/**ass**
gash/**ash**
gasket/**asket**
gasoline/**een**

gasp/**asp**
gassed/**ast**
gastritis/**itis**
gate/**ate**
gather/**ather 1**
gator/**ader**
Gatorade/**ade 1**
gaudy/**ody**
gauge/**age 1**
gaunt/**aunt**
gauze/**ause**
gave/**ave**
gavel/**avel**
gawk/**ock**
gawks/**ox**
gawky/**awky**
gay/**ay**
Gaza Strip/**ip**
gaze/**aze**
gazelle/**ell**
gear/**eer**
gee/**ee**
geek/**eek**
geeky/**eaky**
geese/**ease 2**
geezer/**eezer**
gel/**ell**
gem/**em**
gender/**ender**
gene/**een**
generate/**ate**
generation/**ation**
generator/**ader**
generosity/**ocity**
genetic/**etic**
Genghis Khan/**awn**
genie/**ini**
gent/**ent**
genteel/**eel**
gentle/**ental**
gently/**ently**
gents/**ense**
geographic/**aphic**
geography/**ography**
geological/**ogical**
geologist/**ologist**
geology/**ology**
George/**orge**
Gepetto/**etto**

germ/**erm**
Geronimo/**o**
Gertie/**irty**
gesundheit/**ight**
get/**et, it**
gets/**its**
Gettysburg Address/
   ess
geyser/**izer**
Ghana/**onna**
ghetto/**etto**
ghost/**ost 1**
ghostwriter/**ider**
ghoul/**ool**
giant/**iant**
giants/**iance**
gibe/**ibe**
Gibraltar/**alter**
giddy/**itty**
gift/**ift**
giftwrap/**ap**
gig/**ig**
gigantic/**antic**
giggle/**iggle**
giggly/**iggly**
gill/**ill**
Gina/**ena**
ginger/**inger 2**
gingerbread/**ed**
gingersnap/**ap**
Ginny/**inny**
giraffe/**aff**
girdle/**urdle**
girl/**url**
girlfriend/**end**
girth/**irth**
gist/**ist**
give/**ive 2**
given/**iven**
giver/**iver 2**
gizzard/**izard**
glacial/**acial**
gladder/**atter**
gladiola/**ola**
glance/**ance**
gland/**and**
glare/**air**
glass/**ass**
glassy/**assy**

glaze/aze
gleam/eem
glean/een
glee/ee
glib/ib
glide/ide
glider/ider
glimmer/immer
glint/int
glitch/itch
glitter/itter
glittery/ittery
glitzy/itzy
gloat/ote
glob/ob
global/oble
globe/obe
globetrotter/otter
glockenspiel/eel
gloom/oom
gloomy/oomy
glorified/ide
glorifies/ize
glorify/orify, y
glorious/orious
glory/ory
gloss/oss 2
glossed/ost 2
glossy/ossy
glove/ove 2
glow/o
glowed/ode
glowing/owing
glows/ose 2
glowworm/erm
glue/ew
glued/ude
glues/use 2
glug/ug
glum/um
glut/ut 1
gnash/ash 1
gnat/at 1
gnaw/aw
gnawed/awed
gnome/ome 1
gnu/ew
go/o
goad/ode

goal/ole
goalie/oly
goalpost/ost 1
goaltender/ender
goat/ote
gob/ob
gobble/obble
gobbledygook/
    ook 2, uke
gobbler/obbler
God/awed
godchild/ild
godfather/ather 2
Godiva/iva
godmother/other
goes/ose 2
go-getter/etter
goggle/oggle
going/owing
gold/old
Golden retriever/
    eaver
goldenrod/awed
goldfish/ish
Goldilocks/ox
golly/olly
gone/awn
goner/onor
gong/ong
gonna/onna
goo/ew
good/ood 3
goodwill/ill
gooey/ewy
goof/oof 1
goofball/all
goofy/oofy
goon/oon
goop/oop
goopy/oopy
goose/use 1
gooseflesh/esh
gore/ore
gorge/orge
gorilla/illa
gory/ory
gosh/osh
got/ot
gotten/otten

gourd/ord 1
governmental/ental
gown/own 2
grab/ab 1
grabber/abber
grabby/abby
grace/ace
graced/aste
Gracie/acy
gracious/acious
grad/ad 1
grade/ade 1
graduate/ate, it
graduation/ation
graffiti/eedy
graft/aft
grain/ain
gram/am
Grammy/ammy
Granada/ada
grand/and
granddad/ad 1
granddaddy/atty
grandfather/ather 2
grandiose/ose 1
grandma/aw
grandmother/other
grandpa/aw
grandpappy/appy
grandparent/arent
grandson/un
grandstand/and
granny/anny
grant/ant 1
grants/ance
grape/ape
grapefruit/ute
grapevine/ine 1
graph/aff
graphic/aphic
grapple/apple
grasp/asp
grass/ass
grasshopper/opper
grassy/assy
grate/ate
Grateful Dead/ed
gratifies/ize
gratify/y

gratitude/ude
grave/ave
gravel/avel
graveyard/ard 1
gravitate/ate
gravity/avity
gravy/avy
gray/ay
grayed/ade 1
grayer/ayer
graze/aze
grease/ease 2
greased/east
great/ate
Great Britain/itten
Great Dane/ain
greater/ader
Greece/ease 2
greed/eed
greedy/eedy
Greek/eek
green/een
greenhorn/orn
greet/eet
Greg/eg
gregarious/arious
grenade/ade 1
Gretel/eddle
grew/ew
greyhound/ound
grid/id
griddle/iddle
gridlock/ock
grief/ief
grieve/eave
grill/ill
grilled/illed
grim/im
grime/ime
grimmer/immer
grin/in
grind/ind 1
grindstone/one 1
gringo/ingo
grinned/inned
grinner/inner
grip/ip
gripe/ipe
griper/iper

gristle/istle
grit/it
grits/its
gritty/itty
groan/one 1
grog/og
groggy/oggy
groin/oin
groom/oom
groomer/umor
groove/ove 3
grope/ope
gross/ose 1
grossed/ost 1
grotesque/esque
grotto/otto
grouch/ouch
ground/ound
groundhog/og
groundwork/erk
group/oop
grove/ove 1
grow/o
growing/owing
growl/owl
grown/one 1
grows/ose 2
growth/oth 1
gr-r-r/er
grub/ub
grubby/ubby
grudge/udge
gruel/uel
gruff/uff
gruffer/uffer
grumble/umble
grumbling/umbling
grump/ump
grunt/unt
grunts/unts
guacamole/oly
Guam/om
guarantee/ee
guaranteed/eed
guarantees/eeze
guard/ard 1
guardianship/ip
guerilla/illa
guess/ess

guessed/est
guesser/essor
guesswork/erk
guest/est
guide/ide
guideline/ine 1
guidepost/ost 1
guild/illed
guillotine/een
guilt/ilt
guise/ize
guitar/ar
gull/ull 1
gullibility/ility
gulp/ulp
gum/um
gumdrop/op
gummy/ummy
gumption/
    umption
gumshoes/use 2
gun/un
gung ho/o
Gunga Din/in
gunned/und
gunner/unner
gunnysack/ack
gunshot/ot
gunslinger/inger 1
gunsmith/ith
guppy/uppy
gush/ush 1
gushy/ushy
gust/ust
gusty/usty
gut/ut 1
gutter/utter
guttersnipe/ipe
guy/y
guys/ize
guzzle/uzzle
gymnast/ast, ist
gymnastic/astic
gyp/ip
gypped/ipped
gypsy/ipsy
gyrate/ate

H

habitat/at 1
hack/ack
had/ad 1
hah/aw
ha ha/aw
hail/ale 1
hair/air
hairbrush/ush 1
haircut/ut 1
hairdo/ew
hairdresser/essor
hairline/ine 1
hairpiece/ease 2
hairpin/in
hairy/ary
Haiti/ady
Hal/al
half/aff
halfmast/ast
halfway/ay
halibut/ut 1
hall/all
hallow/allow 1
Halloween/een
hallucinate/ate
hallucination/ation
hallway/ay
hallways/aze
halt/alt
halter/alter
halts/alts
ham/am
hamper/amper
hand/and
handball/all
handbook/ook 2
handcuff/uff
handicap/ap
handiwork/erk
handkerchief/ief
handlebar/ar
handout/out
handpick/ick
handpicked/ict
handshake/ake
handstand/and
handwrite/ight

handwritten/itten
handyman/an
hang/ang
hangman/an
hangnail/ale 1
hangout/out
hangover/over
hankie/anky
hanky-panky/anky
Hans/ons
Hanukkah/onica
happy/appy
hara-kiri/eery
harangue/ang
harass/ass
harassed/ast
hard/ard 1
hard-boil/oil
harder/arter 1
hardhat/at 1
hardhead/ed
hardship/ip
hardy/ardy
hare/air
hark/ark
harm/arm 1
harmonic/onic
harmonica/onica
harmonize/ize
harpoon/oon
harpsichord/ord 1
Harry/ary
has/azz
hash/ash
haste/aste
hasten/ason
hasty/asty
hat/at 1
hatch/atch 1
hate/ate
hater/ader
haughty/ody
haul/all
hauled/alled
haunch/aunch
haunt/aunt
Havana/ana 1
Hawaiian/ion
hawk/ock

hawks/ox
hay/ay
haystack/ack
haystacks/ax
haywire/ire
haze/aze
hazy/azy
he/ee
head/ed
headache/ake
headband/and
headfirst/irst
headhunter/unter
headlight/ight
headline/ine 1
headlined/ind 1
headliner/iner
headlock/ock
headlong/ong
headmaster/aster
headphone/one 1
headstone/one 1
headstrong/ong
headway/ay
heady/etty
heal/eel
healed/ield
heap/eep
hear/eer
heard/erd
hearse/erse
heart/art 1
heartache/ake
heartbeat/eet
heartbreak/ake
heartbroken/oken
heartburn/urn
heartfelt/elt
heartsick/ick
heartstopper/opper
heartthrob/ob
hearty/ardy
heat/eet
heater/eeder
Heather/eather
heatstroke/oke
heave/eave
heave-ho/o
heaven/even

heavyweight/ate
heck/eck
heckle/eckle
Hector/ector
hedge/edge
heed/eed
heel/eel
Heidi/idy
height/ight
heighten/ighten
heir/air
heirloom/oom
heist/iced
held/eld
heliport/ort
hell/ell
hello/ellow, o
help/elp
helpmate/ate
Helsinki/inky
helter-skelter/elter
hem/em
hemisphere/eer
hemline/ine 1
hen/en
her/er
herb/urb
Hercules/eeze
herd/erd
herder/erter
here/eer
hereafter/after
hereditary/ary
heretic/ick
herewith/ith
hero/ero 1
heroic/oic
heroism/ism
heron/aron
herself/elf
hesitant/esident
hesitate/ate
hesitation/ation
hex/ex
hexagon/awn
hexed/ext
hey/ay
hi/y
hibernate/ate

hiccup/up
hiccupped/upt
hicupper/upper
hid/id
hidden/idden
hide/ide
hideous/idious
hi-fi/y
hi-fis/ize
high/y
high-heeled/ield
highlight/ight
highlighter/ider
highs/ize
highway/ay
hijack/ack
hijacked/act
hike/ike
hiker/iker
hilarious/arious
hilarity/arity
hill/ill
hilltop/op
hilly/illy
hilt/ilt
him/im
himself/elf
hindsight/ight
hinge/inge
hint/int
hints/ince
hip/ip
hippie/ippy
hire/ire
his/iz
hiss/iss
hissed/ist
hissy/issy
historic/oric
history/istory
hit/it
hitch/itch
Hitchcock/ock
hitchhike/ike
hitchhiker/iker
hi-tech/eck
hither/ither
hits/its
hitter/itter

hive/ive 1
hoard/ord 1
hoarder/order
hoarse/orse
hoax/okes
hobble/obble
hobbler/obbler
hobby/obby
hobnob/ob
Hoboken/oken
hockey/awky
hodgepodge/odge
hoedown/own 2
hog/og
hogwash/osh
hogwild/ild
hold/old
holdout/out
hole/ole
holey/oly
holiday/ay
holidays/aze
holistic/istic
holler/aller
hollow/allow 2
holly/olly
Hollywood/ood 3
holocaust/ost 2
holster/olster
holy/oly
Holy Grail/ale 1
home/ome 1
homebody/ody
homefront/unt
homegrown/one 1
homeland/and
homemade/ade 1
homeroom/oom
homesick/ick
homespun/un
homestead/ed
homestretch/etch
hometown/own 2
homework/erk
homicidal/idle
homonym/im
hon/un
honcho/oncho
hone/one 1

honey/**unny**
honeybun/**un**
honeybunch/**unch**
honeycomb/**ome 1**
honeymoon/**oon**
honeymooner/**ooner**
honeysuckle/**uckle**
Hong Kong/**ong**
honk/**onk**
honor/**onor**
honorary/**ary**
honorbound/**ound**
hood/**ood 3**
Hood, Robin/**ood 3**
hoodwink/**ink**
hoodwinked/**inct**
hoof/**oof 2**
hook/**ook 2**
hooky/**ookie**
hoop/**oop**
hoopla/**aw**
hoot/**ute**
hop/**op**
hope/**ope**
Hopi/**opey**
hopscotch/**otch**
Horatius/**acious**
hormone/**one 1**
horn/**orn**
horoscope/**ope**
horrific/**ific**
horrified/**ide**
horrifies/**ize**
horrify/**orify, y**
hors d'oeuvre/**erve**
horse/**orse**
horsefly/**y**
horsepower/**our 1**
horseshoe/**ew**
horticulture/**ulture**
hose/**ose 2**
hospital/**iddle**
hospitality/**ality 1**
host/**ost 1**
hostility/**ility**
hot/**ot**
hotel/**ell**
hotfoot/**oot 2**
hotrod/**awed**

hot rodder/**otter**
hotter/**otter**
hotwire/**ire**
Houdini/**ini**
hound/**ound**
hounddog/**og**
hour/**our 1**
hourglass/**ass**
house/**ouse**
housebreak/**ake**
housebroken/**oken**
household/**old**
housekeeper/**eeper**
housewife/**ife**
housework/**erk**
how/**ow 1**
Howard/**owered**
Howdy Doody/**oody**
however/**ever**
howl/**owl**
hub/**ub**
hubbub/**ub**
hubby/**ubby**
hubcap/**ap**
huddle/**uddle**
hue/**ew**
hued/**ude**
hues/**use 2**
huff/**uff**
huffy/**uffy**
hug/**ug**
huge/**uge**
hulk/**ulk**
hull/**ull 1**
hullabaloo/**ew**
hum/**um**
humane/**ain**
humankind/**ind 1**
humble/**umble**
humbling/**umbling**
humbug/**ug**
humdinger/**inger 1**
humdrum/**um**
humidity/**idity**
humiliate/**ate**
humiliation/**ation**
humility/**ility**
hummer/**ummer**
hummingbird/**erd**

humor/**umor**
humorous/**umorous**
hump/**ump**
Hun/**un**
hunch/**unch**
hung/**ung**
hunger/**unger**
hunk/**unk**
hunker/**unker**
hunky-dory/**ory**
hunt/**unt**
hunter/**unter**
hunts/**unts**
hurdle/**urdle**
hurl/**url**
hurrah/**aw**
hurricane/**ain**
hurry/**urry**
hurt/**ert**
hurtle/**urdle**
hush/**ush 1**
hushaby/**y**
husk/**usk**
hustle/**ustle**
hut/**ut 1**
hutch/**utch**
hybrid/**id**
hydraulic/**olic**
hyena/**ena**
hygiene/**een**
hymn/**im**
hype/**ipe**
hyper/**iper**
hyperactive/**active**
hypertension/**ention**
hyphenate/**ate**
hypnotic/**otic**
hypnotism/**ism**
hypnotize/**ize**
hypocrisy/**ocracy**
hypocrite/**it**
hypocrites/**its**
hypocritical/**itical**
hysteria/**area**

I

I/**y**
ice/**ice 1**

iced/**iced**
icepack/**ack**
icicle/**ickle**
icky/**icky**
iconoclast/**ast**
icons/**ons**
icy/**icy**
ID/**ee, idy**
id/**id**
Idaho/**o**
ideal/**eel**
idealism/**ism**
idealistic/**istic**
idealize/**ize**
ideally/**eally**
identified/**ide**
identifies/**ize**
identify/**y**
idiosyncratic/**atic**
idiotic/**otic**
idle/**idle**
idol/**idle**
idolize/**ize**
if/**iff**
iffy/**iffy**
ignite/**ight**
ignition/**ition**
ignore/**ore**
ignored/**ord 1**
iguana/**onna**
ilk/**ilk**
I'll/**ile 1**
ill/**ill**
illegal/**egal**
illegality/**ality 1**
illicit/**icit**
Illinois/**oy**
illogical/**ogical**
illuminate/**ate**
illusion/**usion**
illusive/**usive**
illustrate/**ate**
illustration/**ation**
illustrator/**ader**
I'm/**ime**
imaginary/**ary**
imagination/**ation**
imbibe/**ibe**
imitate/**ate**

imitation/**ation**
imitator/**ader**
immature/**ure**
immaturity/**urity**
immense/**ense**
immensity/**ensity**
immerse/**erse**
immersed/**irst**
immersion/**ersion**
immigrate/**ate**
immigration/**ation**
immobile/**oble**
immoral/**oral**
immorality/**ality 1**
immortality/**ality 1**
immune/**oon**
immunity/**unity**
imp/**imp**
impact/**act**
impair/**air**
impale/**ale 1**
impart/**art 1**
impasse/**ass**
impeach/**each**
impede/**eed**
impeder/**eeder**
imperfection/**ection**
impersonate/**ate**
impersonation/**ation**
impersonator/**ader**
implant/**ant 1**
implement/**ent**
implicit/**icit**
implied/**ide**
implies/**ize**
implode/**ode**
implosion/**osion**
imply/**y**
impolite/**ight**
import/**ort**
importer/**order**
impose/**ose 2**
imposition/**ition**
impossibility/**ility**
impostor/**oster**
impractical/**actical**
impress/**ess**
impressed/**est**
impression/**ession**

impressive/**essive**
imprint/**int**
imprints/**ince**
impromptu/**ew**
improper/**opper**
improve/**ove 3**
improvise/**ize**
improviser/**izer**
impulsive/**ulsive**
impunity/**unity**
impure/**ure**
impurity/**urity**
in/**in**
inability/**ility**
inaction/**action**
inactive/**active**
inattention/**ention**
inborn/**orn**
inbound/**ound**
inbred/**ed**
incense/**ense**
incentive/**entive**
incessant/**escent**
inch/**inch**
incidental/**ental**
incidentally/**ently**
incision/**ision**
incisor/**izer**
incite/**ight**
incline/**ine 1**
include/**ude**
inclusion/**usion**
incognito/**edo**
incomplete/**eet**
inconclusive/**usive**
incorrect/**ect**
increase/**ease 2**
increased/**east**
incurable/**urable**
indecision/**ision**
indeed/**eed**
indent/**ent**
index/**ex**
indexed/**ext**
Indiana/**ana 1**
indicate/**ate**
indicator/**ader**
indict/**ight**
indigestion/**estion**

indirect/**ect**
indiscreet/**eet**
indiscretion/**ession**
individualism/**ism**
individuality/**ality 1**
indoor/**ore**
induce/**use 1**
indulge/**ulge**
industrialism/**ism**
ineffective/**ective**
inefficient/**icient**
inept/**ept**
inequality/**ality 2**
inexcusable/**usable**
inexpensive/**ensive**
infantile/**ile 1**
infect/**ect**
infection/**ection**
infects/**ex**
infer/**er**
inferiority/**ority**
inferred/**erd**
infiltrate/**ate**
infinity/**inity**
inflame/**aim**
inflammation/**ation**
inflate/**ate**
inflation/**ation**
inflection/**ection**
inflict/**ict**
influential/**ential**
info/**o**
inform/**orm 1**
informal/**ormal**
informality/**ality 1**
information/**ation**
informer/**ormer**
infraction/**action**
infrared/**ed**
infringe/**inge**
infuse/**use 2**
ingrate/**ate**
inhale/**ale 1**
inherent/**arent**
inherit/**arrot**
inhibit/**ibit**
inhibition/**ition**
inhumane/**ain**
initial/**icial**

initiate/**ate**
initiation/**ation**
inject/**ect**
injection/**ection**
injects/**ex**
injure/**inger 2**
injurious/**urious**
ink/**ink**
inkblot/**ot**
inked/**inct**
inkwell/**ell**
inmate/**ate**
inn/**in**
innate/**ate**
inner/**inner**
innermost/**ost 1**
innovation/**ation**
innovator/**ader**
inoculate/**ate**
input/**oot 2**
inquire/**ire**
inquisition/**ition**
insane/**ain**
inscribe/**ibe**
inscription/**iption**
insect/**ect**
insecticide/**ide**
insects/**ex**
insecure/**ure**
insecurity/**urity**
insensitivity/**ivity**
insert/**ert**
inside/**ide**
insider/**ider**
insidious/**idious**
insight/**ight**
insincere/**eer**
insincerity/**arity**
insinuate/**ate**
insist/**ist**
insistence/**istance**
insomniac/**ack**
inspect/**ect**
inspection/**ection**
inspector/**ector**
inspects/**ex**
inspiration/**ation**
inspire/**ire**
install/**all**

installed/alled
installer/aller
Instamatic/atic
instead/ed
instigate/ate
instigator/ader
instill/ill
instinct/inct
institute/ute
institution/ution
instruct/uct
instruction/uction
instructive/uctive
instructor/uctor
instrumental/ental
insufficient/icient
insult/ult
insurance/urance
insure/ure
insurgency/urgency
insurgent/ergent
intake/ake
integrate/ate
integration/ation
intellect/ect
intend/end
intense/ense
intensifies/ize
intensify/y
intensity/ensity
intensive/ensive
intent/ent
intention/ention
intently/ently
interact/act
interaction/action
interacts/ax
intercept/ept
interception/eption
interchange/ange
intercom/om
interfere/eer
interferer/earer
interjection/ection
interlaced/aste
interlude/ude
intermission/ition
intern/urn
internal/ernal

internship/ip
interpretation/ation
interracial/acial
interrogate/ate
interrogation/ation
interrupt/upt
interruption/uption
interscholastic/astic
intersect/ect
intersection/ection
intersects/ex
interspaced/aste
intersperse/erse
interstellar/eller
intertwine/ine 1
intertwined/ind 1
intervene/een
intervention/ention
interview/ew
interviewed/ude
interviews/use 2
intimidate/ate
intimidation/ation
into/ew
intoxicate/ate
intoxication/ation
intramural/ural
intrigue/eague
introduce/use 1
introduced/uced
introduction/uction
introvert/ert
intrude/ude
intrusion/usion
intrusive/usive
intuition/ition
invade/ade 1
invader/ader
invasion/asion
invent/ent
invention/ention
inventive/entive
inventor/enter
inverse/erse
invert/ert
invest/est
investigate/ate
investigation/ation
investigator/ader

investor/ester
invigorate/ate
invite/ight
involve/olve
iodine/ine 1
iota/ota
IQ/ew
Iran/awn
Iraq/ack
Irene/een
iridescent/escent
irk/erk
ironclad/ad 1
ironic/onic
ironical/onical
irregularity/arity
irrigate/ate
irritate/ate
irritation/ation
is/iz
Isabel/ell
Isabella/ella
isle/ile 1
isolate/ate
isolation/ation
Israeli/aily
issue/issue
Istanbul/ull 2
it/it
itch/itch
itinerary/ary
its/its
itself/elf
itsy-bitsy/itzy
Ivanhoe/o
I've/ive 1

J

jab/ab 1
jabber/abber
Jabberwocky/awky
jack/ack
jackal/ackle
jackknife/ife
jackpot/ot
jacks/ax
Jacques/ock
Jacques Cousteau/o

jade/ade 1
jag/ag
jaguar/ar
jail/ale 1
jailbird/erd
jailbreak/ake
Jake/ake
jalopy/oppy
jam/am
jamboree/ee
jamborees/eeze
James Bond/ond
Jan/an
Jane/ain
January/ary
Japan/an
Japanese/eeze
jar/ar
jarred/ard 1
Jason/ason
jaunt/aunt
jaw/aw
jawbone/one 1
jaws/ause
jaywalk/ock
jaywalker/ocker
jaywalks/ox
jazz/azz
jazzy/azzy
jealous/ealous
Jean/een
Jeanette/et
Jeanie/ini
jeep/eep
jeer/eer
Jeff/ef
Jekyll/eckle
jell/ell
jelled/eld
Jell-O/ellow
jelly/elly
jellyfish/ish
Jenny/enny
jeopardize/ize
jerk/erk
jerky/erky
Jessie/essy
jest/est
jester/ester

jet/**et**
jetliner/**iner**
jetsetter/**etter**
jewel/**uel**
jeweler/**ooler**
jiffy/**iffy**
jig/**ig**
jiggle/**iggle**
jiggly/**iggly**
jigsaw/**aw**
jigsaws/**ause**
Jill/**ill**
jilt/**ilt**
Jim/**im**
jingle/**ingle**
jitterbug/**ug**
jittery/**ittery**
jive/**ive 1**
Joan/**one 1**
Joan of Arc/**ark**
job/**ob**
Job/**obe**
jock/**ock**
jockey/**awky**
jocks/**ox**
Joe/**o**
Joel/**ole**
Joey/**owy**
jog/**og**
joggle/**oggle**
John/**awn**
John Doe/**o**
Johnny/**awny**
join/**oin**
joint/**oint**
joke/**oke**
joker/**oker**
jokes/**okes**
jolly/**olly**
jolt/**olt**
Jonah/**ona**
Josephine/**een**
josh/**osh**
jot/**ot**
journal/**ernal**
journalism/**ism**
joust/**oust**
joviality/**ality 1**
joy/**oy**

Joyce/**oice**
joyride/**ide**
joys/**oys**
Juanita/**ita**
Judah/**uda**
judge/**udge**
judgmental/**ental**
judicial/**icial**
judicious/**icious**
Judy/**oody**
jug/**ug**
juggle/**uggle**
juggler/**uggler**
juice/**use 1**
juiced/**uced**
jujitsu/**ew**
Jules Verne/**urn**
Juliet/**et**
July/**y**
July Fourth/**orth**
jumble/**umble**
jumbling/**umbling**
jump/**ump**
jumpy/**umpy**
junction/**unction**
June/**oon**
jungle/**ungle**
junk/**unk**
junkheap/**eep**
junky/**unky**
junkyard/**ard 1**
Jupiter/**upiter**
jurisdiction/**iction**
jury/**ury**
just/**ust**
justifiable/**iable**
justification/**ation**
justified/**ide**
justifies/**ize**
justify/**y**
jut/**ut 1**
juvenile/**ile 1**

K

kangaroo/**ew**
kangaroos/**use 2**
kaput/**oot 2**
karate/**ody**

Karen/**aron**
Kate/**ate**
Kathleen/**een**
Katie/**ady**
kayak/**ack**
kayaks/**ax**
kazoo/**ew**
kazoos/**use 2**
keel/**eel**
keen/**een**
keep/**eep**
keeper/**eeper**
keepsake/**ake**
keg/**eg**
Keith/**eath 2**
Kelly/**elly**
kelp/**elp**
Kenny/**enny**
Kentucky/**ucky**
kept/**ept**
kernel/**ernal**
kerosene/**een**
kerplop/**op**
kerplunk/**unk**
kettle/**eddle**
Kevin/**even**
key/**ee**
keyboard/**ord 1**
keyhole/**ole**
keynote/**ote**
keys/**eeze**
Khan, Genghis/**aun**
kibble/**ibble**
kick/**ick**
kicked/**ict**
kicker/**icker**
kickoff/**off**
kicks/**icks**
kickstand/**and**
kid/**id**
kidder/**itter**
kiddie/**itty**
kidnap/**ap**
kill/**ill**
killed/**illed**
killer/**iller**
killjoy/**oy**
killjoys/**oys**
kilometer/

eeder, ometer
kilt/**ilt**
Kim/**im**
kimono/**ona**
kin/**in**
kind/**ind 1**
kindle/**indle**
kinfolk/**oke**
king/**ing**
King Kong/**ong**
King Tut/**ut 1**
kink/**ink**
kinked/**inct**
kinship/**ip**
Kirk/**erk**
kiss/**iss**
kissed/**ist**
kissy/**issy**
kit/**it**
kite/**ight**
kits/**its**
kitten/**itten**
kitty/**itty**
Kleenex/**ex**
knack/**ack**
knapsack/**ack**
knave/**ave**
knead/**eed**
knee/**ee**
kneecap/**ap**
kneed/**eed**
kneel/**eel**
knees/**eeze**
knelt/**elt**
knew/**ew**
knife/**ife**
knight/**ight**
knit/**it**
knits/**its**
knitter/**itter**
knob/**ob**
knobby/**obby**
knock/**ock**
knockabout/**out**
knockdown/**own 2**
knocker/**ocker**
knockout/**out**
knocks/**ox**
knockwurst/**urst**

knoll/ole
knot/ot
knotty/ody
know/o
knowing/owing
knowledge/owledge
known/one 1
knows/ose 2
knuckle/uckle
knucklehead/ed
konk/onk
kook/uke
Kool-Aid/ade 1
kowtow/ow 1
kowtowed/oud
Kriss Kringle/ingle
Kringle, Kriss/ingle
kung fu/ew

L

lab/ab 1
label/able
laboratory/ory
laborious/orious
lace/ace
laced/aste
lack/ack
lacked/act
lackluster/uster
lacks/ax
lacy/acy
lad/ad 1
ladder/atter
lady/ady
ladybird/erd
ladybug/ug
ladylike/ike
lag/ag
lagoon/oon
laid/ade 1
lair/air
lake/ake
lamb/am
lame/aim
lament/ent
lamp/amp
lampoon/oon
lampshade/ade 1

lance/ance
Lancelot/ot
land/and
landlord/ord 1
landlubber/ubber
landmark/ark
Land Rover/over
landscape/ape
landslide/ide
lane/ain
lanky/anky
Laos/ose 1
lap/ap
lapel/ell
Lapland/and
lard/ard 1
large/arge
lark/ark
Larry/ary
laryngitis/itis
lash/ash 1
lass/ass
last/ast
latch/atch 1
late/ate
latecomer/ummer
later/ader
lather/ather 1
Latin/atin
Latino/ino 2
latitude/ude
latter/atter
laugh/aff
laughed/aft
laughingstock/ock
laughter/after
launch/aunch
launder/onder
laundromat/at 1
laurel/oral
Laurie/ory
lavatory/ory
law/aw
lawful/awful
lawman/an
lawn/awn
lawns/ons
laws/ause
lawsuit/ute

lax/ax
lay/ay
layer/ayer
layover/over
layperson/erson
laze/aze
lazy/azy
lead/ed, eed
leader/eeder
leadership/ip
leaf/ief
league/eague
leak/eek
leaky/eaky
lean/een
leap/eep
leapfrog/og
learn/urn
lease/ease 2
least/east
leather/eather
leatherneck/eck
leave/eave
led/ed
ledge/edge
leech/each
leer/eer
leery/eery
left/eft
leftover/over
leg/eg
legal/egal
legality/ality 1
legalize/ize
legendary/ary
legion/egion
legislate/ate
legislation/ation
legislator/ader
legit/it
legwork/erk
lemonade/ade 1
lend/end
lender/ender
length/ength
Lent/ent
lentil/ental
leotard/ard 1
leprechaun/awn

leprechauns/ons
less/ess
lesser/essor
Lester/ester
letdown/own 2
letter/etter
letterhead/ed
level/evel
lever/ever
Levi's/ize
liability/ility
liable/iable
liaison/awn
liberate/ate
liberation/ation
liberator/ader
library/ary
libretto/etto
lice/ice 1
lick/ick
licked/ict
licks/icks
lid/id
lie/y
lied/ide
lies/ize
life/ife
lifeboat/ote
lifeguard/ard 1
lifelike/ike
lifeline/ine 1
lifelong/ong
lifesaver/aver
life-style/ile 1
lifetime/ime
lift/ift
liftoff/off
light/ight
lighten/ighten
lighter/ider
lighthouse/ouse
like/ike
likelihood/ood 3
likewise/ize
lilacs/ax
Lilliput/ut 1
lilt/ilt
lily/illy
limb/im

limbo/**imbo**
lime/**ime**
limelight/**ight**
limitation/**ation**
limousine/**een**
limp/**imp**
line/**ine 1**
lined/**ind 1**
lineup/**up**
linger/**inger 1**
lingo/**ingo**
linguine/**ini**
linguistic/**istic**
link/**ink**
linked/**inct**
lint/**int**
Linus/**inus**
lion/**ion**
lip/**ip**
lippy/**ippy**
lip-read/**eed**
lipstick/**ick**
lipsticks/**icks**
liqueur/**ure**
liquidate/**ate**
liquor/**icker**
lisp/**isp**
lisper/**isper**
list/**ist**
lit/**it**
liter/**eeder**
literary/**ary**
litter/**itter**
litterbag/**ag**
litterbug/**ug**
little/**iddle**
live/**ive 1, ive 2**
livelihood/**ood 3**
liver/**iver 2**
Liverpool/**ool**
livestock/**ock**
Liz/**iz**
lizard/**izard**
llama/**ama**
Lloyd/**oid**
load/**ode**
loaf/**oaf**
loan/**one 1**
lob/**ob**

lobby/**obby**
lobe/**obe**
local/**ocal**
locale/**al**
locality/**ality 1**
locate/**ate**
location/**ation**
Loch Ness/**ess**
lock/**ock**
locker/**ocker**
locket/**ocket**
locks/**ox**
locksmith/**ith**
loco/**oco**
locomotion/**otion**
lodge/**odge**
log/**og**
logical/**ogical**
loin/**oin**
Lola/**ola**
loll/**all**
lolled/**alled**
lollipop/**op**
lollygag/**ag**
lone/**one 1**
lonely/**only**
long/**ong**
Longfellow/**ellow**
longhand/**and**
longitude/**ude**
look/**ook 2**
lookout/**out**
loom/**oom**
loon/**oon**
loop/**oop**
loophole/**ole**
loose/**use 1**
loot/**ute**
looter/**uter**
lop/**op**
lope/**ope**
loquacious/**acious**
lord/**ord 1**
lore/**ore**
Lorraine/**ain**
lose/**use 2**
loser/**user**
loss/**oss 2**
lost/**ost 2**

lot/**ot**
lotion/**otion**
lottery/**ottery**
lotto/**otto**
loud/**oud**
louder/**owder**
loudmouth/**outh 1**
loudspeaker/**eaker**
Louise/**eeze**
Louisiana/**ana 1**
louse/**ouse**
love/**ove 2**
lovebird/**erd**
lovelorn/**orn**
lovesick/**ick**
lovestruck/**uck**
low/**o**
low-cal/**al**
lowdown/**own 2**
Lowell/**ole**
lows/**ose 2**
loyal/**oil**
Loyola/**ola**
luau/**ow 1**
lube/**ube**
lubricate/**ate**
luck/**uck**
lucky/**ucky**
lug/**ug**
Luke/**uke**
lukewarm/**orm 1**
lull/**ull 1**
lullabies/**ize**
lullaby/**y**
lumber/**umber 1**
lumberjack/**ack**
lump/**ump**
lumpy/**umpy**
lunar/**ooner**
lunatic/**ick**
lunch/**unch**
lunchbox/**ox**
lung/**ung**
lunge/**unge**
lurch/**urch**
lure/**ure**
lurk/**erk**
lush/**ush 1**
luster/**uster**

lute/**ute**
luxurious/**urious**
lynch/**inch**

M

ma/**aw**
ma'am/**am**
macabre/**obber**
macaroni/**ony**
macaroon/**oon**
Macbeth/**eath 1**
machete/**etty**
machine/**een**
mad/**ad 1**
madame/**am**
madcap/**ap**
madder/**atter**
made/**ade 1**
mademoiselle/**ell**
Mad Hatter/**atter**
madhouse/**ouse**
madman/**an**
Madrid/**id**
magazine/**een**
Maggie/**aggy**
magician/**ition**
magnetic/**etic**
magnetism/**ism**
magnified/**ide**
magnifies/**ize**
magnify/**y**
magpie/**y**
maid/**ade 1**
mail/**ale 1**
mailbag/**ag**
mailbox/**ox**
maim/**aim**
main/**ain**
Maine/**ain**
mainstream/**eem**
maintain/**ain**
majorette/**et**
majority/**ority**
make/**ake**
makeshift/**ift**
makeup/**up**
malaria/**area**
malcontent/**ent**

male/ale 1
malfunction/unction
Malibu/ew
malicious/icious
mall/all
malnutrition/ition
malt/alt
malts/alts
mama/ama 1
man/an
mañana/onna
mandate/ate
mandatory/ory
mandolin/in
mane/ain
Manhattan/atin
manhole/ole
manhunt/unt
manhunter/unter
maniac/ack
maniacs/ax
manicure/ure
manifest/est
Manila/illa
manipulate/ate
manipulation/ation
manipulator/ader
manner/anner
mannerism/ism
manor/anner
manslaughter/otter
manuscript/ipped
many/enny, inny
map/ap
mar/ar
marathon/awn
marathons/ons
March/arch
march/arch
Mardi Gras/aw
mare/air
Marge/arge
Marie/ee
marina/ina
marine/een
maritime/ime
mark/ark
Mark Twain/ain
Marlene/een

marmalade/ade 1
maroon/oon
marred/ard 1
marrow/arrow
marry/ary
marshmallow/
   allow 1, ellow
mart/art 1
martini/ini
Marty/ardy
martyr/arter 1
Marv/arve
Mary/ary
Mary Jo/o
Masai/y
mascara/ara
mascot/ot
masculinity/inity
mash/ash 1
mask/ask
mason/ason
masquerade/ade 1
masquerader/ader
mass/ass
massacred/erd
massage/age 2
masseur/ure
masseuse/use 1
mast/ast
master/aster
mastermind/ind 1
masterpiece/ease 2
mat/at 1
matador/ore
match/atch 1
mate/ate
materialism/ism
maternal/ernal
matey/ady
math/ath
mathematic/atic
mathematician/ition
matinee/ay
Matisse/ease 2
matrimonial/onial
matrimony/ony
matter/atter
Matterhorn/orn
mature/ure

maturity/urity
maul/all
mauled/alled
Maurice/ease 2
mauve/ove 1
Maxine/een
Maxwell/ell
may/ay
maybe/aby
Maybelline/een
Mayflower/our 1
mayonnaise/aze
mayor/ayer
Mazatlán/awn
maze/aze
me/ee
meadow/etto
meager/eager
meal/eel
mean/een
meant/ent
meantime/ime
meanwhile/ile 1
meany/ini
measure/easure
meat/eet
meatball/all
meaty/eedy
medal/eddle
meddle/eddle
mediator/ader
medicate/
   ate, edicate
medication/ation
mediocre/oker
meditate/ate
meditation/ation
meek/eek
meet/eet
Meg/eg
melancholy/olly
meld/eld
mellow/ellow
melodic/otic
melodious/odious
melodrama/ama
melodramatic/atic
melt/elt
meltdown/own 2

member/ember
membership/ip
memoir/ar
memorial/orial
memorize/ize
men/en, in
mend/end
menorah/ora
mental/ental
mentality/ality 1
mention/ention
mentor/enter, ore
meow/ow 1
meowed/oud
mercenary/ary
merchandise/ice 1
mere/eer
merge/erge
meringue/ang
merit/arrot
mermaid/ade 1
merry/ary
mesh/esh
mesmerize/ize
mess/ess
messed/est
messy/essy
met/et
metal/eddle
metaphor/ore
meteorite/ight
meteorology/ology
meter/eeder
metronome/ome 1
mew/ew
mewed/ude
mews/use 2
Mexico/o
mezzanine/een
Miami/ammy
mic/ike
mice/ice 1
Mickey/icky
microphone/one 1
microscope/ope
microscopic/opic
microwave/ave
midair/air
middle/iddle

midnight/ight
midriff/iff
midsummer/ummer
midterm/erm
midweek/eek
midwinter/inter
miff/iff
miffed/ift
might/ight
mighty/idy
migraine/ain
migrate/ate
migration/ation
mild/ild
mildewy/ewy
mile/ile 1
milestone/one 1
military/ary
milk/ilk
Milk Dud/ud
mill/ill
milled/illed
Millie/illy
milligram/am
million/illion
millionaire/air
Milwaukee/awky
mime/ime
Mimi/eamy
mince/ince
mind/ind 1
mine/ine 1
mined/ind 1
miner/iner
minestrone/ony
mingle/ingle
mini/inny
minimart/art 1
miniscule/ool
miniskirt/ert
minister/inister
mink/ink
Minnesota/ota
Minnie/inny
minor/iner
minority/ority
mint/int
mints/ince
minuet/et

minus/inus
minuscule/ool
minute/ute
mirage/age 2
mirror/earer
mirth/irth
misapprehension/ention
misbehave/ave
miscast/ast
misconception/eption
misconstrue/ew
misconstrued/ude
miscue/ew
miscued/ude
miscues/use 2
misdeal/eel
misdialed/ild
misdo/ew
miser/izer
misfiled/ild
misfit/it
misfits/its
misguide/ide
mishap/ap
mishmash/ash 1
misinform/orm 1
misjudge/udge
mislabel/able
mislead/eed
mismatch/atch 1
misplace/ace
misplaced/aste
misprint/int
misprints/ince
mispronounce/ounce
misquote/ote
misread/ed
misrepresent/ent
miss/iss
missed/ist
missile/istle
mission/ition
missionary/ary
Mississippi/ippy
missive/issive
Missouri/ury, urry
misspeak/eek

misspell/ell
misspelled/eld
misspent/ent
misspoken/oken
missy/issy
mist/ist
mistake/ake
Mister/ister
mistletoe/o
mistook/ook 2
mistreat/eet
mistrust/ust
mistrusted/usted
misunderstand/and
misunderstood/ood 3
misuse/use 1, use 2
mitt/it
mitten/itten
mitts/its
Mitzi/itzy
mix/icks
moan/one 1
moat/ote
mob/ob
Mobil/oble
mobile/oble, eel
mobility/ility
mobilize/ize
Moby Dick/ick
mock/ock
mockingbird/erd
mocks/ox
mod/awed
mode/ode
model/oddle
moderation/ation
moderator/ader
modernize/ize
modified/ide
modifies/ize
modify/y
module/ool
Mohawk/ock
Mohawks/ox
molar/olar
mold/old
mole/ole
molecule/ool
Molly/olly

mom/om
momentary/ary
mommy/ommy
Mona/ona
monarch/ark
monastery/ary
money/unny
mongoose/use 1
monk/unk
monkey/ee, unky
monkeys/eeze
monocle/onical
monologue/og
monopolize/ize
monorail/ale 1
monotone/one 1
monsoon/oon
monstrosity/ocity
Montana/ana 1
months/once
Montreal/all
monumental/ental
moo/ew
mooch/ooch
moocher/uture
mood/ude
moody/oody
mooed/ude
moon/oon
moonbeam/eem
moonchild/ild
moonlight/ight
moonlighter/ider
moonlit/it
moonstruck/uck
moos/use 2
moose/use 1
moot/ute
mop/op
mope/ope
moped/ed
mopey/opey
moral/oral
morale/al
morality/ality 1
moratorium/orium
morbidity/idity
more/ore
morn/orn

morning/**orning**
moronic/**onic**
morons/**ons**
morose/**ose 1**
Morse Code/**ode**
mortality/**ality 1**
mortar/**order**
mortifies/**ize**
mortify/**ortify, y**
mortuary/**ary**
Moscow/**ow 1**
mosey/**osy**
moss/**oss 2**
mossy/**ossy**
most/**ost 1**
motel/**ell**
moth/**oth 2**
mother/**other**
Mother Goose/**use 1**
motherhood/**ood 3**
motif/**ief**
motion/**otion**
motivate/**ate**
motivation/**ation**
motorbike/**ike**
motto/**otto**
mound/**ound**
mount/**ount**
mountaintop/**op**
mounts/**ounce**
mourn/**orn**
mourning/**orning**
mouse/**ouse**
mouseketeer/**eer**
mousetrap/**ap**
mousse/**use 1**
mouth/**outh 1**
mouthwash/**osh**
move/**ove 3**
mow/**o**
mowed/**ode**
mowing/**owing**
mows/**ose 2**
Mozart/**art 1**
mozzarella/**ella**
Ms./**iz**
much/**utch**
muck/**uck**
mucky/**ucky**

mud/**ud**
muddle/**uddle**
muddy/**uddy**
mudhole/**ole**
muff/**uff**
muffle/**uffle**
mug/**ug**
mukluk/**uck**
mule/**ool**
multiplication/**ation**
multiplied/**ide**
multiplies/**ize**
multiply/**y**
multitude/**ude**
mum/**um**
mumble/**umble**
mumbling/**umbling**
mummify/**y**
mummy/**ummy**
munch/**unch**
mundane/**ain**
municipality/**ality 1**
mural/**ural**
murder/**erter**
murky/**erky**
muscle/**ustle**
musclebound/**ound**
muse/**use 2**
muser/**user**
mush/**ush 1**
mushroom/**oom**
musicale/**al**
musician/**ition**
musk/**usk**
musketeer/**eer**
muskrat/**at 1**
muss/**us**
mussed/**ust**
mussel/**ustle**
must/**ust**
mustache/**ash 1**
mustang/**ang**
muster/**uster**
musty/**usty**
mute/**ute**
mutilate/**ate**
mutilation/**ation**
mutineer/**eer**
mutt/**ut 1**

mutter/**utter**
muumuu/**ew**
muumuus/**use 2**
muzzle/**uzzle**
my/**y**
myself/**elf**
mysterious/**erious**
mystery/**istory**
mystic/**istic**
mysticism/**ism**
mystifies/**ize**
mystify/**y**
mystique/**eek**
myth/**ith**
mythological/**ogical**
mythology/**ology**

N

nab/**ab 1**
Nabisco/**isco**
nadir/**ader**
nag/**ag**
nail/**ale 1**
naive/**eave**
name/**aim**
namesake/**ake**
name-tag/**ag**
Nan/**an**
nanny/**anny**
nap/**ap**
napalm/**alm**
narcotic/**otic**
narrate/**ate**
narrator/**ader**
narrow/**arrow**
nation/**ation**
nationality/**ality 1**
nationalize/**ize**
nativity/**ivity**
naughty/**ody**
nauseate/**ate**
Navajo/**o**
navigate/**ate**
navigator/**ader**
navy/**avy**
nay/**ay**
nays/**aze**
Neanderthal/**all**

near/**eer**
nearby/**y**
Near East/**east**
nearer/**earer**
neat/**eet**
neaten/**eaten**
neater/**eeder**
neat-o/**edo**
necessary/**ary**
neck/**eck**
neckline/**ine 1**
necks/**ex**
necktie/**y**
neckties/**ize**
nectar/**ector**
nectarine/**een**
need/**eed**
needle/**eedle**
needlepoint/**oint**
needy/**eedy**
neglect/**ect**
neglects/**ex**
negotiator/**ader**
neigh/**ay**
neighborhood/**ood 3**
neighed/**ade 1**
Nell/**ell**
Nellie/**elly**
neophyte/**ight**
Neptune/**oon**
nerdy/**urdy**
Nero/**ero 1**
nerve/**erve**
nest/**est**
net/**et**
network/**erk**
neurotic/**otic**
neuter/**uter**
neutrality/**ality 1**
neutralize/**ize**
neutrons/**ons**
never/**ever**
nevermore/**ore**
nevertheless/**ess**
new/**ew**
newborn/**orn**
newcomer/**ummer**
New Delhi/**elly**
newfound/**ound**

New Guinea/**inny**
newly/**uly**
newlywed/**ed**
New Mexico/**o**
Newport/**ort**
news/**use 2**
newsbreak/**ake**
newscast/**ast**
newscaster/**aster**
newsletter/**etter**
newsprint/**int**
newsreel/**eel**
newt/**ute**
New York/**ork 1**
next/**ext**
NFL/**ell**
nib/**ib**
nibble/**ibble**
nice/**ice 1**
nicey-nicey/**icy**
niche/**itch**
nick/**ick**
nicked/**ict**
nickel/**ickle**
nickname/**aim**
nicks/**icks**
Nicky/**icky**
nicotine/**een**
niece/**ease 2**
nifty/**ifty**
Nigeria/**eria**
night/**ight**
nightclub/**ub**
nightfall/**all**
nightgown/**own 2**
nightie/**idy**
nightingale/**ale 1**
nightlife/**ife**
nightmare/**air**
nightshirt/**ert**
nighttime/**ime**
nil/**ill**
Nile/**ile 1**
nimble/**imble**
nincompoop/**oop**
nine/**ine 1**
ninny/**inny**
nip/**ip**
nipped/**ipped**

nippy/**ippy**
nitpick/**ick**
nitpicked/**ict**
nitpicker/**icker**
nitpicks/**icks**
nitwit/**it**
nitwits/**its**
nix/**icks**
no/**o**
Nobel Prize/**ize**
nobility/**ility**
noble/**oble**
nobody/**ody**
nocturnal/**ernal**
nocturne/**urn**
nod/**awed**
Noel/**ell**
noise/**oys**
Nolan/**olen**
nomad/**ad 1**
nominate/**ate**
nomination/
    ation, omination
nominee/**ee**
nominees/**eeze**
nonbeliever/**eaver**
nonchalant/**aunt**
noncommittal/**iddle**
nondescript/**ipped**
none/**un**
nonetheless/**ess**
nonfat/**at 1**
nonfiction/**iction**
nonplus/**us**
nonplussed/**ust**
nonsense/**ense**
nonstop/**op**
nonuser/**user**
noodle/**oodle**
nook/**ook 2**
noon/**oon**
noose/**oose**
nope/**ope**
nor/**ore**
Nora/**ora**
norm/**orm 1**
normal/**ormal**
normality/**ality 1**
north/**orth**

North Carolina/**ina 2**
North Dakota/**ota**
North Pole/**ole**
Norway/**ay**
Norwegian/**egion**
nose/**ose 2**
nosebleed/**eed**
nosedive/**ive 1**
nose-thumber/
    ummer
nosh/**osh**
nosy/**osy**
not/**ot**
notch/**otch**
note/**ote**
notebook/**ook 2**
notification/**ation**
notified/**ide**
notifies/**ize**
notify/**y**
notion/**otion**
notoriety/**iety**
notorious/**orious**
Notre Dame/**aim**
noun/**own 2**
November/**ember**
Novocain/**ain**
now/**ow 1**
nowadays/**aze**
nowhere/**air**
nubby/**ubby**
nude/**ude**
nudge/**udge**
nuke/**uke**
null/**ull 1**
nullify/**y**
numb/**um**
number/**umber 1**
numerous/**umorous**
numskull/**ull 1**
nun/**un**
nurse/**erse**
nursed/**irst**
nursemaid/**ade 1**
nut/**ut 1**
nutrition/**ition**
nutritious/**icious**
nutshell/**ell**
nutty/**uddy**

nuzzle/**uzzle**

O

oaf/**oaf**
Oahu/**ew**
oak/**oke**
oaken/**oken**
oaks/**okes**
oar/**ore**
oat/**ote**
oath/**oth 1**
oatmeal/**eel**
obese/**ease 2**
obey/**ay**
obeyed/**ade 1**
obeys/**aze**
obituary/**ary**
object/**ect**
objection/**ection**
objective/**ective**
objectivity/**ivity**
objects/**ex**
obligation/**ation**
obligatory/**ory**
oblique/**eek**
oblong/**ong**
O'Brien/**ion**
obscene/**een**
obscure/**ure**
obscurity/**urity**
observation/**ation**
observatory/**ory**
observe/**erve**
obsessed/**est**
obsession/**ession**
obsessive/**essive**
obstetrician/**ition**
obstruct/**uct**
obstruction/**uction**
obtain/**ain**
obtrusive/**usive**
occasion/**asion**
occult/**ult**
occupation/**ation**
occupied/**ide**
occupies/**ize**
occupy/**y**
occur/**er**

occurred/**erd**
ocean/**otion**
oceanography/
   ography
o'clock/**ock**
octagon/**awn**
octopus/**uss 1**
odd/**awed**
oddball/**all**
odder/**otter**
ode/**ode**
odious/**odious**
odometer/**ometer**
Oedipus/**uss 1**
of/**ove 2**
off/**off**
offend/**end**
offender/**ender**
offense/**ense**
offensive/**ensive**
offhand/**and**
official/**icial**
officiate/**ate**
offspring/**ing**
offstage/**age 1**
offtrack/**ack**
often/**often**
ogle/**oggle**
oh/**o**
oil/**oil**
okay/**ay**
okayed/**ade 1**
okays/**aze**
okey-doke/**oke**
Oklahoma/**oma**
old/**old**
older/**older**
old King Cole/**ole**
Oldsmobile/**eel**
oldster/**olster**
Olympiad/**ad 1**
Omaha/**aw**
omit/**it**
omniscient/**icient**
on/**awn**
once/**unts**
one/**un**
ongoing/**owing**
only/**only**

ooze/**use 2**
opaque/**ake**
operate/**ate**
operation/**ation**
operator/**ader**
opossum/**ossum**
opportune/**oon**
opportunistic/**istic**
opportunity/**unity**
oppose/**ose 2**
oppress/**ess**
oppressed/**est**
oppression/**ession**
oppressive/**essive**
oppressor/**essor**
optician/**ition**
optimism/**ism**
optimistic/**istic**
option/**option**
or/**ore**
oral/**oral**
orangoutang/**ang**
orangutan/**an**
ordeal/**eel**
order/**order**
ordinary/**ary**
Oreo/**o**
Oreos/**ose 2**
organism/**ism**
organization/**ation**
organize/**ize**
organizer/**izer**
origami/**ommy**
originality/**ality 1**
oriole/**orial**
Orion/**ion**
ornamental/**ental**
ornate/**ate**
orthodox/**ox**
orthopedic/**edic**
ostentatious/**acious**
ostracize/**ize**
other/**other**
otherwise/**ize**
otter/**otter**
ouch/**ouch**
ought/**ot**
ounce/**ounce**
our/**our 1**

oust/**oust**
out/**out**
outbid/**id**
outbound/**ound**
outbreak/**ake**
outburst/**irst**
outcast/**ast**
outclassed/**ast**
outcome/**um**
outcries/**ize**
outcry/**y**
outdid/**id**
outdo/**ew**
outdone/**un**
outdoor/**ore**
outdraw/**aw**
outfit/**it**
outfits/**its**
outfox/**ox**
outgoing/**owing**
outgrew/**ew**
outgrossed/**ost 1**
outgrow/**o**
outguess/**ess**
outguessed/**est**
outhouse/**ouse**
outlast/**ast**
outlaw/**aw**
outlawed/**awed**
outlaws/**ause**
outline/**ine 1**
outlined/**ind 1**
outlive/**ive 2**
outlook/**ook 2**
outloud/**oud**
outnumber/**umber 1**
outpost/**ost 1**
output/**oot 2**
outrage/**age 1**
outrageous/**ageous**
outran/**an**
outrank/**ank**
outreach/**each**
outright/**ight**
outrun/**un**
outscore/**ore**
outscored/**ord 1**
outshine/**ine 1**
outshone/**one 1**

outshoot/**ute**
outside/**ide**
outsider/**ider**
outsmart/**art 1**
outspoken/**oken**
outswam/**am**
outtalk/**ock**
outvote/**ote**
outwear/**air**
outweighed/**ade 1**
outweighs/**aze**
outwit/**it**
outwits/**its**
outworn/**orn**
ovation/**ation**
over/**over**
overachiever/**eaver**
overact/**act**
overactive/**active**
overacts/**ax**
overall/**all**
overate/**ate**
overbite/**ight**
overboard/**ord 1**
overbuild/**illed**
overcame/**aim**
overcast/**ast**
overcharge/**arge**
overcoat/**ote**
overcome/**um**
overcrowd/**oud**
overdid/**id**
overdo/**ew**
overdone/**un**
overdrawn/**awn**
overdress/**ess**
overdressed/**est**
overdue/**ew**
overeager/**eager**
overeat/**eet**
overeater/**eeder**
overexert/**ert**
overexpose/**ose 2**
overfed/**ed**
overfeed/**eed**
overflow/**o**
overflowed/**ode**
overflowing/**owing**
overflows/**ose 2**

overgrown/**one 1**
overgrowth/**oth 1**
overhang/**ang**
overhaul/**all**
overhauled/**alled**
overhead/**ed**
overhear/**eer**
overheard/**erd**
overindulge/**ulge**
overjoy/**oy**
overjoyed/**oid**
overkill/**ill**
overlap/**ap**
overload/**ode**
overlook/**ook 2**
overmuch/**utch**
overnight/**ight**
overpaid/**ade 1**
overpass/**ass**
overpower/**our 1**
overpowered/
   owered
overpriced/**iced**
overprotective/**ective**
overran/**an**
overrate/**ate**
overreact/**act**
overreacts/**ax**
overridden/**idden**
overripe/**ipe**
overrule/**ool**
overseas/**eeze**
oversee/**ee**
oversees/**eeze**
overshoot/**ute**
oversight/**ight**
oversleep/**eep**
overslept/**ept**
overspend/**end**
overstate/**ate**
overstep/**ep**
overstepped/**ept**
overstuff/**uff**
overt/**ert**
overtake/**ake**
overtime/**ime**
overtire/**ire**
overture/**ure**
overturn/**urn**

overweight/**ate**
overwork/**erk**
overzealous/**ealous**
ow/**ow 1**
owe/**o**
owed/**ode**
owes/**ose 2**
owl/**owl**
own/**one 1**
ownership/**ip**
ox/**ox**
ozone/**one 1**

P

pa/**aw**
pace/**ace**
paced/**aste**
pachyderm/**erm**
Pacific/**ific**
pacified/**ide**
pacifies/**ize**
pacifism/**ism**
pacify/**y**
pack/**ack**
packed/**act**
packs/**ax**
Pac-Man/**an**
pact/**act**
pad/**ad 1**
paddle/**attle**
padlock/**ock**
page/**age 1**
pagoda/**ota**
paid/**ade 1**
pail/**ale 1**
pain/**ain**
pair/**air**
pajama/
   ama 1, ama 2
Pakistan/**an**
pal/**al**
pale/**ale 1**
Palestine/**ine 1**
palindrome/**ome 1**
pallbearer/**arer**
palm/**alm, om**
palomino/**ino 2**
Pam/**am**

pamper/**amper**
pan/**an**
Panama/**aw**
Panasonic/**onic**
pancake/**ake**
pane/**ain**
panic-stricken/**icken**
panned/**and**
panorama/**ama 2**
pant/**ant 1**
pantomime/**ime**
pants/**ance**
paperback/**ack**
paperweight/**ate**
papoose/**use 1**
pappy/**appy**
par/**ar**
parachute/**ute**
parade/**ade 1**
paradise/**ice 1**
paradox/**ox**
paragon/**awn**
paragons/**ons**
paragraph/**aff**
Paraguay/**y**
parakeet/**eet**
parallel/**ell**
paralyze/**ize**
paramount/**ount**
paranoid/**oid**
paraphrase/**aze**
parasite/**ight**
parasitic/**itic**
parasol/**all**
paratrooper/**ooper**
parch/**arch**
Parcheesi/**easy**
parent/**arent**
parental/**ental**
Parisian/**ision**
park/**ark**
parmesan/**awn**
parole/**ole**
paroled/**old**
parolee/**oly**
parrot/**arrot**
part/**art 1**
participate/**ate**
participation/**ation**

party/**ardy**
partygoing/**owing**
Pasadena/**ena**
pass/**ass**
passed/**ast**
passerby/**y**
passport/**ort**
password/**erd**
past/**ast**
paste/**aste**
pastel/**ell**
pasteurize/**ize**
pastime/**ime**
pastor/**aster**
pastoral/**oral**
pastrami/**ommy**
pat/**at 1**
patch/**atch 1**
patchwork/**erk**
patchy/**atchy**
paternal/**ernal**
path/**ath**
pathetic/**etic**
pathology/**ology**
patriotic/**otic**
patriotism/**ism**
patrol/**ole**
patrolled/**old**
patroller/**olar**
patronize/**ize**
patty/**atty**
Paul/**all**
Paulette/**et**
Paul Revere/**eer**
paunch/**aunch**
pauper/**opper**
pause/**ause**
pave/**ave**
pavilion/**illion**
paw/**aw**
pawed/**awed**
pawn/**awn**
pawnbroker/**oker**
pawned/**ond**
pawns/**ons**
pawnshop/**op**
paws/**ause**
pay/**ay**
paycheck/**eck**

payoff/**off**
payola/**ola**
payroll/**ole**
pays/**aze**
pea/**ee**
peace/**ease 2**
Peace Corps/**ore**
peacetime/**ime**
peach/**each**
peacock/**ock**
peacocks/**ox**
peak/**eek**
peanutty/**uddy**
pear/**air**
pearl/**url**
pearly/**urly**
peas/**eeze**
peashooter/**uter**
pebble/**ebble**
pecan/**awn**
pecans/**ons**
peck/**eck**
pecks/**ex**
peculiarity/**arity**
pedal/**eddle**
peddle/**eddle**
pediatrician/**ition**
pedicure/**ure**
pedigree/**ee**
pedigrees/**eeze**
peek/**eek**
peek-a-boo/**ew**
peeker/**eaker**
peel/**eel**
peeled/**ield**
peep/**eep**
peephole/**ole**
peer/**eer**
peewee/**ee**
peg/**eg**
pelt/**elt**
pen/**en**
penalize/**ize**
pencil/**encil**
penetrate/**ate**
penmanship/**ip**
penned/**end**
penny/**enny**
pension/**ention**

pensive/**ensive**
pentagon/**awn**
penthouse/**ouse**
pep/**ep**
pepped/**ept**
peppermint/**int**
pepperoni/**ony**
Pepsi-Cola/**ola**
per/**er**
perceive/**eave**
percent/**ent**
percents/**ense**
perception/**eption**
perch/**urch**
percolate/**ate**
percussion/**ussion**
perfect/**ect**
perfection/**ection**
perfects/**ex**
perform/**orm 1**
performer/**ormer**
perfume/**oom**
perfumy/**oomy**
periscope/**ope**
perish/**erish**
periwinkle/**inkle**
perk/**erk**
perky/**erky**
perm/**erm**
permission/**ition**
permissive/**issive**
permit/**it**
permits/**its**
perpetrator/**ader**
perplex/**ex**
perplexed/**ext**
persecute/**ute**
persecution/**ution**
persecutor/**uter**
persevere/**eer**
Persian/**ersion**
persist/**ist**
persistence/**istance**
person/**erson**
personality/**ality 1**
personified/**ide**
personifies/**ize**
personify/**y**
personnel/**ell**

perspective/**ective**
perspiration/**ation**
perspire/**ire**
persuade/**ade 1**
persuader/**ader**
persuasion/**asion**
pert/**ert**
perturb/**urb**
Peru/**ew**
peruse/**use 2**
pessimism/**ism**
pest/**est**
pester/**ester**
pet/**et**
petal/**eddle**
Pete/**eet**
Peter/**eeder**
Peter Pan/**an**
petite/**eet**
petition/**ition**
petrified/**ide**
petrify/**y**
petticoat/**ote**
petty/**etty**
pew/**ew**
pewter/**uter**
pharaoh/**arrow**
phase/**aze**
Ph.D./**ee**
phenomenon/**awn**
Phil/**ill**
phone/**one 1**
phonetic/**etic**
phonic/**onic**
phonograph/**aff**
phony/**ony**
phony-baloney/**ony**
phooey/**ewy**
photograph/**aff**
photographed/**aft**
photographic/**aphic**
photography/
  ography
phrase/**aze**
physician/**ition**
physique/**eek**
piccolo/**o**
pick/**ick**
picked/**ict**

picker/**icker**
picker-upper/**upper**
picket/**icket**
pickle/**ickle**
pickpocket/**ocket**
picks/**icks**
pickup/**up**
picky/**icky**
picnic/**ick**
picnicked/**ict**
picnicker/**icker**
picnics/**icks**
pictorial/**orial**
picturesque/**esque**
piddle/**iddle**
pie/**y**
piece/**ease 2**
pieced/**east**
piecemeal/**eel**
pier/**eer**
Pierre/**air**
pies/**ize**
piety/**iety**
pig/**ig**
pigeonhole/**ole**
pigeonholed/**old**
pigeon-toed/**ode**
piggyback/**ack**
pigpen/**en**
pigskin/**in**
pigsties/**ize**
pigsty/**y**
pigtail/**ale 1**
pike/**ike**
pile/**ile 1**
piled/**ild**
pill/**ill**
pillar/**iller**
pillow/**illow**
pimple/**imple**
pin/**in**
piñata/**ada**
pinball/**all**
pinch/**inch**
pine/**ine 1**
pinecone/**one 1**
pined/**ind**
ping/**ing**
Ping-Pong/**ong**

pink/**ink**
pinkie/**inky**
pinned/**inned**
Pinocchio/**o**
pinochle/**uckle**
pinpoint/**oint**
pinpricks/**icks**
pinstripe/**ipe**
pioneer/**eer**
pip/**ip**
pipe/**ipe**
pipeline/**ine**
piper/**iper**
pip-squeak/**eek**
pique/**eek**
piranha/**onna**
pirouette/**et**
pistachio/**o**
pit/**it**
pita/**ita**
pitch/**itch**
pitchfork/**ork 1**
pitfall/**all**
pits/**its**
pitter-patter/**atter 1**
pity/**itty**
pizzazz/**azz**
place/**ace**
placed/**aste**
plagiarism/**ism**
plagiarize/**ize**
plaid/**ad 1**
plain/**ain**
plainspoken/**oken**
plan/**an**
plane/**ain**
planetary/**ary**
plank/**ank**
planned/**and**
planner/**anner**
plant/**ant 1**
plantation/**ation**
plants/**ance**
plaque/**ack**
plaques/**ax**
plaster/**aster**
plastic/**astic**
plate/**ate**
platform/**orm 1**

Platonic/**onic**
platoon/**oon**
platter/**atter**
platypus/**uss 1**
play/**ay**
played/**ade 1**
player/**ayer**
playground/**ound**
playmate/**ate**
play-off/**off**
playpen/**en**
plays/**aze**
plaything/**ing**
playwright/**ight**
plea/**ee**
plead/**eed**
pleas/**eeze**
please/**eeze**
pleasure/**easure**
pleat/**eet**
pledge/**edge**
pliable/**iable**
pliant/**iant**
plight/**ight**
plod/**awed**
plop/**op**
plot/**ot**
plotter/**otter**
plow/**ow 1**
plowed/**oud**
ploy/**oy**
ploys/**oys**
pluck/**uck**
plucked/**uct**
plucks/**ucks**
plucky/**ucky**
plug/**ug**
plum/**um**
plumber/**ummer**
plume/**oom**
plump/**ump**
plunder/**under**
plunge/**unge**
plunk/**unk**
plural/**ural**
plus/**us**
plush/**ush 1**
P.M. /**em**
pneumonia/**onia**

poach/**oach**
pocket/**ocket**
pod/**awed**
poem/**ome 1**
poetic/**etic**
point/**oint**
poise/**oys**
poke/**oke**
poker/**oker**
pokes/**okes**
polar/**olar**
Polaroid/**oid**
pole/**ole**
police/**ease 2**
policed/**east**
polish/**olish**
polite/**ight**
political/**itical**
politician/**ition**
politics/**icks**
poll/**ole**
polled/**old**
pollster/**olster**
pollute/**ute**
polluter/**uter**
pollution/**ution**
Polly/**olly**
Pollyanna/**ana 1**
polo/**olo**
poltergeist/**iced**
polyester/**ester**
pompom/**om**
poncho/**oncho**
pond/**ond**
ponder/**onder**
ponds/**ons**
pontoon/**oon**
pony/**ony**
pooch/**ooch**
poodle/**oodle**
poof/**oof 1**
poofy/**oofy**
pooh/**ew**
poohed/**ude**
pool/**ool**
poop/**oop**
pooper/**ooper**
poor/**ore, ure**
pop/**op**

popcorn/**orn**
pope/**ope**
Popeye/**y**
popper/**opper**
poppy/**oppy**
poppycock/**ock**
Popsicle/**ickle**
Pop Tart/**art 1**
popularity/**arity**
popularize/**ize**
populate/**ate**
population/**ation**
porch/**orch**
porcupine/**ine 1**
pore/**ore**
por favor/**or**
pork/**ork 1**
port/**ort**
porter/**order**
portfolio/**o**
porthole/**ole**
portion/**ortion**
portrayed/**ade 1**
portrays/**aze**
pose/**ose 2**
posh/**osh**
position/**ition**
posse/**ossy**
possess/**ess**
possessed/**est**
possession/**ession**
possessive/**essive**
possessor/**essor**
possibility/**ility**
possum/**ossum**
post/**ost 1**
postcard/**ard 1**
posterity/**arity**
postmark/**ark**
postmaster/**aster**
postpone/**one 1**
postscript/**ipped**
postwar/**ore**
pot/**ot**
potbelly/**elly**
potential/**ential**
pothole/**ole**
potion/**otion**
potluck/**uck**

potter/**otter**
pottery/**ottery**
potty/**ody**
pouch/**ouch**
pounce/**ounce**
pound/**ound**
pour/**ore**
poured/**ord** 1
pout/**out**
pouter/**owder**
pow/**ow** 1
powder/**owder**
power/**our** 1
power-driven/**iven**
powered/**owered**
powerhouse/**ouse**
powwow/**ow**
pox/**ox**
practical/**actical**
practicality/**ality** 1
prairie/**ary**
praise/**aze**
prance/**ance**
prank/**ank**
prattle/**attle**
pray/**ay**
prayed/**ade** 1
prayer/**air**
prays/**aze**
preach/**each**
preacher/**eacher**
prearrange/**ange**
precarious/**arious**
precautionary/**ary**
precede/**eed**
precinct/**inct**
precise/**ice** 1
precision/**ision**
precocious/**ocious**
precut/**ut** 1
predecessor/**essor**
predict/**ict**
prediction/**iction**
predictor/**ictor**
predicts/**icks**
preemie/**eamy**
prefer/**er**
preferential/**ential**
preferred/**erd**

prehistoric/**oric**
prejudge/**udge**
prejudicial/**icial**
preliminary/**ary**
premature/**ure**
premier/**eer**
premonition/**ition**
preoccupied/**ide**
preoccupies/**ize**
preoccupy/**y**
prep/**ep**
preparation/**ation**
prepare/**air**
preposition/**ition**
preschool/**ool**
preschooler/**ooler**
prescribe/**ibe**
prescription/**iption**
present/**ent**
presentation/**ation**
presenter/**enter**
presents/**ense**
preservation/**ation**
preserve/**erve**
preshrunk/**unk**
president/**esident**
presidential/**ential**
press/**ess**
pressed/**est**
presume/**oom**
presumption/
    umption
preteen/**een**
pretend/**end**
pretender/**ender**
pretense/**ense**
pretension/**ention**
pretty/**iddy**
prevail/**ale** 1
prevent/**ent**
prevention/**ention**
preventive/**entive**
prey/**ay**
price/**ice** 1
priced/**iced**
pricey/**icy**
prick/**ick**
pricked/**ict**
prickly/**ickly**

pricks/**icks**
pride/**ide**
pried/**ide**
priest/**east**
prim/**im**
prima donna/**onna**
primary/**ary**
primate/**ate**
prime/**ime**
primp/**imp**
prince/**ince**
principality/**ality** 1
print/**int**
printer/**inter**
prints/**ince**
priority/**ority**
Priscilla/**illa**
prism/**ism**
prissy/**issy**
prize/**ize**
prizefight/**ight**
prizewinner/**inner**
pro/**o**
probability/**ility**
probation/**ation**
probe/**obe**
problematic/**atic**
proceed/**eed**
procession/**ession**
processor/**essor**
procrastinate/**ate**
procrastination/**ation**
procrastinator/**ader**
prod/**awed**
prodder/**otter**
produce/**use** 1
produced/**uced**
production/**uction**
productive/**uctive**
productivity/**ivity**
profane/**ain**
profess/**ess**
professed/**est**
profession/**ession**
professionalism/**ism**
professor/**essor**
profile/**ile** 1
profound/**ound**
program/**am**

progress/**ess**
progressed/**est**
progression/**ession**
progressive/**essive**
prohibit/**ibit**
prohibition/**ition**
project/**ect**
projector/**ector**
projects/**ex**
prolific/**ific**
prologue/**og**
prolong/**ong**
prom/**om**
promenade/
    ade 1, **awed**
promote/**ote**
promotion/**otion**
promotional/**otional**
prone/**one** 1
pronoun/**own** 2
pronounce/**ounce**
pronto/**onto**
pronunciation/**ation**
proof/**oof** 1
proofread/**ed, eed**
proofreader/**eeder**
prop/**op**
propel/**ell**
propelled/**eld**
propeller/**eller**
proper/**opper**
proportion/**ortion**
proposal/**osal**
propose/**ose** 2
proposition/**ition**
propriety/**iety**
pros/**ose** 2
prose/**ose** 2
prosecute/**ute**
prosecution/**ution**
prosecutor/**uter**
prospect/**ect**
prospects/**ex**
prosperity/**arity**
protect/**ect**
protection/**ection**
protector/**ector**
protects/**ex**
protégé/**ay**

protein/een
protest/est
protestor/ester
protocol/all
prototype/ipe
protrude/ude
protrusion/usion
proud/oud
prouder/owder
prove/ove 3
proverb/urb
provide/ide
provider/ider
provision/ision
provoke/oke
provoker/oker
provokes/okes
prowl/owl
proxy/oxy
prude/ude
prudent/udent
prune/oon
pry/y
psalm/alm, om
pseudonym/im
psych/ike
psychological/ogical
psychologist/ologist
psychology/ology
psychopath/ath
psychosomatic/atic
psychotic/otic
PTA/ay
P.U./ew
pub/ub
publicity/icity
publicize/ize
puck/uck
pucker/ucker
pucks/ucks
puddle/uddle
pueblo/o
puff/uff
puffy/uffy
pug/ug
puke/uke
pull/ull 2
pulley/ully
pulp/ulp

pulsate/ate
pump/ump
pumpernickel/ickle
pumpkin/umpkin
pun/un
punch/unch
punctuality/ality 1
punctuate/ate
punctuation/ation
punk/unk
punker/unker
punky/unky
punned/und
punner/unner
punt/unt
punter/unter
punts/unts
pup/up
pupil/uple
puppy/uppy
pure/ure
purebred/ed
purgatory/ory
purge/erge
purify/y
purity/urity
purloin/oin
Purple Heart/art 1
purr/er
purred/erd
purse/erse
pursue/ew
pursued/ude
pursues/use 2
pursuit/ute
pus/us
push/ush 2
pushover/over
pushy/ushy
puss/uss 1
pussycat/at 1
pussyfoot/oot 2
put/oot 2
put-down/own 2
putt/ut 1
putter/utter
putty/uddy
puzzle/uzzle
pyramid/id

python/awn
pythons/ons

Q

Q-Tip/ip
quack/ack
quacked/act
quacks/ax
quad/awed
quadruple/uple
quail/ale 1
quake/ake
qualification/ation
qualified/ide
qualifies/ize
qualify/y
quality/ality 2
qualm/alm, om
quarantine/een
quarrel/oral
quarry/ory
quart/ort
quarter/order
quarterback/ack
quartet/et
quash/osh
queasy/easy
Quebec/eck
queen/een
quelled/eld
quench/ench
quencher/enture
query/eery
quest/est
question/estion
questionnaire/air
quibble/ibble
quick/ick
quicken/icken
quicker/icker
quickie/icky
quickly/ickly
quicksand/and
quiet/iet
quilt/ilt
quip/ip
quipped/ipped
quirk/erk

quirky/erky
quit/it
quite/ight
quits/its
quitter/itter
quiver/iver 2
quiz/iz
quota/ota
quotation/ation
quote/ote

R

rabbi/y
rabble/abble
raccoon/oon
race/ace
raced/aste
racehorse/orse
racetrack/ack
racial/acial
racism/ism
rack/ack
racketeer/eer
racks/ax
radiate/ate
radiation/ation
radiator/ader
radio/o
radioactive/active
radioactivity/ivity
radios/ose 2
raft/aft
rafter/after
rag/ag
rage/age 1
ragtag/ag
raid/ade 1
raider/ader
rail/ale 1
railroad/ode
railway/ay
railways/aze
rain/ain
rainbow/o
rainbows/ose 2
raincheck/eck

raincoat/ote
raindrop/op
rainfall/all
rainswept/ept
raise/aze
raisin/azon
rake/ake
rally/alley
ram/am
Rama/ama 1
Ramon/one 1
ramp/amp
rampage/age 1
rampageous/ageous
ramshackle/ackle
ran/an
rang/ang
range/ange
Rangoon/oon
rank/ank
ransack/ack
ransacked/act
rant/ant 1
rap/ap
Raphael/ell
rapport/ore
Raquel/ell
rare/air
rarer/arer
rarity/arity
rash/ash 1
rasp/asp
raspberry/ary
rat/at 1
rate/ate
rather/ather 1
ratifies/ize
ratify/y
ratio/o
rationale/al
rationality/ality 1
rattle/attle
rattlesnake/ake
ratty/atty
ravage/avage
rave/ave
ravine/een
ravioli/oly
raw/aw

ray/ay
rays/aze
razz/azz
razzmatazz/azz
reach/each
react/act
reaction/action
reactive/active
reacts/ax
read/ed, eed
reader/eeder
ready/etty
real/eel
realism/ism
realistic/istic
reality/ality 1
realization/ation
realize/ize
really/eally
ream/eem
reap/eep
reaper/eeper
reappear/eer
rear/eer
rearrange/ange
reason/eason
reassurance/urance
reassure/ure
reattach/atch 1
rebate/ate
rebel/ebble, ell
rebelled/eld
rebirth/irth
reborn/orn
rebound/ound
rebuff/uff
rebuild/illed
rebuke/uke
rebut/ut 1
recall/all
recalled/alled
recap/ap
recede/eed
receipt/eet
receive/eave
receiver/eaver
reception/eption
recess/ess
recessed/est

recession/ession
recharge/arge
reciprocity/ocity
recital/idle
recite/ight
reclaim/aim
recline/ine 1
recliner/iner
recluse/use 1
reclusive/usive
recognition/ition
recognize/ize
recoil/oil
recollect/ect
recollection/ection
recommend/end
recommendation/
   ation
reconcile/ile 1
reconsider/itter
reconstruct/uct
reconstruction/
   uction
record/ecord, ord 1
recorder/order
recreation/ation
recruit/ute
recruiter/uter
rectify/y
recuperate/ate
red/ed
redder/etter
redeem/eem
red-faced/aste
redhead/ed
redid/id
redo/ew
redone/un
redshirt/ert
reduce/use 1
reduced/uced
reduction/uction
redwood/ood 3
Reeboks/ox
reed/eed
reef/ief
reek/eek
reel/eel
reelect/ect

reelects/ex
reeled/ield
reenter/enter
ref/ef
refer/er
referee/ee
refereed/eed
referees/eeze
referred/erd
refill/ill
refine/ine 1
refined/ind 1
reflect/ect
reflection/ection
reflective/ective
reflector/ector
reflects/ex
reflex/ex
reform/orm 1
reformatory/ory
reformer/ormer
refrain/ain
refresh/esh
refreshen/ession
refrigerator/ader
refuge/uge
refugee/ee
refund/und
refuse/use 1, use 2
refute/ute
regain/ain
regal/egal
regard/ard 1
regatta/ada
regime/eem
region/egion
registrar/ar
registration/ation
regress/ess
regret/et
regroup/oop
regrowth/oth 1
regularity/arity
regulate/ate
regulation/ation
regulator/ader
rehab/ab 1
rehearse/erse
rehearsed/irst

reign/ain
reimburse/erse
reimbursed/irst
rein/ain
reindeer/eer
reinforce/orse
reiterate/ate
reject/ect
rejection/ection
rejects/ex
rejoice/oice
rejoin/oin
relate/ate
relation/ation
relativity/ivity
relax/ax
relaxation/ation
relay/ay
release/ease 2
released/east
reliable/iable
reliance/iance
reliant/iant
relied/ide
relief/ief
relies/ize
relieve/eave
relive/ive 2
rely/y
remain/ain
remake/ake
remark/ark
remarry/ary
Rembrandt/ant 1
remember/ember
remind/ind 1
reminisced/ist
remorse/orse
remote/ote
remove/ove 3
render/ender
rendezvous/ew
rendezvoused/ude
rendition/ition
renegade/ade 1
renege/eg
renew/ew
renewal/uel
renewed/ude

Reno/ino 2
Renoir/ar
renounce/ounce
renown/own 2
renowned/ound
rent/ent
rental/ental
reoccurred/erd
reorganize/ize
repaid/ade 1
repair/air
repay/ay
repays/aze
repeat/eet
repeater/eeder
repel/ell
repelled/eld
repent/ent
repercussion/ussion
repetition/ition
repetitious/icious
rephrase/aze
replace/ace
replaced/aste
replied/ide
replies/ize
reply/y
report/ort
reporter/order
repossess/ess
represent/ent
represents/ense
repress/ess
repressed/est
repression/ession
reprimand/and
reproach/oach
reproduce/use 1
reproduced/uced
reproduction/uction
reproductive/uctive
reptile/ile 1
reptilian/illion
repulsive/ulsive
reputation/ation
repute/ute
request/est
rerun/un

research/urch
resemble/emble
resent/ent
resents/ense
reservation/ation
reserve/erve
reservoir/ar, ore
reset/et
reshape/ape
reside/ide
resident/esident
residential/ential
residue/ew
resign/ine 1
resignation/ation
resigned/ind 1
resist/ist
resistance/istance
resolute/ute
resolution/ution
resolve/olve
resort/ort
resource/orse
respect/ect
respects/ex
respond/ond
responds/ons
responsibility/ility
rest/est
restart/art 1
restaurant/aunt, unt
restore/ore
restored/ord 1
restrain/ain
restrict/ict
restriction/iction
restricts/icks
result/ult
resurrection/ection
retail/ale 1
retain/ain
retaliate/ate
retaliation/ation
retch/etch
retell/ell
rethink/ink
retire/ire
retold/old
retouch/utch

retrace/ace
retraced/aste
retreat/eet
retribution/ution
retrieve/eave
retroactive/active
retrospective/ective
return/urn
reunion/union
reunite/ight
reusable/usable
reveal/eel
revealed/ield
revel/evel
revelation/ation
revenue/ew
revenues/use 2
reverberate/ate
Revere, Paul/eer
reverse/erse
reversed/irst
review/ew
reviewed/ude
reviews/use 2
revise/ize
revision/ision
revitalize/ize
revival/ival
revive/ive 1
revolt/olt
revolution/ution
revolutionary/ary
revolve/olve
revue/ew
reward/ord 1
rewrote/ote
rhinestone/one 1
rhino/ino 1
rhyme/ime
rib/ib
rice/ice 1
rich/itch
ricocheted/ade 1
ricotta/ota
rid/id
riddle/iddle
ride/ide
rider/ider
ridge/idge

ridicule/**ool**
riffraff/**aff**
rift/**ift**
rig/**ig**
rigatoni/**ony**
right/**ight**
rigor/**igger**
rile/**ile 1**
riled/**ild**
rim/**im**
rind/**ind 1**
ring/**ing**
ringer/**inger 1**
ringleader/**eeder**
Ringo/**ingo**
rink/**ink**
rinky-dink/**ink**
rinky-dinky/**inky**
rinse/**ince**
Rin Tin Tin/**in**
Rio de Janeiro/**arrow**
Rio Grande/**and**
riot/**iet**
rip/**ip**
ripe/**ipe**
rip-off/**off**
ripped/**ipped**
ripple/**ipple**
riptide/**ide**
Rip Van Winkle/**inkle**
rise/**ize**
riser/**izer**
risk/**isk**
risky/**isky**
Rita/**ita**
rite/**ight**
ritualistic/**istic**
ritzy/**itzy**
rival/**ival**
river/**iver 2**
roach/**oach**
road/**ode**
roadblock/**ock**
roadblocks/**ox**
roadrunner/**unner**
roadside/**ide**
roam/**ome 1**
roar/**ore**
roared/**ord 1**

roast/**ost 1**
rob/**ob**
robber/**obber**
robe/**obe**
Robin Hood/**ood 3**
robot/**ot**
robust/**ust**
rock/**ock**
rockaby/**y**
Rockefeller/**eller**
rocker/**ocker**
rocket/**ocket**
rocks/**ox**
rocky/**awky**
rod/**awed**
rode/**ode**
rodeo/**o**
rodeos/**ose 2**
rogue/**ogue 1**
role/**ole**
roll/**ole**
rolled/**old**
roller/**olar**
Rolls-Royce/**oice**
roly-poly/**oly**
romance/**ance**
romantic/**antic**
romanticism/**ism**
romanticize/**ize**
Rome/**ome 1**
Romeo/**o**
romp/**omp**
Ron/**awn**
roof/**oof 1, oof 2**
rooftop/**op**
rook/**ook 2**
rookie/**ookie**
room/**oom**
roomy/**oomy**
roost/**uced**
rooster/**ooster**
root/**oot 2, ute**
rooter/**uter**
rope/**ope**
rose/**ose 2**
Rose Bowl/**ole**
rosebud/**ud**
rosebush/**ush 2**
Rosemarie/**ee**

Rosemary/**ary**
Rose Parade/**ade 1**
Rosie/**osy**
Ross/**oss 2**
roster/**oster**
rosy/**osy**
rot/**ot**
rotate/**ate**
rotation/**ation**
rotten/**otten**
rouge/**uge**
rough/**uff**
rougher/**uffer**
roughhouse/**ouse**
roughneck/**eck**
round/**ound**
roundabout/**out**
roundup/**up**
roust/**oust**
rout/**out**
route/**out, ute**
routine/**een**
rover/**over**
row/**o, ow 1**
rowboat/**ote**
rowed/**ode**
rowing/**owing**
rows/**ose 2**
Roy/**oy**
royal/**oil**
rub/**ub**
rubber/**ubber**
rubberneck/**eck**
rubbernecks/**ex**
rubble/**ouble**
rudder/**utter**
rude/**ude**
rue/**ew**
rued/**ude**
ruffle/**uffle**
rug/**ug**
rule/**ool**
ruler/**ooler**
rum/**um**
rumble/**umble**
rumbling/**umbling**
rummy/**ummy**
rumor/**umor**
rumormonger/**unger**

rump/**ump**
Rumpelstiltskin/**in**
run/**un**
runabout/**out**
runaround/**ound**
runaway/**ay**
runaways/**aze**
rung/**ung**
runner/**unner**
runny/**unny**
runt/**unt**
runts/**unts**
runway/**ay**
rural/**ural**
ruse/**use 2**
rush/**ush 1**
Russell/**ustle**
Russian/**ussion**
rust/**ust**
rusted/**usted**
rustle/**ustle**
rusty/**usty**
rut/**ut 1**
Ruth/**ooth**
Ruth, Babe/**ooth**
RV/**ee**
Ryan/**ion**
rye/**y**

S

sable/**able**
sabotage/**age 2**
saboteur/**ure**
sack/**ack**
sacked/**act**
sacks/**ax**
sacrifice/**ice 1**
sacrificed/**iced**
sad/**ad 1**
sadder/**atter**
saddle/**attle**
saddlebag/**ag**
safari/**arry 2**
safeguard/**ard 1**
sag/**ag**
sagacity/**acity**
sage/**age 1**
saggy/**aggy**

Sagittarius/**arious**
Sahara/**ara**
said/**ed**
Saigon/**awn**
sail/**ale 1**
St. Bernard/**ard 1**
St. Jude/**ude**
St. Nick/**ick**
St. Patrick's Day/**ay**
St. Peter/**eeder**
sainthood/**ood 3**
sake/**ake**
sale/**ale 1**
salesmanship/**ip**
saliva/**iva**
Sally/**alley**
salon/**awn**
saloon/**oon**
salt/**alt**
Salt Lake City/**itty**
salts/**alts**
salute/**ute**
Sam/**am**
same/**aim**
samurai/**y**
sanctimony/**ony**
sanctuary/**ary**
sand/**and**
sandbag/**ag**
sandblast/**ast**
sandblaster/**aster**
sandbox/**ox**
San Jose/**ay**
sandman/**an**
sandpiper/**iper**
sane/**ain**
San Francisco/**isco**
sang/**ang**
sanitary/**ary**
sank/**ank**
Santa Anita/**ita**
Santa Claus/**ause**
Santa Fe/**ay**
Santa Monica/**onica**
sap/**ap**
sapphire/**ire**
sappy/**appy**
Sarah/**ara**
sarcasm/**asm**

sarcastic/**astic**
sardine/**een**
sarge/**arge**
sari/**arry 2**
sarong/**ong**
sash/**ash 1**
sashimi/**eamy**
Saskatchewan/**awn**
sass/**ass**
sassafras/**ass**
sassed/**ast**
sassy/**assy**
sat/**at 1**
satellite/**ight**
satin/**atin**
satire/**ire**
satirize/**ize**
satisfaction/**action**
satisfied/**ide**
satisfies/**ize**
satisfy/**y**
sauce/**oss 2**
saucy/**ossy**
Saudi/**ody**
sauerkraut/**out**
Saul/**all**
sauna/**onna**
savage/**avage**
Savannah/**ana 1**
save/**ave**
savor/**aver**
savory/**avery**
saw/**aw**
sawdust/**ust**
sawed/**awed**
sax/**ax**
saxophone/**one 1**
say/**ay**
scab/**ab 1**
scald/**alled**
scale/**ale 1**
scaly/**aily**
scam/**am**
scamp/**amp**
scamper/**amper**
scan/**an**
scanner/**anner**
scant/**ant 1**
scapegoat/**ote**

scar/**ar**
scare/**air**
scarecrow/**o**
scarecrows/**ose 2**
scarf/**arf 1**
scarred/**ard 1**
scary/**ary**
scatter/**atter**
scatterbrain/**ain**
scene/**een**
scent/**ent**
scents/**ense**
scheme/**eem**
schism/**ism**
schlep/**ep**
scholar/**aller**
scholarship/**ip**
scholastic/**astic**
school/**ool**
schoolbell/**ell**
schoolmaster/**aster**
schoolwork/**erk**
schooner/**ooner**
schuss/**uss 1**
science/**iance**
scientific/**ific**
sci-fi/**y**
scoff/**off**
scold/**old**
scoop/**oop**
scooper/**ooper**
scoot/**ute**
scooter/**uter**
scope/**ope**
scorch/**orch**
score/**ore**
scoreboard/**ord 1**
scorecard/**ard 1**
scored/**ord 1**
scorn/**orn**
Scot/**ot**
Scotch/**otch**
Scottie/**ody**
scour/**our 1**
scoured/**owered**
scout/**out**
scoutmaster/**aster**
scowl/**owl**
Scrabble/**abble**

scram/**am**
scrap/**ap**
scrapbook/**ook 2**
scrape/**ape**
scrappy/**appy**
scratch/**atch 1**
scratchy/**atchy**
scrawl/**all**
scrawled/**alled**
scrawny/**awny**
scream/**eem**
screech/**each**
screecher/**eacher**
screen/**een**
screw/**ew**
screwdriver/**iver 1**
screws/**use 2**
screwy/**ewy**
scribble/**ibble**
scribe/**ibe**
script/**ipped**
scroll/**ole**
Scrooge/**uge**
scrub/**ub**
scrubber/**ubber**
scruff/**uff**
scrunch/**unch**
scruple/**uple**
scrutinize/**ize**
scud/**ud**
scuff/**uff**
scuffle/**uffle**
scum/**um**
scummy/**ummy**
scurry/**urry**
scuttle/**uddle**
scuttlebutt/**ut 1**
sea/**ee**
seafarer/**arer**
seafood/**ude**
seal/**eel**
sealed/**ield**
seam/**eem**
seaport/**ort**
search/**urch**
searchlight/**ight**
seas/**eeze**
seashore/**ore**
seasick/**ick**

season/eason
seat/eet
Seattle/attle
seaweed/eed
seclude/ude
seclusion/usion
seclusive/usive
secondary/ary
secondhand/and
secretary/ary
secrete/eet
sect/ect
section/ection
securable/urable
secure/ure
security/urity
sedan/an
sedate/ate
sedentary/ary
see/ee
seed/eed
seedy/eedy
seek/eek
seem/eem
seen/een
seep/eep
sees/eeze
seesaw/aw
seesawed/awed
seesaws/ause
seethe/eethe
segregate/ate
segregation/ation
seize/eeze
select/ect
selection/ection
selective/ective
selects/ex
self/elf
sell/ell
seller/eller
semester/ester
semiautomatic/atic
semicolon/olen
semiformal/ormal
seminar/ar
send/end
sender/ender
senile/ile 1

senility/ility
seniority/ority
señor/ore
señora/ora
señorita/ita
sensationalism/ism
sense/ense
sensibility/ility
sensitivity/ivity
sensitize/ize
sent/ent
sentimental/ental
sentimentality/
   ality 1
separate/ate, it
separation/ation
September/ember
serape/oppy
serenade/ade 1
serenader/ader
serene/een
serf/urf
serious/erious
serpentine/een
serve/erve
servitude/ude
Sesame Street/eet
session/ession
set/et
setback/ack
settle/eddle
setup/up
seven/even
seventeen/een
7-Up/up
sever/ever
severe/eer
severer/earer
severity/arity
sew/o
sewed/ode
sewing/owing
sewn/one 1
sews/ose 2
sex/ex
shabby/abby
shack/ack
shackle/ackle
shacks/ax

shade/ade 1
shadowbox/ox
shady/ady
shaft/aft
shag/ag
shaggy/aggy
shake/ake
Shake 'n Bake/ake
Shakespeare/eer
shall/al
shallow/allow 1
sham/am
shame/aim
shampoo/ew
shampooed/ude
shampoos/use 2
shamrock/ock
shamrocks/ox
Shanghai/y
shape/ape
share/air
sharecropper/opper
shareholder/older
shark/ark
Sharon/aron
sharpshooter/uter
shatter/atter
shave/ave
shaver/aver
shawl/all
she/ee
shed/ed
sheen/een
sheep/eep
sheepskin/in
sheer/eer
sheet/eet
shelf/elf
shell/ell
shelled/eld
Shelley/elly
shelter/elter
shelve/elve
Sherlock/ock
shied/ide
shield/ield
shies/ize
shift/ift
shifty/ifty

shillelagh/aily
shimmer/immer
shin/in
shindig/ig
shine/ine 1
shiner/iner
shingle/ingle
shiny/iny
ship/ip
shipped/ipped
shipper/ipper
shipshape/ape
shipwreck/eck
shipwrecked/ect
shipyard/ard 1
shirk/erk
Shirley/urly
shirt/ert
shirtsleeve/eave
shirttail/ale 1
shish kebab/ob
shiver/iver 2
shock/ock
shocker/ocker
shocks/ox
shockwave/ave
shoddy/ody
shoe/ew
shoehorn/orn
shoelace/ace
shoes/use 2
shoeshine/ine 1
shoeshiner/iner
shoestring/ing
shone/one 1
shook/ook 2
shoot/ute
shooter/uter
shop/op
shoplift/ift
shopper/opper
shore/ore
short/ort
shortcake/ake
shortchange/ange
shortcut/ut 1
shorter/order
shorthand/and
shortstop/op

shorty/orty
Shoshone/ony
shot/ot
shotgun/un
shotput/oot 2
should/ood 3
shoulder/older
shout/out
shouter/owder
shove/ove 2
show/o
showbiz/iz
showed/ode
shower/our 1
showered/owered
showing/owing
shown/one 1
show-off/off
shows/ose 2
showtime/ime
showy/owy
shrank/ank
shred/ed
shredder/etter
shrewd/ude
shriek/eek
shrill/ill
shrilly/illy
shrimp/imp
shrimpy/impy
shrine/ine 1
shrink/ink
shrivel/ivel
shroud/oud
shrub/ub
shrug/ug
shrunk/unk
shrunken/unken
shucks/ucks
shudder/utter
shuffle/uffle
shun/un
shunned/und
shush/ush 1
shut/ut 1
shutter/utter
shuttle/uddle
shy/y
shyness/inus

Siamese/eeze
Siberia/eria
Sibyl/ibble
Sicilian/illion
sick/ick
sickbed/ed
sicken/icken
sicker/icker
sickle/ickle
sickly/ickly
Sid/id
side/ide
sidekick/ick
sideline/ine 1
sidesaddle/attle
sideshow/o
sideshows/ose 2
sidestep/ep
sidestepped/ept
sideswipe/ipe
sidetrack/ack
sidetracked/act
sidewalk/ock
sideways/aze
sieve/ive 2
sift/ift
sigh/y
sighed/ide
sighs/ize
sight/ight
sightsee/ee
sign/ine 1
signed/ind 1
signifies/ize
signify/y
signpost/ost 1
silhouette/et
silicon/awn
silk/ilk
silkworm/erm
sill/ill
silly/illy
Silly Putty/uddy
silverware/air
similarity/arity
simmer/immer
simple/imple
simplicity/icity
simplifies/ize

simplify/y
simplistic/istic
sin/in
Sinbad/ad 1
since/ince
sincere/eer
sincerer/earer
sincerity/arity
sing/ing
Singapore/ore
singe/inge
singer/inger 1
single/ingle
Sing Sing/ing
sinister/inister
sink/ink
sinned/inned
sinner/inner
sinus/inus
sip/ip
sipped/ipped
sipper/ipper
sir/er
sire/ire
sirloin/oin
sis/iss
sissy/issy
sister/ister
sisterhood/ood 3
sit/it
sitcom/om
site/ight
sits/its
sitter/itter
Sitting Bull/ull 2
situate/ate
situation/ation
six/icks
sixteen/een
size/ize
sizzle/izzle
skate/ate
skateboard/ord 1
skater/ader
skedaddle/attle
skepticism/ism
sketch/etch
ski/ee
skid/id

skied/eed
skies/ize
skill/ill
skilled/illed
skim/im
skimp/imp
skimpy/impy
skin/in
skinned/inned
skinny/inny
skintight/ight
skip/ip
skipped/ipped
skipper/ipper
Skippy/ippy
skirt/ert
skis/eeze
skit/it
skits/its
skittery/ittery
skulk/ulk
skull/ull 1
skunk/unk
sky/y
skydive/ive 1
skydiver/iver1
skylark/ark
skyline/ine 1
skyrocket/ocket
slack/ack
slacks/ax
slain/ain
slam/am
slang/ang
slant/ant 1
slap/ap
slaphappy/appy
slapstick/ick
slash/ash 1
slate/ate
slaughter/otter
slave/ave
slavery/avery
slay/ay
slays/aze
sled/ed
sleek/eek
sleep/eep
sleepaholic/olic

sleeper/eeper
Sleepy Beauty/oody
sleepwalk/ock
sleepwalker/ocker
sleepwalks/ox
sleepy/eepy
sleepyhead/ed
sleet/eet
sleeve/eave
sleigh/ay
sleighbell/ell
slender/ender
slept/ept
sleuth/ooth
slew/ew
slice/ice 1
sliced/iced
slick/ick
slicked/ict
slicker/icker
slid/id
slide/ide
slight/ight
slighter/ider
slim/im
slime/ime
slimmer/immer
sling/ing
slingshot/ot
slink/ink
slinky/inky
slip/ip
slipped/ipped
slipper/ipper
slipshod/awed
slit/it
slither/ither
slits/its
sliver/iver 2
slob/ob
slobber/obber
sloop/oop
slop/op
slope/ope
sloppy/oppy
Sloppy Joe/o
slosh/osh
slot/ot
sloth/oth 2

slouch/ouch
slow/o
slowdown/own 2
slowed/ode
slowly/oly
slowpoke/oke
slows/ose 2
sludge/udge
slug/ug
slum/um
slumber/umber 1
slumlord/ord 1
slump/ump
slunk/unk
slur/er
slurp/urp
slurred/erd
slush/ush 1
sly/y
slyness/inus
smack/ack
smacked/act
smacks/ax
small/all
smaller/aller
smallish/olish
smart/art 1
smarter/arter
smarty/ardy
smash/ash 1
smear/eer
smell/ell
smelly/elly
smelter/elter
smile/ile 1
smiled/ild
smirk/erk
smith/ith
smitten/itten
smock/ock
smocks/ox
smoggy/oggy
smoke/oke
smoker/oker
smokes/okes
smokescreen/een
Smokey the Bear/air
smolder/older
smooch/ooch

smorgasbord/ord 1
smother/other
smudge/udge
smug/ug
smuggle/uggle
smuggler/uggler
Smurf/urf
smut/ut 1
snack/ack
snacked/act
snacks/ax
snafu/ew
snag/ag
snaggletooth/ooth
snail/ale 1
snake/ake
snakebite/ight
snakeskin/in
snap/ap
snappy/appy
snapshot/ot
snare/air
snatch/atch 1
snazzy/azzy
sneak/eek
sneaker/eaker
sneaky/eaky
sneer/eer
sneeze/eeze
sneezy/easy
snide/ide
sniff/iff
sniffed/ift
snigger/igger
snip/ip
sniper/iper
snipped/ipped
snippy/ippy
snitch/itch
snivel/ivel
snob/ob
snobby/obby
snoop/oop
snooper/ooper
snoopy/oopy
snoot/ute
snooty/oody
snooze/use 2
snoozer/user

snore/ore
snored/ord 1
snort/ort
snot/ot
snotty/ody
snout/out
snow/o
snowball/all
snowballed/alled
snowbound/ound
snowdrift/ift
snowed/ode
snowfall/all
snowflake/ake
snowing/owing
snowplow/ow 1
snows/ose 2
snowstorm/orm 1
Snow White/ight
snowy/owy
snub/ub
snuff/uff
snuffle/uffle
snug/ug
snuggle/uggle
snuggler/uggler
so/o
soak/oke
soap/ope
soapy/opey
soar/ore
soared/ord 1
sob/ob
sobber/obber
soccer/ocker
socialism/ism
socialite/ight
socialize/ize
society/iety
sociologist/ologist
sociology/ology
sock/ock
socket/ocket
socks/ox
Socrates/eeze
soda/ota
soften/often
soggy/oggy
soil/oil

sojourn/urn
solar/olar
Solarcaine/ain
sold/old
sole/ole
solely/oly
solicit/icit
solidarity/arity
solidifies/ize
solidify/y
solitaire/air
solitary/ary
solitude/ude
solo/olo
solution/ution
solve/olve
sombrero/arrow
some/um
somebody/ody
somehow/ow 1
someone/un
somersault/alt
somersaults/alts
something/ing
sometime/ime
someway/ay
somewhat/ot, ut 1
somewhere/air
son/un
song/ong
songbird/erd
songwriter/ider
Sonia/onia
sonic/onic
sonny/unny
Sony/ony
soon/oon
sooner/ooner
soot/oot 2
soothsayer/ayer
sophistication/ation
sophomore/ore
sophomoric/oric
sore/ore
sorority/ority
sorry/arry 2
sort/ort
s.o.s./ess
sought/ot

soul/ole
sound/ound
soundproof/oof 1
soundtrack/ack
soup/oop
soupy/oopy
sour/our 1
source/orse
sourdough/o
soured/owered
sourpuss/uss 1
south/outh 1
South Carolina/ina 2
South Dakota/ota
southpaw/aw
souvenir/eer
Soviet/et
sow/ow 1
sox/ox
soy/oy
spa/aw
space/ace
spacecraft/aft
spaced/aste
spaceship/ip
spacey/acy
spacious/acious
spackle/ackle
spade/ade 1
spaghetti/etty
Spain/ain
span/an
spank/ank
spanned/and
spar/ar
spare/air
sparerib/ib
spark/ark
sparred/ard 1
sparrow/ero 2
spasm/asm
spastic/astic
spat/at 1
spatial/acial
spawn/awn
speak/eek
speaker/eaker
spear/eer
spearhead/ed

spearmint/int
specialize/ize
specific/ific
specifies/ize
specify/y
speck/eck
spectator/ader
specter/ector
speculate/ate
speculation/ation
speculator/ader
sped/ed
speech/each
speed/eed
speeder/eeder
speedometer/ometer
speed-read/eed
speedy/eedy
spell/ell
spellbound/ound
spelled/eld
speller/eller
spend/end
spendthrift/ift
spent/ent
spewed/ude
sphere/eer
spice/ice 1
spiced/iced
spicy/icy
spider/ider
spied/ide
spies/ize
spiffy/iffy
spike/ike
spill/ill
spilled/illed
spillover/over
spilt/ilt
spin/in
spindle/indle
spine/ine 1
spinner/inner
spiny/iny
spire/ire
spiritualism/ism
spit/it
spitball/all
spite/ight

spitfire/ire
spits/its
spitter/itter
spittoon/oon
splash/ash 1
splashdown/own 2
splashy/ashy
splat/at 1
splatter/atter
splendor/ender
splice/ice 1
splint/int
splinter/inter
split/it
splits/its
splurge/erge
spoil/oil
spoilsport/ort
Spokane/an
spoke/oke
spoken/oken
spokes/okes
spokesperson/erson
sponge/unge
spoof/oof 1
spoofy/oofy
spook/uke
spool/ool
spoon/oon
spoonfed/ed
sport/ort
sportsmanship/ip
sporty/orty
spot/ot
spot-check/eck
spotlight/ight
spotty/ody
spouse/ouse
spout/out
sprain/ain
sprang/ang
sprawl/all
sprawled/alled
spray/ay
sprayed/ade 1
sprays/aze
spread/ed
spree/ee
sprees/eeze

spring/**ing**
springtime/**ime**
springy/**ingy 1**
sprinkle/**inkle**
sprint/**int**
sprinter/**inter**
sprints/**ince**
sprite/**ight**
spritz/**its**
sprout/**out**
spruce/**use 1**
spruced/**uced**
sprung/**ung**
spry/**y**
spryness/**inus**
spud/**ud**
spun/**un**
spunk/**unk**
spunky/**unky**
spur/**er**
spurred/**erd**
spurt/**ert**
sputter/**utter**
spy/**y**
spyglass/**ass**
squabble/**obble**
squabbler/**obbler**
squad/**awed**
squall/**all**
squalled/**alled**
squalor/**aller**
squander/**onder**
square/**air**
squash/**osh**
squat/**ot**
squawk/**ock**
squawks/**ox**
squeak/**eek**
squeaky/**eaky**
squeal/**eel**
squeezer/**eezer**
squelch/**elch**
squid/**id**
squiggle/**iggle**
squiggly/**iggly**
squint/**int**
squire/**ire**
squirm/**erm**
squirrel/**url**

squirt/**ert**
squirter/**erter**
squirty/**irty**
squish/**ish**
stab/**ab 1**
stabilize/**ize**
stability/**ility**
stable/**able**
stack/**ack**
stacked/**act**
stacks/**ax**
staff/**aff**
staffed/**aft**
stag/**ag**
stage/**age 1**
stagecoach/**oach**
stagestruck/**uck**
stagnate/**ate**
stain/**ain**
stair/**air**
staircase/**ace**
stairway/**ay**
stake/**ake**
stakeout/**out**
stale/**ale 1**
stalemate/**ate**
stall/**all**
stalled/**alled**
stamp/**amp**
stampede/**eed**
Stan/**an**
stance/**ance**
stand/**and**
standby/**y**
standout/**out**
standstill/**ill**
star/**ar**
starch/**arch**
stardust/**ust**
stare/**air**
stargaze/**aze**
stark/**ark**
starlight/**ight**
starred/**ard 1**
starry/**arry 2**
starstruck/**uck**
start/**art 1**
starter/**arter 1**
Star Trek/**eck**

starvation/**ation**
starve/**arve**
stash/**ash 1**
state/**ate**
static/**atic**
station/**ation**
stationary/**ary**
stationery/**ary**
statistic/**istic**
status quo/**o**
staunch/**aunch**
stay/**ay**
stayed/**ade 1**
stays/**aze**
steadfast/**ast**
steady/**etty**
steak/**ake**
steal/**eel**
steam/**eem**
steamboat/**ote**
steamroll/**ole**
steamrolled/**old**
steamroller/**olar**
steamy/**eamy**
steed/**eed**
steel/**eel**
steep/**eep**
steeper/**eeper**
steer/**eer**
Stella/**ella**
stellar/**eller**
stem/**em**
stench/**ench**
stencil/**encil**
step/**ep**
stepchild/**ild**
stepdaughter/**otter**
stepmother/**other**
stepped/**ept**
stepsister/**ister**
stereo/**o**
stereophonic/**onic**
stereos/**ose 2**
stereotype/**ipe**
sterilize/**ize**
stern/**urn**
stethoscope/**ope**
Steve/**eave**
stew/**ew**

stewed/**ude**
stews/**use 2**
stick/**ick**
sticker/**icker**
sticks/**icks**
stickup/**up**
sticky/**icky**
stiff/**iff**
stiletto/**etto**
still/**ill**
stilled/**illed**
stilt/**ilt**
stimulate/**ate**
stimulation/**ation**
sting/**ing**
stinger/**inger 1**
stingray/**ay**
stingy/**ingy 2**
stink/**ink**
stinkaroo/**ew**
stinky/**inky**
stint/**int**
stir/**er**
stirred/**erd**
stitch/**itch**
stock/**ock**
stockbroker/**oker**
Stockholm/**ome 1**
stockpile/**ile 1**
stockpiled/**ild**
stocks/**ox**
stocky/**awky**
stoic/**oic**
stoke/**oke**
stokes/**okes**
stole/**ole**
stolen/**olen**
stomachache/**ake**
stomp/**omp**
stone/**one 1**
stonewall/**all**
stony/**ony**
stood/**ood 3**
stooge/**uge**
stool/**ool**
stoolie/**uly**
stoop/**oop**
stop/**op**
stoplight/**ight**

stopper/**opper**
stopwatch/**otch**
store/**ore**
stored/**ord 1**
stork/**ork 1**
storm/**orm 1**
story/**ory**
storyline/**ine 1**
stout/**out**
stouter/**owder**
stove/**ove 1**
stow/**o**
stowaway/**ay**
stowed/**ode**
straddle/**attle**
straight/**ate**
straighter/**ader**
strain/**ain**
strait/**ate**
straitlaced/**aste**
strand/**and**
strange/**ange**
stranglehold/**old**
strangulate/**ate**
strap/**ap**
stratosphere/**eer**
straw/**aw**
strawberry/**ary**
straws/**ause**
stray/**ay**
strays/**aze**
streak/**eek**
stream/**eem**
streamline/**ine 1**
streamlined/**ind 1**
street/**eet**
streetcar/**ar**
strength/**ength**
strep/**ep**
stress/**ess**
stressed/**est**
stressful/**essful**
stretch/**etch**
strewn/**oon**
stricken/**icken**
strict/**ict**
stricter/**ictor**
stride/**ide**
strife/**ife**

strike/**ike**
striker/**iker**
string/**ing**
strip/**ip**
stripe/**ipe**
stripped/**ipped**
strive/**ive 1**
striven/**iven**
strode/**ode**
stroganoff/**off**
stroke/**oke**
strokes/**okes**
stroll/**ole**
strolled/**old**
stroller/**olar**
strong/**ong**
stronghold/**old**
struck/**uck**
strudel/**oodle**
struggle/**uggle**
struggler/**uggler**
strum/**um**
strummer/**ummer**
strut/**ut 1**
stub/**ub**
stubble/**ouble**
stubby/**ubby**
stuck/**uck**
student/**udent**
studio/**o**
study/**uddy**
stuff/**uff**
stuffy/**uffy**
stumble/**umble**
stumbling/**umbling**
stump/**ump**
stumpy/**umpy**
stun/**un**
stung/**ung**
stunk/**unk**
stunned/**und**
stunner/**unner**
stunt/**unt**
stunts/**unts**
stupefies/**ize**
stupefy/**y**
stupid/**upid**
stupider/**upiter**
stupidity/**idity**

stupor/**ooper**
sturdy/**urdy**
stutter/**utter**
sty/**y**
style/**ile 1**
styled/**ild**
sub/**ub**
subdue/**ew**
subdued/**ude**
subdues/**use 2**
subject/**ect**
subjective/**ective**
subjects/**ex**
sublime/**ime**
submarine/**een**
submerge/**erge**
submerse/**erse**
submersion/**ersion**
submission/**ition**
submissive/**issive**
submit/**it**
subpoena/**ena**
subscribe/**ibe**
subscription/**iption**
subside/**ide**
substitute/**ute**
substitution/**ution**
subterfuge/**uge**
subtitle/**idle**
subtle/**uddle**
subtopic/**opic**
subtract/**act**
subtraction/**action**
subtracts/**ax**
suburb/**urb**
subvert/**ert**
subway/**ay**
subways/**aze**
succeed/**eed**
success/**ess**
successful/**essful**
succession/**ession**
successor/**essor**
succinct/**inct**
succotash/**ash 1**
succumb/**um**
such/**utch**
suck/**uck**
sucked/**uct**

sucker/**ucker**
sucks/**ucks**
suction/**uction**
Sudafed/**ed**
sue/**ew**
sued/**ude**
suede/**ade 1**
sues/**use 2**
Suess, Dr./**use 1**
suffer/**uffer**
suffice/**ice 1**
sufficed/**iced**
sufficient/**icient**
suffocate/**ate**
suffragette/**et**
sugarcoat/**ote**
suggest/**est**
suggestion/**estion**
suit/**ute**
suitcase/**ace**
suite/**eet**
suitor/**uter**
sulk/**ulk**
sum/**um**
summarize/**ize**
summation/**ation**
summer/**ummer**
summertime/**ime**
sun/**un**
sunbeam/**eem**
sunblock/**ock**
sunburn/**urn**
sunburst/**irst**
sundown/**own 2**
sung/**ung**
sunk/**unk**
sunken/**unken**
sunlight/**ight**
sunlit/**it**
sunned/**und**
sunny/**unny**
sunrise/**ize**
sunscreen/**een**
sunset/**et**
Sunset Strip/**ip**
sunshine/**ine 1**
sunstroke/**oke**
suntan/**an**
suntanned/**and**

super/**ooper**
superb/**urb**
supercool/**ool**
Superdome/**ome 1**
super-duper/**ooper**
superficial/**icial**
superiority/**ority**
superman/**an**
supermom/**om**
superpower/**our 1**
supersede/**eed**
supersonic/**onic**
superstar/**ar**
superstition/**ition**
superstitious/**icious**
supervise/**ize**
supervision/**ision**
supervisor/**izer**
supper/**upper**
supplant/**ant 1**
supplied/**ide**
supplies/**ize**
supply/**y**
support/**ort**
supporter/**order**
suppose/**ose 2**
suppress/**ess**
suppressed/**est**
suppression/**ession**
supreme/**eem**
Supreme Court/**ort**
sure/**ure**
surefire/**ire**
surety/**urity**
surf/**urf**
surfboard/**ord 1**
surge/**erge**
surly/**urly**
surname/**aim**
surpass/**ass**
surpassed/**ast**
surprise/**ize**
surrender/**ender**
surround/**ound**
survey/**ay**
surveyed/**ade 1**
surveyor/**ayer**
surveys/**aze**
survival/**ival**

survive/**ive 1**
survivor/**iver 1**
Susanna/**ana 1**
suspect/**ect**
suspects/**ex**
suspend/**end**
suspender/**ender**
suspense/**ense**
suspension/**ention**
suspicion/**ition**
suspicious/**icious**
sustain/**ain**
suture/**uture**
svelte/**elt**
Svengali/**olly**
swab/**ob**
Swahili/**eally**
swallow/**allow 2**
swam/**am**
swami/**ommy**
swamp/**omp**
swan/**awn**
swanky/**anky**
swans/**ons**
swap/**op**
swarm/**orm 1**
swashbuckle/**uckle**
swat/**ot**
swatch/**otch**
sway/**ay**
swayed/**ade 1**
sways/**aze**
swear/**air**
swearword/**erd**
sweat/**et**
sweater/**etter**
sweaty/**etty**
sweep/**eep**
sweeper/**eeper**
sweet/**eet**
sweeten/**eaten**
sweeter/**eeder**
sweetheart/**art 1**
sweetie/**eedy**
swell/**ell**
swelter/**elter**
swept/**ept**
swerve/**erve**
swift/**ift**

swig/**ig**
swim/**im**
swimmer/**immer**
swindle/**indle**
swine/**ine 1**
swing/**ing**
swipe/**ipe**
swirl/**url**
swirly/**urly**
swish/**ish**
Swiss/**iss**
switch/**itch**
switcheroo/**ew**
swivel/**ivel**
swollen/**olen**
swoon/**oon**
swoop/**oop**
sword/**ord 1**
swore/**ore**
sworn/**orn**
swung/**ung**
symbol/**imble**
symbolic/**olic**
symbolism/**ism**
sympathetic/**etic**
sympathize/**ize**
symphonic/**onic**
symptomatic/**atic**
synagogue/**og**
syndrome/**ome 1**
synonym/**im**
synthetic/**etic**
Syria/**eria**
syringe/**inge**
syrup/**urp**
systematic/**atic**
Szechwan/**awn**

T

tab/**ab 1**
Tabasco/**asco**
tabby/**abby**
tabernacle/**ackle**
table/**able**
tabloid/**oid**
taboo/**ew**
taboos/**use 2**
tack/**ack**

tacked/**act**
tackle/**ackle**
tact/**act**
tactical/**actical**
tad/**ad 1**
tadpole/**ole**
tag/**ag**
tagalong/**ong**
Tahiti/**eedy**
tail/**ale 1**
tailgate/**ate**
tailgater/**ader**
tailpipe/**ipe**
tailspin/**in**
tailwind/**inned**
Taipei/**ay**
Taiwan/**awn**
Taj Mahal/**all**
take/**ake**
tale/**ale 1**
talk/**ock**
talkathon/**awn**
talker/**ocker**
talks/**ox**
tall/**all**
Tallahassee/**assy**
taller/**aller**
tallish/**olish**
tally/**alley**
tamale/**olly**
tambourine/**een**
tame/**aim**
Tammy/**ammy**
tamper/**amper**
tan/**an**
Tang/**ang**
tangerine/**een**
tank/**ank**
tanned/**and**
tanner/**anner**
tantalize/**ize**
tantamount/**ount**
tap/**ap**
tape/**ape**
tar/**ar**
tardy/**ardy**
tarred/**ard 1**
tarry/**ary**
tart/**art 1**

Tartar/arter 1
tarter/arter 1
task/ask
taste/aste
tasty/asty
tatter/atter
tattle/attle
tattletale/ale 1
tattoo/ew
tattooed/ude
tattoos/use 2
taught/ot
taunt/aunt
taupe/ope
taut/ot
tauter/otter
tawny/awny
tax/ax
taxation/ation
taxi/axi
taxicab/ab 1
taxpayer/ayer
tea/ee
teach/each
teacher/eacher
teacup/up
teakettle/eddle
teal/eel
team/eem
teamwork/erk
teapot/ot
tear/air,eer
teardrop/op
tearful/earful
tearstain/ain
teary/eery
teas/eeze
tease/eeze
technicality/ality 1
technician/ition
technique/eek
technology/ology
Ted/ed
Teddy/etty
tee/ee
teem/eem
teen/een
teenage/age 1
teeny/ini

teenybopper/opper
teeny weeny/ini
teepee/ee
teepees/eeze
teeter/eeder
teeth/eath 2
teethe/eethe
Tel Aviv/eave
telecast/ast
telegram/am
telegraph/aff
telephone/one 1
telephonic/onic
telescope/ope
telescopic/opic
televise/ize
television/ision
tell/ell
teller/eller
telltale/ale 1
Tell, William/ell
temperamental/ental
temporary/ary
tempt/empt
ten/en
tenacious/acious
tenacity/acity
tend/end
tender/ender
tenderfoot/oot 2
tenderize/ize
tenderloin/oin
Tennessee/ee
tense/ense
tension/ention
tent/ent
tents/ense
tepee/eepy
tepees/eeze
teriyaki/awky
term/erm
terminate/ate
terminator/ader
terminology/ology
termite/ight
terrain/ain
terrific/ific
terrified/ide
terrifies/ize

terrify/y
territorial/orial
territory/ory
terror/arer
terrorism/ism
terrorize/ize
Terry/ary
terse/erse
Tess/ess
test/est
tester/ester
testify/y
testimonial/onial
testimony/ony
tether/eather
text/ext
textbook/ook 2
Thailand/and
than/an, en
thank/ank
that/at 1
thatch/atch 1
thaw/aw
theft/eft
their/air
them/em
theme/eem
then/en
Theodore/ore
theorize/ize
theory/eery
there/air
thereafter/after
therefore/ore
thermometer/
   ometer
thermostat/at 1
these/eeze
they/ay
thick/ick
thicken/icken
thicker/icker
thicket/icket
thickly/ickly
thief/ief
thigh/y
thighs/ize
thimble/imble
thin/in

thing/ing
thingamabob/ob
thingamajig/ig
think/ink
thinned/inned
thinner/inner
third/erd
thirst/irst
thirteen/een
thirty/irty
this/iss
thistle/istle
thong/ong
thorn/orn
thoroughbred/ed
those/ose 2
though/o
thought/ot
thrash/ash 1
thread/ed
threadbare/air
threat/et
three/ee
threshold/old
threw/ew
thrift/ift
thrifty/ifty
thrill/ill
thrilled/illed
thriller/iller
thrive/ive 1
throat/ote
throb/ob
throne/one 1
throng/ong
throttle/oddle
through/ew
throughout/out
throw/o
throwaway/ay
throwing/owing
thrown/one 1
throws/ose 2
thrust/ust
thud/ud
thug/ug
thumb/um
thumbnail/ale 1
thumbtack/ack

thumbtacks/**ax**
thump/**ump**
thunder/**under**
thundercloud/**oud**
thunderstorm/**orm 1**
thunderstruck/**uck**
thus/**us**
thwart/**ort**
thyme/**ime**
Tibet/**et**
tick/**ick**
ticked/**ict**
ticker/**icker**
ticket/**icket**
tickle/**ickle**
tickly/**ickly**
ticks/**icks**
Tic Tac/**ack**
ticktock/**ock**
ticktocks/**ox**
tidal/**idle**
tidbits/**its**
tide/**ide**
tidepool/**ool**
tidy/**idy**
tie/**y**
tied/**ide**
tier/**eer**
ties/**ize**
tiff/**iff**
tight/**ight**
tighten/**ighten**
tighter/**ider**
tight-lipped/**ipped**
tightrope/**ope**
tightwad/**awed**
Tijuana/**onna**
tile/**ile 1**
tiled/**ild**
till/**ill**
tilled/**illed**
tilt/**ilt**
Tim/**im**
Timbuktu/**ew**
time/**ime**
timekeeper/**eeper**
timepiece/**ease 2**
time-saver/**aver**
timetable/**able**

timeworn/**orn**
timidity/**idity**
tin/**in**
Tina/**ena**
tinfoil/**oil**
tinge/**inge**
tingle/**ingle**
Tinkertoys/**oys**
tinny/**inny**
tint/**int**
tints/**ince**
tiny/**iny**
tip/**ip**
tipped/**ipped**
tipper/**ipper**
tippytoe/**o**
tipsy/**ipsy**
tiptoe/**o**
tiptoed/**ode**
tiptoeing/**owing**
tiptoes/**ose 2**
tiptop/**op**
tirade/**ade 1**
tire/**ire**
'tis/**iz**
tissue/**issue**
titanosaur/**ore**
title/**idle**
titter/**itter**
tizzy/**izzy**
to/**ew**
toad/**ode**
toadstool/**ool**
toast/**ost 1**
today/**ay**
Todd/**awed**
toddle/**oddle**
toe/**o**
toehold/**old**
toenail/**ale 1**
toes/**ose 2**
together/**eather**
toil/**oil**
token/**oken**
Tokyo/**o**
told/**old**
Toledo/**edo**
tolerate/**ate**
toll/**ole**

tom/**om**
tomahawk/**ock**
tomahawks/**ox**
tomb/**oom**
tombstone/**one 1**
tomcat/**at 1**
Tommy/**ommy**
ton/**un**
tone/**one 1**
tongue/**ung**
tonic/**onic**
tonight/**ight**
tonsillitis/**itis**
Tonto/**onto**
Tony/**ony**
too/**ew**
toodle-oo/**ew**
took/**ook 2**
tool/**ool**
toot/**ute**
tooth/**ooth**
toothache/**ake**
toothbrush/**ush 1**
toothpaste/**aste**
toothpick/**ick**
toothpicks/**icks**
top/**op**
topaz/**azz**
topic/**opic**
topmost/**ost 1**
topnotch/**otch**
topper/**opper**
torch/**orch**
torchbearer/**arer**
tore/**ore**
torment/**ent**
tormentor/**enter**
torn/**orn**
Toronto/**onto**
torpedo/**edo**
torrential/**ential**
tortellini/**ini**
toss/**oss 2**
tossed/**ost 2**
tostada/**ada**
tot/**ot**
totality/**ality 1**
tote/**ote**
totter/**otter**

touch/**utch**
touchdown/**own**
tough/**uff**
tougher/**uffer**
toughie/**uffy**
tour/**ure**
tow/**o**
toward/**ord 1**
towed/**ode**
towel/**owl**
tower/**our 1**
towered/**owered**
towing/**owing**
town/**own 2**
towrope/**ope**
tows/**ose 2**
toxicity/**icity**
toy/**oy**
toyed/**oid**
Toyota/**ota**
toys/**oys**
trace/**ace**
traced/**aste**
track/**ack**
tracked/**act**
tracks/**ax**
tract/**act**
traction/**action**
Tracy/**acy**
trade/**ade 1**
trademark/**ark**
trader/**ader**
tradition/**ition**
traffic/**aphic**
trail/**ale 1**
trailblaze/**aze**
train/**ain**
trait/**ate**
traitor/**ader**
tram/**am**
tramp/**amp**
trampoline/**een**
trance/**ance**
tranquilize/**ize**
tranquillity/**ility**
transact/**act**
transaction/**action**
transatlantic/**antic**
transcend/**end**

transcendental/ental
transcribe/ibe
transcript/ipped
transferred/erd
transfix/icks
transform/orm 1
transformer/ormer
transfusion/usion
transistor/ister
transition/ition
translate/ate
translator/ader
transmission/ition
transmit/it
transmits/its
transmittal/iddle
transparent/arent
transpire/ire
transplant/ant 1
transplants/ance
transport/ort
transportation/ation
transporter/order
transverse/erse
trap/ap
trapdoor/ore
trapeze/eeze
trash/ash 1
trashcan/an
trashy/ashy
trauma/ama 1
traumatic/atic
traumatize/ize
travel/avel
travelogue/og
tray/ay
trays/aze
tread/ed
treadmill/ill
treason/eason
treasure/easure
treat/eet
treaty/eedy
treble/ebble
tree/ee
treed/eed
trees/eeze
treetop/op
trek/eck

trekked/ect
treks/ex
tremble/emble
trench/ench
trend/end
trendsetter/etter
trespass/ass
Trevor/ever
trial/ile 1
tribe/ibe
tribute/ute
trick/ick
tricked/ict
trickle/ickle
tricks/icks
tricky/icky
tricycle/ycle
tried/ide
tries/ize
trigger/igger
trill/ill
trilled/illed
trillion/illion
trim/im
trimmer/immer
Trinidad/ad 1
trinity/inity
trip/ip
triple/ipple
tripod/awed
tripped/ipped
tripper/ipper
trite/ight
triviality/ality 1
trod/awed
troll/ole
trolley/olly
trombone/one 1
tromp/omp
troop/oop
trooper/ooper
tropic/opic
trot/ot
trotter/otter
troubadour/ore
trouble/ouble
troubleshoot/ute
troubleshooter/uter
trough/off

trounce/ounce
troupe/oop
trouper/ooper
trout/out
Troy/oy
truce/use 1
truck/uck
trucked/uct
trucker/ucker
truckload/ode
trucks/ucks
trudge/udge
Trudy/oody
true/ew
truffle/uffle
truism/ism
truly/uly
trump/ump
trunk/unk
trust/ust
trusted/usted
trustee/usty
truth/ooth
try/y
tryout/out
tsk tsk/isk
tsunami/ommy
tub/ub
tube/ube
tucked/uct
Tucson/awn
tug/ug
tuition/ition
tumble/umble
tumbleweed/eed
tumbling/umbling
tummy/ummy
tumor/umor
tumult/ult
tune/oon
tuner/ooner
tunnel/unnel
turf/urf
Turk/erk
turkey/erky
turmoil/oil
turn/urn
turncoat/ote
turnover/over

turnstile/ile 1
turquoise/oice, oys
turtle/urdle
turtledove/ove 2
turtleneck/eck
tusk/usk
tussle/ustle
Tut, King/ut 1
tutor/uter
tutorial/orial
tutti-frutti/oody
tutu/ew
tux/ucks
tuxedo/edo
TVs/eeze
TWA/ay
twang/ang
tweak/eek
tweed/eed
tweet/eet
tweezer/eezer
twelve/elve
twice/ice 1
twiddle/iddle
twig/ig
twilight/ight
twin/in
twine/ine 1
twined/ind 1
twinge/inge
Twinkie/inky
twinkle/inkle
twirl/url
twirly/urly
twist/ist
twister/ister
twitch/itch
twitter/itter
two/ew
two-seater/eeder
tycoon/oon
tyke/ike
Tylenol/all
type/ipe
typecast/ast
typewriter/ider
typewritten/itten
typhoon/oon

U

udder/**utter**
ugh/**ug**
Ukraine/**ain**
ukulele/**aily**
umbrella/**ella**
ump/**ump**
umpire/**ire**
unable/**able**
unafraid/**ade 1**
unapparent/**arent**
unaware/**air**
unbend/**end**
unborn/**orn**
unbroken/**oken**
uncanny/**anny**
unchain/**ain**
uncivil/**ivel**
unclear/**eer**
unclench/**ench**
uncontrolled/**old**
uncouth/**ooth**
uncut/**ut 1**
undeniable/**iable**
under/**under**
underachiever/**eaver**
underarm/**arm 1**
undercut/**ut 1**
underdog/**og**
underdone/**un**
underfed/**ed**
underfoot/**oot 2**
undergrad/**ad 1**
underground/**ound**
underlie/**y**
underline/**ine 1**
underlined/**ind 1**
undermine/**ine 1**
undermined/**ind 1**
underneath/**eath 2**
underpaid/**ade 1**
underpants/**ance**
underrate/**ate**
underscore/**ore**
undershirt/**ert**
understand/**and**
understood/**ood 3**
understudy/**uddy**

undertow/**o**
underwater/**otter**
underway/**ay**
underwear/**air**
underweight/**ate**
underwent/**ent**
undo/**ew**
undone/**un**
undress/**ess**
undressed/**est**
unearth/**irth**
uneasy/**easy**
unemotional/**otional**
unemployed/**oid**
unexplored/**ord 1**
unfair/**air**
unfit/**it**
unfold/**old**
unfulfilled/**illed**
unfurl/**url**
unglued/**ude**
unhappy/**appy**
unheard/**erd**
unhitch/**itch**
unholy/**oly**
unhook/**ook 2**
unhurt/**ert**
unicorn/**orn**
unifies/**ize**
uniform/**orm 1**
unify/**y**
unimpressed/**est**
union/**union**
unique/**eek**
unite/**ight**
unity/**unity**
universe/**erse**
university/**ersity**
unjust/**ust**
unkind/**ind 1**
unknown/**one 1**
unlace/**ace**
unlaced/**aste**
unlatch/**atch 1**
unlawful/**awful**
unless/**ess**
unlike/**ike**
unload/**ode**
unlock/**ock**

unlocks/**ox**
unlucky/**ucky**
unmade/**ade 1**
unnecessary/**ary**
unnerve/**erve**
unobtrusive/**usive**
unofficial/**icial**
unorthodox/**ox**
unpack/**ack**
unpacked/**act**
unpacks/**ax**
unpaid/**ade 1**
unparalleled/**eld**
unpin/**in**
unplug/**ug**
unproductive/**uctive**
unravel/**avel**
unreal/**eel**
unrealistic/**istic**
unrefined/**ind 1**
unrehearsed/**irst**
unreliable/**iable**
unripe/**ipe**
unroll/**ole**
unromantic/**antic**
unruly/**uly**
unsaid/**ed**
unsatisfied/**ide**
unsavory/**avery**
unscrew/**ew**
unseen/**een**
unsettle/**eddle**
unskilled/**illed**
unspoken/**oken**
unstable/**able**
unsteady/**etty**
unsung/**ung**
unsure/**ure**
unsurpassed/**ast**
untidy/**idy**
untie/**y**
untied/**ide**
unties/**ize**
until/**ill**
unto/**ew**
untold/**old**
untrue/**ew**
untruth/**ooth**
unusable/**usable**

unveil/**ale 1**
unwed/**ed**
unwell/**ell**
unwind/**ind 1**
unwise/**ize**
unwrap/**ap**
unwritten/**itten**
unzip/**ip**
up/**up**
upbeat/**eet**
update/**ate**
upend/**end**
upgrade/**ade 1**
upheld/**eld**
uphill/**ill**
uplift/**ift**
upon/**awn**
upped/**upt**
uppercut/**ut 1**
upright/**ight**
uproar/**ore**
uproarious/**orious**
uproot/**ute**
upscale/**ale 1**
upset/**et**
upstage/**age 1**
upstart/**art 1**
uptight/**ite**
up-to-date/**ate**
upturn/**urn**
urge/**erge**
urgency/**urgency**
urgent/**ergent**
urn/**urn**
Uruguay/**y**
us/**us**
USA/**ay**
usable/**usable**
use/**use 1, use 2**
user/**user**
usurp/**urp**
Utah/**aw**
utensil/**encil**
utility/**ility**
utilize/**ize**
utmost/**ost 1**
utopia/**opia**
utter/**utter**

V

vacate/ate
vacation/ation
vaccinate/ate
vaccine/een
vagabond/ond
vagabonds/ons
vain/ain
valentine/ine 1
validate/ate
validity/idity
valley/alley
vamoose/use 1
vamoosed/uced
vamp/amp
vampire/ire
van/an
vandalism/ism
vane/ain
vanguard/ard 1
vanilla/illa
Van Winkle, Rip/
   inkle
vaporizer/izer
variation/ation
variety/iety
various/arious
vary/ary
vase/ace
Vaseline/een
vast/ast
vaster/aster
vat/at 1
vaudeville/ill
vault/alt
vaulter/alter
vaults/altz
VCR/ar
veal/eel
veer/eer
veg/edge
vegetarianism/ism
vehicle/ickle
veil/ale 1
vein/ain
velocity/ocity
velour/ure
vendor/ender

vent/ent
ventilator/ader
vents/ense
venture/enture
veracity/acity
verb/urb
verbalize/ize
verbose/ose 1
verge/erge
verification/ation
verified/ide
verifies/ize
verify/y
Vermont/aunt
Verne, Jules/urn
Veronica/onica
versatility/ility
verse/erse
version/ersion
verve/erve
very/ary
vest/est
vet/et
veto/edo
vex/ex
vexed/ext
viable/iable
vibrate/ate
vibration/ation
vicarious/arious
vice/ice 1
vicinity/inity
vicious/icious
Vicki/icky
victimize/ize
victor/ictor
victorious/orious
video/o
videos/ose 2
vied/ide
Vietnam/om
view/ew
viewed/ude
viewpoint/oint
views/use 2
vigor/igger
vile/ile 1
villa/illa
vindicate/ate

vine/ine 1
viola/ola
violate/ate
violation/ation
violin/in
VIP/ee
viper/iper
vise/ize
vision/ision
visionary/ary
visor/izer
visualize/ize
vital/idle
vitality/ality 1
vitalize/ize
vivacious/acious
vocabulary/ary
vocal/ocal
vocalize/ize
vogue/ogue 1
voice/oice
void/oid
volley/olly
volleyball/all
voluntary/ary
volunteer/eer
volunteerism/ism
voodoo/ew
vote/ote
vouch/ouch
vow/ow 1
vowed/oud
vowel/owl
vulgarity/arity
vulture/ulture

W

wad/awed
waddle/oddle
wade/ade 1
waffle/awful
wag/ag
wage/age 1
wail/ale 1
waist/aste
wait/ate
waiter/ader
waive/ave

waiver/aver
wake/ake
walk/ock
walker/ocker
walkie-talkie/awky
walks/ox
wall/all
walled/alled
wallflower/our 1
wallow/allow 2
Wally/olly
Walter/alter
waltz/alts
wand/ond
wander/onder
wanderlust/ust
wands/ons
wane/ain
wanna/onna
want/aunt
war/ore
ward/ord 1
wardrobe/obe
ware/air
warehouse/ouse
warfare/air
warlike/ike
warm/orm 1
warmer/ormer
warmonger/unger
warn/orn
warning/orning
warpath/ath
warred/ord 1
wart/ort
wartime/ime
warty/orty
wary/ary
was/uzz
wash/osh
washboard/ord 1
Washington, D.C./ee
washrag/ag
waste/aste
wasteland/and
watch/otch
watchdog/og
watchword/erd
water/otter

waterbed/**ed**
waterfall/**all**
Waterloo/**ew**
watery/**ottery**
wave/**ave**
waver/**aver**
wavy/**avy**
wax/**ax**
waxy/**axi**
way/**ay**
wayfarer/**arer**
ways/**aze**
we/**ee**
weak/**eek**
weaker/**eaker**
wear/**air**
weary/**eery**
weather/**eather**
weatherbeaten/
   eaten
weathervane/**ain**
weatherworn/**orn**
weave/**eave**
weaver/**eaver**
wed/**ed**
wedge/**edge**
weed/**eed**
weeder/**eeder**
weedy/**eedy**
week/**eek**
weekday/**ay**
weep/**eep**
weeper/**eeper**
weepy/**eepy**
weigh/**ay**
weighed/**ade 1**
weighs/**aze**
weight/**ate**
weighty/**ady**
welch/**elch**
weld/**eld**
welfare/**air**
well/**ell**
well-versed/**irst**
welt/**elt**
went/**ent**
wept/**ept**
were/**er**
west/**est**

wet/**et**
wetter/**etter**
we've/**eave**
whack/**ack**
whacked/**act**
whale/**ale 1**
wham/**am**
whammy/**ammy**
wharf/**arf 2**
what/**ot, ut 1**
whatever/**ever**
whatnot/**ot**
wheat/**eet**
wheedle/**eedle**
wheel/**eel**
wheelbarrow/**arrow**
wheelchair/**air**
wheelie/**eally**
wheeze/**eeze**
when/**en**
whenever/**ever**
where/**air**
wherever/**ever**
whet/**et**
whether/**eather**
which/**itch**
whichever/**ever**
whiff/**iff**
whiffed/**ift**
while/**ile 1**
whim/**im**
whine/**ine 1**
whined/**ind 1**
whiner/**iner**
whinny/**inny**
whiny/**iny**
whip/**ip**
whiplash/**ash 1**
whipped/**ipped**
whippoorwill/**ill**
whirl/**url**
whirlpool/**ool**
whirlwind/**inned**
whisk/**isk**
whiskey/**isky**
whisper/**isper**
whistle/**istle**
white/**ight**
whiten/**ighten**

whiter/**ider**
whitewash/**osh**
whittle/**iddle**
whiz/**iz**
who/**ew**
whoa/**o**
whoever/**ever**
whole/**ole**
wholesale/**ale 1**
wholly/**oly**
whom/**oom**
whomp/**omp**
whoop/**oop**
whoopee/**oopy**
whoosh/**ush 2**
whopper/**opper**
whose/**use 2**
why/**y**
Wichita/**aw**
wicker/**icker**
wicket/**icket**
wicks/**icks**
wide/**ide**
wider/**ider**
widespread/**ed**
wienie/**ini**
wife/**ife**
wig/**ig**
wiggle/**iggle**
wiggly/**iggly**
wigwam/**om**
wild/**ild**
wildcat/**at 1**
wildebeest/**east**
wildflower/**our 1**
wildlife/**ife**
will/**ill**
willed/**illed**
William Tell/**ell**
willow/**illow**
willpower/**our 1**
willy-nilly/**illy**
wilt/**ilt**
wimp/**imp**
wimpy/**impy**
win/**in**
wince/**ince**
wind/**ind 1, inned**
windbag/**ag**

windblown/**one 1**
windmill/**ill**
windowpane/**ain**
windowsill/**ill**
windpipe/**ipe**
windshield/**ield**
windswept/**ept**
wine/**ine 1**
wing/**ing**
wingding/**ing**
wingdinger/**inger 1**
wink/**ink**
winked/**inct**
winner/**inner**
Winnie the Pooh/**ew**
Winnipeg/**eg**
winter/**inter**
wipe/**ipe**
wiper/**iper**
wire/**ire**
wiretap/**ap**
wise/**ize**
wisecrack/**ack**
wisecracked/**act**
wisecracks/**ax**
wiser/**izer**
wish/**ish**
wishbone/**one 1**
wisp/**isp**
wit/**it**
witch/**itch**
witchcraft/**aft**
with/**ith**
withdraw/**aw**
withdrawn/**awn**
withdrew/**ew**
wither/**ither**
withheld/**eld**
withhold/**old**
within/**in**
without/**out**
wits/**its**
witticism/**ism**
witty/**itty**
wizard/**izard**
Wizard of Oz/**ause**
wobble/**obble**
wobbler/**obbler**
woe/**o**

woebegone/awn
woes/ose 2
wok/ock
woke/oke
woks/ox
womb/oom
wombat/at 1
won/un
wonder/under
won ton/awn
woo/ew
wood/ood 3
woodblock/ock
woodchopper/opper
woodchuck/uck
woodcutter/utter
woodpile/ile 1
woodwind/inned
woodwork/erk
wooed/ude
woof/oof 2
wool/ull 2
woolly/ully
word/erd
wordy/urdy
wore/ore
work/erk
workaholic/olic
workload/ode
workout/out
workplace/ace
workshop/op
worldwide/ide
worm/erm
worn/orn
worry/urry
worrywart/ort
worse/erse
worsen/erson
worst/irst
worth/irth
worthwhile/ile 1
would/ood 3
wound/ound
wove/ove 1
wow/ow 1
wowed/oud
wrap/ap
wrath/ath

wreath/eath 2
wreck/eck
wrecked/ect
wrecks/ex
wrench/ench
wretch/etch
wring/ing
wrinkle/inkle
wrist/ist
wristwatch/otch
write/ight
writer/ider
written/itten
wrong/ong
wrote/ote
wrung/ung
wry/y
Wyatt Earp/urp

X

Xerox/ox
x-ray/ay
x-rayed/ade 1
x-rays/aze
xylophone/one 1

Y

yacht/ot
yak/ack
yakked/act
yaks/ax
Yale/ale 1
yam/am
yank/ank
Yankee/anky
Yankee Doodle/
   oodle
yap/ap
yard/ard 1
yardstick/ick
yarn/arn
yawn/awn
yawned/ond
yawner/onor
yawns/ons
year/eer
yearn/urn

yeast/east
yell/ell
yelled/eld
yeller/eller
yellow/ellow
Yellowstone/one 1
yelp/elp
yen/en
yep/ep
yes/ess
yesterday/ay
yet/et
yield/ield
yippee/ippy
yokel/ocal
Yokohama/ama 1
yolk/oke
yolks/okes
yonder/onder
yoo-hoo/ew
you/ew
young/ung
younger/unger
your/ore, ure
you're/ure
yourself/elf
youth/ooth
you've/ove 3
yo-yo/o
yo-yos/ose 2
yuck/uck
yucky/ucky
Yukon/awn
yule/ool
yum/um
yummy/ummy
yuppie/uppy
Yvonne/awn

Z

zag/ag
Zambezi/easy
Zanzibar/ar
zap/ap
zeal/eel
zealous/ealous
zero/ero 1
zest/est

Zeus/use 1
zigzag/ag
zillion/illion
zinc/ink
zing/ing
zinger/inger 1
zingy/ingy 1
zip/ip
zipped/ipped
zipper/ipper
zippy/ippy
zit/it
zither/ither
zits/its
zone/one 1
zonk/onk
zoo/ew
zoologist/ologist
zoology/ology
zoom/oom
zoos/use 2
zucchini/ini